"When Margaret O'Gara was welcomed at the eternal banquet of our Lord on August 16, 2012, we lost a treasured colleague at the tables of ecumenical dialogue. As we remember her with thanksgiving, we are grateful that she gives us now in *No Turning Back* an insightful legacy—a legacy that calls us and our churches to embrace in both faith and practice the prayer of Jesus that 'they may all be one.'

"She understood that persistent prayer is at the heart of the ecumenical movement. She recognized that the nurturing of mutual trust is essential for the ongoing quest. And she was concerned—as are so many others at dialogue tables—over the procrastination of our churches in receiving the ecumenical discoveries that already have emerged.

"With personal gentleness and profound conviction, Margaret demonstrated ecumenical imagination in searching for new insights on lingering issues of division. She was persistent in the quest for ways to reflect more deeply the unity that we have been granted in Christ through baptism. She recognized that the unity of the church is not ours to create. It is a gift.

"Most in the first generation and many in the second generation of scholars in a half-century of profound ecumenical dialogues have been called by their Creator and Redeemer to eternal life. Now others must come to those crucial tables. Dr. O'Gara offers superb guidance for them, reminding our churches that, indeed, there can be no turning back."

> — Rev. Lowell G. Almen
> Secretary, Evangelical Lutheran Church in America, 1987–2007
> U.S. Lutheran–Roman Catholic Dialogue, 1998–present

"During the eight years I was privileged to be Margaret O'Gara's colleague in Canada, I experienced her deep passion for Christian unity and her relentless pursuit of it through theological research, ecumenical dialogue, and (not least) humble prayer. I am convinced that readers of *No Turning Back* will experience something of what I did."

> — Prof. Pablo Argarate
> Institute for Ecumenical Theology, Eastern Orthodoxy, and Patristics
> University of Graz, Austria

"*No Turning Back* shows Margaret O'Gara's great command of the ecumenical literature, especially in ecclesiology. Her essays are well organized and thorough. She is honest, insightful, even-handed, occasionally provocative, and always lucid."

> — Rev. John W. Crossin, OSFS
> Executive Director, Secretariat for Ecumenical and Interreligious
> Affairs
> United States Conference of Catholic Bishops

"Drawing on decades of experience, and writing at times in strikingly personal terms, Margaret O'Gara introduces the reader to the practice of ecumenical dialogue, a practice that she readily qualifies as a form of asceticism rooted in common prayer, attentive listening, and rigorous theological study. With a clear vision and penetrating insight, she surveys the often-neglected achievements and complex challenges facing the next generation of ecumenical scholars. This highly readable book by one of North America's most accomplished ecumenists is required reading for anyone interested in ecumenical theology and ecclesiology."

> — Prof. Catherine E. Clifford
> Saint Paul University, Ottawa
> Anglican–Roman Catholic Dialogue of Canada, 1993–present

"No Turning Back reflects the breadth and depth of Margaret O'Gara's ecumenical experience, gifts and passion. In its convergence text *The Church: Towards a Common Vision*, the Commission on Faith and Order proposes that a 'certain kind of authority' can be recognised in ecumenical dialogues 'when they reflect a common search for and the discovery of the truth in love, urge believers to seek the Lord's will for ecclesial communion, and invite ongoing *metanoia* and holiness of life.' This 'certain kind of authority' shone in Margaret O'Gara's teaching, writing, and engagement in ecumenical dialogue. And it shines through the pages of this book."

> — Rev. Canon John Gibaut
> Director, Commission on Faith and Order
> World Council of Churches, Geneva

"No Turning Back is a fitting memorial to Margaret O'Gara's committed life and work, especially because of her deeply engaged and creative contribution to ecumenism. Through the gentle force of her personality and in the clear grace of a vocation, she illumined what ecumenism must mean as an imperative shaping the church and expanding the horizons of Catholic faith. In a world where meetings can be onerous, documents dry, and exchanges paper thin, she will ever be remembered as a bright spirit, bringing warmth and clarity to everything she touched. Thanks be also to her husband, Michael Vertin, for his editor's introduction—a loving appreciation of Margaret along with judicious selection from her mature writings. Readers can nourish the memory of Margaret through the beautiful portrait included in this book, while her writings live on as an essential reference for those who, in shared hope, pray with her in the communion of saints, that we may be one. With her gone before us into the Light, there can be no turning back."

> — Rev. Anthony J. Kelly, CSsR
> Australian Catholic University
> International Theological Commission, 2004–present

(endorsements continued on page 255)

No Turning Back

The Future of Ecumenism

Margaret O'Gara

Edited by *Michael Vertin*

Forewords by
Bishop Richard J. Sklba
and
Professor David M. Thompson

A Michael Glazier Book

LITURGICAL PRESS
Collegeville, Minnesota

www.litpress.org

A Michael Glazier Book published by Liturgical Press

Cover design by Jodi Hendrickson.

Quotations and citations from the documents of the Second Vatican Council are taken from *The Documents of Vatican II*, ed. Walter M. Abbott (New York: America Press, 1966).

1	2	3	4	5	6	7	8	9

Library of Congress Cataloging-in-Publication Data

O'Gara, Margaret, 1947–
    No turning back : the future of Ecumenism / Margaret O'Gara ; edited by Michael Vertin.
        pages   cm
    Includes index.
    "A Michael Glazier book."
    ISBN 978-0-8146-8313-2 — ISBN 978-0-8146-8338-5 (ebook)
    1. Ecumenical movement.   2. Catholic Church—Relations.   3. Christian union—Catholic Church.   I. Vertin, Michael, 1939– editor of compilation.   II. Title.

BX1785.O34   2014
280'.042—dc23
                                                              2014010554

Contents

Part One
Introducing the Ecumenical Perspective

Part Two
Deepening the Ecumenical Perspective

Foreword by
Bishop Richard J. Sklba

For the dozen years during which I was privileged to serve as the Catholic Co-Chair of the U.S. Lutheran–Roman Catholic Dialogue, Professor Margaret O'Gara was an ardent and remarkable member of every conversation. Whether intensely focused on the theological issue of the moment in the formal sessions of the Dialogue or casually engaged in darning socks during more relaxed hours of after-dinner social discussion, Margaret was always respectfully involved and eventually willing to share her wisdom. She invariably participated in the group's patient theological search for ecclesial reconciliation without ever dominating the exchange. If anything, she seemed to prefer a touch of quiet reflection in her thoughtful consideration of other members' comments. It was a joy and an inspiration to witness her at work.

From my own vantage point during the tenth round, dedicated to "The Church as *Koinonia* of Salvation" (1998–2004), and the eleventh, summarizing round on "The Hope of Eternal Life" (2005–2010), I witnessed the manner in which the officially appointed group of scholars sought fresh starting points for addressing longstanding disagreements and then carefully brought them to new levels of theological resolution. There was always a certain thrill to watching how Margaret quietly wove her research and knowledge into the conversation.

I confess that I learned a great deal from the way Margaret often tested an idea or a tentative suggestion privately during the coffee break before bringing the thought to the full body of delegates. It seemed as if her probing mind was constantly seeking the right phrase and the most understandable approach to the question. I always found her to be dialogic to the core, perhaps the modern epitome of how theological dialogue should be conducted responsibly and fruitfully. The task is truly an enterprise of teamwork at every level and at every stage.

The papers selected for this collection exhibit the wide range of topics Margaret treated during the final decade and a half of her mature productive work. But in one way or another all the papers address serious theological and ecumenical questions of ecclesiology, as she sought ever to serve a church broken and yet yearning for the level of healing that only God's grace can effect. In each case her thinking had been crystallized for presentation in some professional venue. In bringing together the various results, this volume well illustrates the inner logic and intellectual dynamism of that thinking. Perhaps only in retrospect, then, can a current reader understand the way in which the formal dialogues truly benefited from the cross-pollination of ecumenical conversation. The faith of every participant was deepened and developed in the process.

Margaret knew only too well that ecumenical pilgrimage requires hard work. Ever careful and creative, but always thoroughly Catholic, she was convinced of the gift that Catholics bring to such exchanges from our tradition. She understood that these theological "meals," whether elaborate banquets or less formal picnics, must inevitably be "pot luck" by nature, with a menu in which each tradition serves its best and awaits the complementary offerings of the other invited guests.

Margaret's soul mate and intellectual companion through several (although alas, from our limited human perspective, too few) decades, Michael Vertin, has done us all a great service in bringing this collection of talks and essays to formal publication. The topics are interrelated, and the whole is surely greater than the sum of its parts.

I am honored to have been invited to contribute this modest foreword from my own perspective and experience. My confident hope and persistent prayer remains that the work of Margaret's lifetime may continue to nourish the thought of future ecumenical efforts. Indeed, there can be "No Turning Back!"

Richard J. Sklba

Auxiliary Bishop Emeritus of Milwaukee
Co-Chair, 1998–2010, U.S. Lutheran–Roman Catholic Dialogue
January 1, 2014

Foreword by
Professor David M. Thompson

The published work of an active ecumenist is almost inevitably dictated by circumstances. Much time is spent writing position papers for meetings or presenting lectures, shorter addresses, and summary talks; there is little time to write substantial books. Those working in universities depend very much on sympathetic department heads. The way this pattern has affected those who have been involved regularly in international and national theological dialogues for the last thirty years is only just becoming apparent as the first generation passes the torch to the next. Margaret O'Gara was taken from us prematurely with much still to give, despite the substantial amount she had already given. I welcome Michael Vertin's invitation to write a foreword for this posthumous collection of her writings for ecumenical occasions over the last sixteen years.

The title, *No Turning Back*, reflects Margaret's absolute commitment to the goal of visible unity and the process of ecumenical dialogue as a means to that end. In several papers she notes the value of long-term commitment to dialogue, and the fruit that the work of even a few committed souls can bring. Typically for one who had the gift of friendship to a remarkable degree, she affirmed the theological significance of friendship in the ecumenical movement—a theme already noticed by other historians of ecumenism. Constant prayer is the spiritual dimension of such friendship and transformation; "pray without ceasing" is a necessary text for the ecumenist, who is often more aware of sorrows than joys. Her abiding theme is teaching authority in the church. The First Vatican Council was the subject of Margaret's first book: the discussion of papal primacy (the neglected paragraph in *Pastor Aeternus*), a paper on the teaching of the magisterium, and another on the convergences between Catholics, Disciples of Christ, and Lutherans on teaching authority show that the teaching of Vatican I, crucially modulated by Vatican II, remained a key concern for her. Finally, her commitment to the next generation of ecumenists was not just on paper: it was the driving motive of her teaching, which she both loved and enjoyed, and was her own contribution to continuing ecumenical engagement.

Reading these papers, I recalled her quiet insistence on a historical approach to the understanding of doctrine—and the way in which she always carefully distinguished that from the relativism condemned by recent popes. I find it no coincidence that, as we have become more accustomed to understand doctrine as inseparable from its historical context, we have found more opportunities for convergence and agreement. For the church today lives in very different times from key eras of the past, whether patristic, scholastic, Reformation, or Enlightenment. Our world has both expanded and contracted so that, for example, the Western church cannot now ignore the Oriental Orthodox churches with which it parted company 1,500 years ago; indeed, with current political turbulence farther east we may even find them living next door to us.

I also detected (and share) her controlled impatience in these papers with the churches' unwillingness to recognize that things have changed, that convergences and agreements have been reached, but that readiness to act on those agreements is still hard to find. All ecumenists know that they may well not live to see the fruit of their labors, and in any case the unity of the church is not primarily a matter of human achievement. Still, sometimes the latter point becomes an excuse for inaction. Might this not be to take the name of the Holy Spirit in vain? Margaret's patience sometimes seemed infinite, and these papers are an appropriate way to remember (in the full sense of *anamnesis*) her commitment to the ecumenical quest. "Making Peace for Peacemaking" is deeply parabolic, and *No Turning Back* is both a summary and a motto.

David M. Thompson

Emeritus Professor of Modern Church History, Cambridge University
Disciples Member and Lead Disciples Drafter,
Disciples of Christ–Roman Catholic International Commission
for Dialogue, 1980–present
January 1, 2014

Editor's Introduction

The title chosen by Margaret O'Gara for this book is inspired by a Christian hymn that originated in mid-nineteenth-century India. The first stanza is the following, with the final line repeated at the end of every subsequent stanza:

I have decided to follow Jesus;
I have decided to follow Jesus;
I have decided to follow Jesus;
No turning back, no turning back.

Ecumenism is the collaborative effort of Christians to foster the visible unity of Jesus' church. During Margaret's more than three decades as a Roman Catholic ecumenical theologian she became convinced that there is no turning back from ecumenism for those who would follow Jesus today. Her conviction came from conclusions about Jesus' desire for his church, the fidelity of Christians to that desire thus far, and what fidelity requires of them going forward.

In the first part of this introduction I will give some historical background and then explain Margaret's three conclusions. In later parts I will summarize her contributions to the ecumenical enterprise and indicate the aim and structure of this book.

1. No Turning Back

To be a Christian is to judge that Jesus of Nazareth is the concrete historical self-manifestation of the triune God, and to strive to live as Jesus did—a life of totally self-transcending love.

Like other *human* persons, Christians are actively oriented toward the ultimate, toward whatever would totally satisfy their wondering minds and restless hearts. Like other *spiritual* persons, Christians experientially, though not always knowingly, encounter something of the ultimate, something of what is sometimes labeled "the divine."

Like other *religious* persons, Christians make the judgment that this or that event or person is a revelation of the divine in human history, and decide to live in accord with what that revelation entails. But what distinguishes Christians is their judgment that Jesus of Nazareth is the revelation of the divine—and, indeed, not the mere revelation but the divine self-gift, the gift in which God both models concretely what fully human living is and invites everyone concretely to live in that way.[1]

Of course, anyone who has even a passing familiarity with Christian history knows that Christians have not been entirely successful at living as Jesus did. Disagreements resulting in divisions and sometimes violence have often marked the relations not only between Christians and others but even between Christians themselves. Four examples confirm the point. Already in the biblical period, the controversy about whether Gentiles who became Christians were required to adopt Jewish ritual practices sharply divided the Christian community. The patristic disputes about the exact relationship of Jesus to God the Father raged not just for decades but for centuries. The medieval argument between Eastern and Western Christians about the procession of the Holy Spirit within the Trinity became so serious that the two groups condemned each other and broke off further relations. Within the Western church, the early modern clash between Reformers and Rome about the nature of justification by grace was a key theological factor in centuries of European wars.

On the other hand, divisions within the Christian community are not necessarily permanent. As recounted in Acts 15, the controversy about the requirements faced by Gentile Christians was successfully resolved. The Councils of Nicea I, Ephesus, and Chalcedon settled the christological disputes. Eastern and Western Christians remain somewhat at odds, but the 1964 meeting between Pope Paul VI and Athenagoras, Patriarch of Constantinople, led to retraction of the

---

[1] For the Roman Catholic doctrinal background of this paragraph, see Vatican Council II, *Nostra Aetate* (Declaration on the Relationship of the Church to Non-Christian Religions), nn. 1–4, and *Lumen Gentium* (Dogmatic Constitution on the Church), nn. 13–16. For the foundational methodological background, see Bernard Lonergan, *Method in Theology* (New York: Herder & Herder, 1972), especially chap. 4. For the interreligious implications, see Frederick Crowe, "Son of God, Holy Spirit, and World Religions," 324–43 in Crowe, *Appropriating the Lonergan Idea*, ed. Michael Vertin (Washington, DC: Catholic University of America Press, 1989).

earlier mutual condemnations and in 1965 to the irenic *Joint Catholic-Orthodox Declaration*. And in 1999 the Roman Catholic Church and the Lutheran World Federation, in their *Joint Declaration on the Doctrine of Justification*, affirmed that the differences, at least today, between Catholic and Lutheran teachings about justification are not church dividing.

The two joint declarations just mentioned illustrate a sea change that has taken place within the community of Christians during the past century or so, a development that has given rise to the modern ecumenical movement. This development involves elements of communal recognition and communal response, and although those elements are multiple and diverse, a few instances will indicate the emerging trend.

In 1910, at the World Missionary Conference in Edinburgh, Scotland, Christian missionaries began taking serious account of the obstacle presented to credible proclamation of the Gospel in places such as Africa by the scandalous spectacle of diverse Christian churches fiercely competing with each other for converts. During the 1930s and 1940s some German Protestants and Catholics began recognizing that their longstanding differences paled in comparison to the deeper commonalities on which they drew in opposing Hitler. In the 1950s and 1960s increasing numbers of Christians from diverse denominations discovered themselves working together in opposing apartheid in South Africa, protesting civil rights abuses in the southern United States, and marching against the Vietnam War.

Increasing acknowledgment of such shared commitments engendered the beginnings of a striking shift of institutional emphasis within the Christian community as a whole—away from defending even divisive differences and toward first exploring and then encouraging their elimination in the forthright pursuit of full communion. Small and inconsequential at first, this shift has gained magnitude and authority with the passage of time. The Life and Work movement and the complementary Faith and Order movement, with their respective social and doctrinal emphases, were initiated during the years preceding the Second World War. They contributed in turn to the establishment in 1948 of the World Council of Churches. Initially a mainly Protestant organization, the WCC eventually was augmented by reciprocal relationships with the Roman Catholic and Orthodox Churches, and its world assemblies approximately every seven years attract representatives from virtually all the Christian churches. On the Roman Catholic side all the bishops worldwide, together with official Protestant and Orthodox observers, gathered for the Second Vatican Council from 1962 through 1965; and significant ecumenical endorsements and commitments appear in the sixteen documents the council produced.

The fifty years since Vatican II have seen continued progress by the Christian churches toward increased solidarity, greater mutuality, and fuller communion with one another. It has become increasingly common for Christians to pray together and even to welcome one another to participate in some parts of their respective worship services. The collaboration of Christian churches in such societal initiatives as promoting racial justice, opposing the use of military force to resolve international conflicts, and providing disaster relief has become more and more familiar. Moreover, numerous bilateral agreements, along with some multilateral ones, have been reached by the many official ecumenical dialogues established after the council— agreements on various aspects of what Christians believe about the church itself and about such central ecclesial matters as baptism, eucharist, ministry, and authority to teach and govern.

Of course, it must be admitted that not all the churches, let alone all the members of any church, are equally enthusiastic about these developments. For a variety of reasons, in this or that quarter of the Christian community there is unease about or even rejection of steps that have been taken, and reluctance about or even outright resistance to taking further steps in the direction of total solidarity, complete mutuality, full communion. But in any case the remarkable growth in the magnitude and authority of the ecumenical movement from one hundred years ago to today is difficult to deny.

Against the background of this historical sketch I can readily explain Margaret's conviction, like that of virtually every other ecumenical theologian, that there is *no turning back* from ecumenism for those who would follow Jesus today. The conviction rests on three conclusions that, in and through the developments I have recounted, the community of Christians has learned to recognize with greater clarity and affirm with greater certainty.

The first conclusion is a general one. It is a reflection of Jesus' prayer on behalf of his of followers "that all may be one. As you, Father are in me and I am in you, may they also be one in us" (John

17:21). The prayer manifests the divine will that Christians *be* one in order that collectively they both share in and express the loving communion of Father, Son, and Spirit. And therefore, since the church is divided, God wills that it *become* one.[2] Of course, church unity, like any other good, is fundamentally a divine gift. But insofar as Christians themselves can cooperate with God in the realization of that gift, God bids them do so. God wills that they unreservedly undertake the ecumenical enterprise—that there *be* no turning back from the pursuit of full communion.

The second conclusion is implied by the first, and it regards the past. It is that, insofar as Christians have been faithful to the divine will thus far, their actions are uniquely good in the sense that God endorses and blesses them. To the extent that Christians throughout history and more deliberatively during the past century have striven for unity—that there *has been* no turning back—God endorses and blesses their undertaking.

The third conclusion, also implied by the first one, regards the future. It is that, insofar as Christians now renew and subsequently keep their commitment of fidelity to the divine will, their actions are uniquely good in the sense just noted. To the extent that Christians vigorously dedicate themselves to maintaining and extending their ecumenical pilgrimage toward full communion—that *henceforth there be* no turning back—God will endorse and bless their endeavor.

An addendum to this explanation is that just as Jesus' proclamation of, and invitation of all into, the community of divine love stands at the very heart of his mission, so too a commitment to ecumenism is not a peripheral matter for those who would be his followers. On the contrary, it is central to Christian living.[3] For the visible unity of the church both strengthens its witness to the world and foreshadows the communion of saints around the banquet table of the Lamb.

A further addendum is that from the Christian standpoint the pursuit of ecumenism is not at odds with cultivating interreligious relations. Exploring and promoting communion among people insofar as they are Christian and doing so insofar as they are religious—or spiritual, or human—are complementary rather than opposed

---

[2] John Paul II, encyclical *Ut Unum Sint*, n. 9.
[3] Ibid.

undertakings. In Christian eyes, the human, the spiritual, the religious, and the Christian features of concrete living are successively more determinate signs of the divine ground and goal of all that is. Consequently, to explore and promote communion among people on the basis of any of those features is always *thoroughly* valuable. Nonetheless, Christians understand their beliefs and practices not as mere signs of the divine but as directly informed by the utterly gratuitous self-gift of the divine, the self-gift that is simultaneously an invitation to participate in the inner life of God—Father, Son, and Spirit. Hence, to explore and promote communion among people on the basis of Christian beliefs and practices—to pursue ecumenism—is *supremely* valuable.

At the same time, some (though not all) Christians also maintain that Christians cannot exclude the possibility that, for God's own reasons, the current diversity of world religions is part of God's providential design of universal history. On this view, to explore and promote communion with the adherents of other religions may give Christians a fuller knowledge and deeper appreciation of God, what God has wrought, and what God wills. And precisely for that reason, interreligious engagement by Christians no longer remains just an optional complement to ecumenism but becomes an essential one.[4]

2. Margaret O'Gara as Ecumenical Theologian

Margaret O'Gara was born in Chicago in 1947. The vigorous Christian commitment she eventually developed owed much to her parents. Joan Smith and James O'Gara first met in a discussion group organized by the Catholic Worker movement. Not long after they married, and Margaret and Monica, her younger sister, were born, the family moved to New York. James had accepted a position with *Commonweal* magazine, a lay Catholic journal of opinion. He ultimately served the journal for more than three decades, first as managing editor and then as editor.

---

[4] Besides the items above in note 1, see Vatican Council II, *Lumen Gentium* (Dogmatic Constitution on the Church), nn. 13–16. Cf. Frederick Crowe, "Lonergan's Universalist View of Religion," 111–41, in Crowe, *Developing the Lonergan Legacy*, ed. Michael Vertin (Toronto: University of Toronto Press, 2004).

Her familial milieu oriented Margaret quite early not just to devout Christian living but also to thoughtful reflection on that living, namely, doing theology. That early orientation became enriched with theological learning during her undergraduate studies at Trinity College in Washington, DC, master's studies at the Yale Divinity School, and doctoral studies at the University of St. Michael's College, Toronto. She would eventually publish her doctoral dissertation under the title *Triumph in Defeat: Infallibility, Vatican I, and the French Minority Bishops.*[5] In 1976, near the end of her doctoral program, she was appointed to the Faculty of Theology at St. Michael's, and she served there as a creative, committed, and energetic faculty member for the next thirty-six years. She entered the realm of eternal life in 2012, after suffering from cancer for two years.

Margaret's teaching assignments were those of a professor in systematic theology. She happily handled the introductory course, Foundations of Theology, virtually every year she taught. Among her other frequent offerings were Theological Anthropology, Trinitarian Theology, Christology, and various courses on Karl Rahner's theology. However, starting very early in her teaching career she regularly sought and received assignments in what quickly became the central focus of her professional interest and commitment: ecumenical theology, the personally engaged study of the divisions between the Christian churches for the sake of overcoming them. Courses explicitly devoted wholly or at least partly to ecumenical themes are more numerous than any other group on her cumulative course list, appearing under such headings as Christian Theologies in Dialogue, Anglican and Roman Catholic Theologies in Convergence, Ecumenical Dialogue on Authority, Four Movements Reforming Theology, Breakthroughs and Barriers in Ecumenical Dialogue, and New Directions in Magisterial Teaching. Not surprisingly, ecumenical issues and insights indirectly influenced her other courses as well.

Like most theology professors, Margaret accepted invitations to service in the wider community beyond her own institution. Besides extensive public lecturing, she played an active role in several academic and ecclesiastical organizations and enterprises, especially those with an ecumenical dimension. She served as president of the

---

[5] Margaret O'Gara, *Triumph in Defeat: Infallibility, Vatican I, and the French Minority Bishops* (Washington, DC: The Catholic University of America Press, 1988).

North American Academy of Ecumenists (1987–1989) and the Catholic Theological Society of America (2007–2008). She was a member of the Toronto Archdiocesan Ecumenical Commission (1988–2012). She was a board member of the Collegeville Institute for Ecumenical and Cultural Research (1990–2012). She served as the anglophone theological advisor to the delegation from the Canadian Conference of Catholic Bishops at the World Synod of Bishops (2001).

Perhaps most importantly, however, Margaret served on five official national or international dialogues between the Roman Catholic Church and other churches: the Anglican–Roman Catholic Dialogue of Canada (1976–1993), the Disciples of Christ–Roman Catholic International Commission for Dialogue (1983–2012), the U.S. Lutheran–Roman Catholic Dialogue (1994–2012), the Lutheran–Roman Catholic International Commission on Unity (1995–2007), and the Evangelical–Roman Catholic Dialogue of Canada (2008–2012). She was also a long-time member of Bridgefolk, a North American organization for dialogue between Roman Catholics and Mennonites (2002–2012).[6]

3. This Book: Its Aim and Structure

In 1998 Margaret published *The Ecumenical Gift Exchange*, a collection of ten of her papers on ecumenical themes.[7] She envisioned *No Turning Back: The Future of Ecumenism* as a sequel. She intended it, like the earlier book, for all Christians who take seriously Jesus' prayer "that all may be one" (John 17). More precisely, the purpose of this work, like that of the previous one, would be threefold. It would illustrate the broad lines of ecumenism for general readers; it would share certain concrete details of recent ecumenical developments with specialist readers; and it would encourage both groups of readers in their commitment to the pursuit of full communion among the Christian churches. Margaret had selected most of the papers she wished

---

[6] Obviously Margaret often served on more than one dialogue at the same time, and her work in one would commonly both facilitate and enrich her contributions to the others. Nonetheless, her cumulative service of eighty-nine dialogue years is unusual, even within the ranks of dedicated ecumenical theologians.

[7] Margaret O'Gara, *The Ecumenical Gift Exchange* (Collegeville, MN: Liturgical Press, 1998).

to include and had begun editing them for a unified collection, but her illness forced her to set the project aside. The present volume completes that project in line with her intentions.

The volume contains seventeen papers that collectively span the years from 1996 to 2012, plus a complete list of Margaret's publications.[8] Ten of the papers have already appeared in print, while seven are published here for the first time. Sixteen papers are divided into two groups of eight each, with their order in each group being roughly chronological; one stands as the collection's epilogue.

The first group of papers is presented here as *introducing* the ecumenical perspective to general readers, such as students of religious studies or theology and reflective members of the broader Christian community. The papers of this group are relatively short and accessible, deal with familiar topics, and typically originated as popular talks. They indicate something of the basic rationale and motivating spirit of the ecumenical enterprise, the wide variety of occasions and topics on which ecumenists may be invited to offer observations and recommendations, and the personal traits required for ecumenical work and the personal changes nurtured by it.

The second group is presented as potentially *deepening* the perspective of ecumenical specialists, whether academic or ecclesiastical. The papers of this group are longer and more demanding, deal with somewhat technical subjects, and often originated as scholarly lectures. They manifest the painstaking research and careful argumentation that characterize ecumenical scholarship, and they communicate recent results of just such scholarship on certain of Margaret's favorite themes, including the exercise of teaching authority in Christ's church, the ecclesial character of infallibility, the theology and practice of ordained ministry, and concrete strategies for fostering ecumenical progress.

Of course, both groups of papers will be of interest to some generalist readers and some specialist ones. Taken collectively, they illuminate various facets of Margaret's work as a Roman Catholic ecumenical theologian. They show the diverse ecclesial communities with which she was in dialogue, especially Anglicans, Disciples of Christ, Evangelicals, Lutherans, and Mennonites. They suggest the

---

[8] For Margaret's *curriculum vitae* and additional information about her, visit http://stmikes.utoronto.ca/theology/margaret-ogara/default.asp.

xxii *No Turning Back*

broad range of tasks she performed, including historical and theoretical research, writing, dialoguing, teaching, advising, public lecturing, and preaching. They highlight the intrinsically collaborative character of ecumenical endeavor. And they illustrate how Margaret's lifetime of ecumenical labor was in effect a contribution to the broader project of "harvesting the fruits" that is outlined by Cardinal Walter Kasper, former head of the Pontifical Council for Promoting Christian Unity: interpreting the ecumenical work that has already been done, showing why it must be carried forward, and cultivating that forward movement.[9]

Finally, two features of the book's text deserve explanation. First, in any group of papers that a given writer composed for different audiences, certain key ideas are apt to appear more than once. Moreover, the words, images, and anecdotes employed to express those ideas in different papers may be similar or occasionally even identical. Such is the case with the papers gathered for this collection. Since eliminating such repetitions editorially would usually damage the integrity of individual papers, most of the repetitions have been allowed to remain.

Second, given the special importance of the word "church" in a book about ecumenism, a remark is in order about capitalization practices for that word here. Except for direct quotations (which exactly reproduce the original), the word is *capitalized* when it refers to a specific denomination as a whole (e.g., "the Roman Catholic Church," "the Evangelical Lutheran Church in America") or when it is part of an official name or title (e.g., "the wedding took place at St. Mark's Church"). In most other cases the word is *not capitalized*. In particular, it is lowercase in reference to the whole body of Christians, worldwide or throughout time (e.g., "We pray for the church throughout the world"), the Christian faith (e.g., "She returned to the church when she had children"), or the body of Christians constituting one congregation or living in any particular place (e.g., "She always belonged to this church," "Paul was eager to visit the church at Ephesus").[10]

---

[9] Walter Kasper, *Harvesting the Fruits: Aspects of Christian Faith in Ecumenical Dialogue* (London and New York: Continuum, 2009).

[10] This paragraph, including its examples, draws heavily on the *Liturgical Press Style Guide*, 7th ed. (Collegeville, MN: Liturgical Press, 2008).

4. Expressions of Gratitude

It is my happy task to conclude this introduction with several expressions of gratitude.

First, I thank the following journals and other copyright holders for permission to use material that previously appeared in the form indicated by the introductory notes to the respective chapters: *Benedictine Bridge*, for chapter 3; *Bondings*, for chapter 5; *Canon Law Society of America Proceedings*, for chapter 10; *Catholic Theological Society of America Proceedings*, for chapters 11 and 16; *Commonweal*, for chapter 7; *Ecumenism*, for chapter 2; *The Jurist*, for chapter 9; *Origins*, for chapter 16; the United States Conference of Catholic Bishops, for chapter 14; and University Press of America, for chapter 6.

Second, I warmly thank Hans Christoffersen and his colleagues at Liturgical Press for their enthusiasm about this project from the very beginning, and for their discerning guidance and friendly support at every step along the way.

Third, I convey my heartfelt appreciation to Dr. Daniel Monsour, erstwhile member of the editorial staff at the Lonergan Research Institute at Regis College, Toronto. By his meticulous reading of the manuscript and his indefatigable checking, updating, and supplementing its many references, Danny has made a capital contribution to the resulting volume's technical quality.

Fourth, I offer my profound gratitude to Bishop Richard Sklba and Professor David Thompson for their insightful, generous, and beautifully wrought forewords, and for the long collegial friendships with Margaret that their words reflect.

Fifth, I gratefully and fondly remember Brother Jeffrey Gros, who among his many ecumenical contributions served for fourteen years as an ecumenical officer for the U. S. Conference of Catholic Bishops. In May 2013 I sought Jeff's candid opinion on the potential value of Margaret's project and whether I should try to bring it to completion. He responded immediately with strong encouragement and astute advice. He also volunteered further assistance on particular issues—an especially (but typically) generous offer, since he was suffering from terminal cancer. We had additional exchanges during the following weeks, and his last message to me, a ten-point reply to a short question, was written less than three weeks before his death in August 2013. The publication of this volume owes a great deal to him.

Finally and most centrally, in my dual role as her academic colleague and—for thirty-six years, three months, and twenty-three days—her providentially graced husband, with unique gratitude and affection I remember Margaret O'Gara, the light of my life.

Michael Vertin
Professor Emeritus, Philosophy, Study of Religion, Theology
St. Michael's College, University of Toronto
February 1, 2014

Abbreviations

AC   Lutheran–Roman Catholic Commission on Unity, and Pontifical Council for Promoting Christian Unity. *The Apostolicity of the Church: Study Document of the Lutheran–Roman Catholic Commission on Unity [of] The Lutheran World Federation [and] Pontifical Council for Promoting Christian Unity.* Minneapolis, MN: Lutheran University Press, 2006.

CCC   Disciples of Christ–Roman Catholic International Commission for Dialogue. "The Church as Communion in Christ: Report of the Disciples of Christ/Roman Catholic International Commission for Dialogue." In Jeffrey Gros et al., eds. *Growth in Agreement II: Report and Agreed Statements of Ecumenical Conversations on a World Level, 1982–1998.* Geneva: WCC Publications; Grand Rapids: Eerdmans, 2000, 386–98.

CCM   Evangelical Lutheran Church in America, Churchwide Assembly. *Called to Common Mission: A Lutheran Proposal for a Revision of the Concordat of Agreement.* Chicago: Evangelical Lutheran Church in America, 1999.

CTP   Willard Roth and Gerald W. Schlabach, eds. *Called Together to Be Peacemakers: Report of the International Dialogue between the Catholic Church and Mennonite World Conference, 1998–2003,* abridged edition. Kitchener, ON: Pandora Press, 2005.

DS   Henricus Denzinger and Adolfus Schönmetzer. *Enchiridion Symbolorum: definitionum et declarationum de rebus fidei et morum,* 32nd ed. Freiburg: Herder, 1963. The translation used is from Karl Rahner, ed., *The Teaching of the Catholic Church.* Translated into English from German by Geoffrey Stevens. Staten Island, NY: Alba House, 1967.

Mansi   J. D. Mansi. *Sacrorum conciliorum nova et amplissima collectio* . . . Florence: Expensis Antonii Zatta Veneti, 1759–1798. Reprint and continuation Paris and Leipzig: Welter, 1901–1927.

NR   Anglican–Lutheran International Continuation Committee. *The Niagara Report: Report of the Anglican–Lutheran Consultation on Episcope, Niagara Falls, September 1987.* London: Published for the Anglican Consultative Council and the Lutheran World Federation [by] Church House Publishing, 1988.

PCS   Conversations between the British and Irish Anglican Churches and the Nordic and Baltic Lutheran Churches. *The Porvoo Common Statement* (1992). London: Council for Christian Unity of the General Synod of the Church of England, 1993.

RHF   Disciples of Christ–Roman Catholic International Commission for Dialogue. "Receiving and Handing on the Faith: the Mission and Responsibility of the Church (1993–2002)." In *Mid-Stream* 41/4 (October 2002): 51–79.

Part One

Introducing
the
Ecumenical Perspective

1

The Catholic Church in the World Today[1]

I am delighted to be at this conference and to learn about the Mennonite tradition and grasp more deeply what gifts Catholics and Mennonites can offer and receive from one another. I was asked to say something about the strengths and weaknesses of my church in the world today. So let me sketch what I see as one important strength of the Roman Catholic Church and one of its important weaknesses.

1. One Important Strength

Last fall I had a new experience: I served as a theological advisor to the five Canadian bishops who attended the 2001 World Synod of Bishops. The Canadian bishops pride themselves on being consultative. So they invited two theologians to assist their five delegates with advice as they gathered for a month in Rome with some 250 other bishops from around the world to address the topic of this

[1] First presented on July 12, 2002, as "Being a Global Church: Strengths and Challenges," at a Mennonite–Roman Catholic conference on peacemaking and worship, Saint John's Abbey, Collegeville, MN. Posted on www.bridgefolk.net on April 16, 2009.

synod, the ministry of bishops. I was privileged to be one of those two advisors.[2]

The synod was a rich and dramatic example of Roman Catholic solidarity at the international level. And I think it also showed how ecclesial solidarity can encourage and confirm ecclesial commitment to global justice and peace.

For starters, the timing of our stay in Rome turned out to be pretty unusual. The synod began on September 29, 2001, less than three weeks after the 9/11 attack on the World Trade Center in New York. It got under way with a beautiful celebration of the eucharist in St. Peter's Basilica. A week later, in response to 9/11, the United States and its allies attacked the Taliban and al-Qaeda forces in Afghanistan. So the remaining weeks of the synod coincided with the onset of the Afghanistan war.

While the first half of the synod was devoted to individual presentations by the delegates, the second half was spent in workshops and discussions. Especially striking to me were the small-group discussions, where ten or twelve bishops from all over the world sat together and talked about what it means to be a bishop. For the bishops, these discussions were remarkable experiences of solidarity. They not only shared ideas for addressing their common challenges, but they also supported one another in facing the differing challenges the international hostilities presented to different bishops.[3]

You may remember how at the start of the war in Afghanistan it seemed that many nations might become involved, and all were being asked to choose: you're either with the United States or against it. Here were these bishops, all in one church, celebrating the eucharist together each day but simultaneously realizing that their countries could soon

---

[2] The other adviser was Father Gilles Routhier, Professor of Theology at Laval University, Quebec City. For the five delegates' report on the synod to the church in Canada, see http://www.cccb.ca/site/Files/CdnSynod.html.

[3] In an e-mail message to me on November 26, 2013, Father Routhier sketched just how the two theological advisors followed the synod's events. Although they were not present at the bishops' individual presentations, workshops, or discussions, each day they received a summary of the interventions that had been made. They analyzed each summary and entered the results into an electronic database; thus they were readily able to see which topics were receiving the most attention. This information was filled out at their daily midday meal with the five Canadian bishops, who would share their sense of the meaning and direction of the events. Finally, the two advisors often would join the bishops at an evening reception, to assist them as they formed their judgments on the topics under discussion. (Ed.)

be at war with each other. The countries of some bishops were threatening to attack the cities where other bishops might be preaching to their congregations, to bomb the people that others might be baptizing. In the middle of the synod, Cardinal Edward Egan of New York went home for a time to take part in a service honoring the victims of the World Trade Center attack. Shortly afterward, Bishop Anthony Lobo of Islamabad, Pakistan, left permanently to be with the people of his diocese, people whom he feared might be killed by random bombs or as the result of military mistakes in nearby Afghanistan.

The situation in which the bishops found themselves was absurd, but they confronted it in sacramentally based solidarity with one another. They felt themselves strongly compelled to denounce the terrorist acts of 9/11, and they did so. After expressing sympathy for the victims and their families, they continued: "We absolutely condemn terrorism, which nothing can justify."[4] But they also recognized that terrorism often stems from gross injustice and the hopelessness it fosters. So they spoke out as well against extreme poverty and the social structures of poverty in which the rich nations are complicit. "Some endemic evils, when they are too long ignored, can produce despair in entire populations."[5] In short, the bishops asserted what has become a classic Catholic teaching in our time: "To achieve peace, work for justice."

I think these developments during the synod illustrate a Roman Catholic strength: the tendency of sacramentally based solidarity to encourage and confirm an ecclesial commitment to justice and peace for the entire world.

2. One Important Weakness

My example of a weakness in the Roman Catholic tradition shows itself in something we've heard a lot about during the past few years: the sexual abuse crisis. Perhaps it's not so surprising that some clergy have sinned, although victimization of children is especially lamentable. What's more surprising is how those sins have been handled by

---

[4] Message of the Tenth Ordinary General Assembly of the Synod of Bishops (26 October 2001): http://www.vatican.va/news_services/press/sinodo/documents/bollettino_20_x-ordinaria-2001/02_inglese/b29_02.html, n. 9.

[5] Ibid., n. 11; cf. n. 10.

church authorities. I think this crisis illustrates a serious problem in the Roman Catholic tradition: the lack of episcopal accountability.

First of all, the bishops are not properly accountable to their own local church. Christopher Ruddy speaks about the lack of synodality, i.e., the lack of relationship within and among the local churches, which contributes to the sense that the bishop cannot really be called to account by members of the laity in his own diocese.[6] Of course, laypeople certainly ought to be involved in accountability today, but the structures of accountability that should already have been in place were lacking. Also lacking is accountability of the bishops to one another. The Vatican sometimes makes such mutual accountability— which Catholics have discussed under the term "collegiality"—more difficult. In fact, the Vatican often isolates the bishops from one another so that they are left to operate as lone rangers. And this in turn has sometimes led the bishops, as they've responded to the sexual abuse situation, to go from one extreme to the other, from laxity to harshness.

People often say the Roman Catholic Church has too many structures, but in some respects just the opposite is true. We need more or at least better structures of episcopal accountability, and I think that has been shown somewhat dramatically in this sad crisis. Although we Roman Catholics commit ourselves to global justice, this structural deficiency can prevent us from serving justice within our own church, thus putting us in a position of self-contradiction.

Here is one place where Roman Catholics have something to learn from the Mennonite tradition. Mennonites have long envisioned ecclesial responsibility, including mutual accountability, as a duty that is shared by everyone in the church. We could profit greatly from their example.

I have sketched an important strength of the Roman Catholic Church in the world and also an important weakness. And I have indicated a Mennonite strength that I suggest could serve to correct that Catholic weakness. This brief account illustrates my conviction that we Roman Catholics have gifts to offer and gifts to receive in our encounter with the Mennonite tradition.

---

[6] Christopher Ruddy, "The American Church's Sexual Abuse Crisis," *America* 186 (June 3, 2002): 9–10.

2

Ecumenical Dialogue in Canada Today[1]

What is the situation of ecumenical dialogue in Canada today? I want to draw attention to three points that help answer this question. Each illuminates the texture of church life in Canada and helps us understand why ecumenical dialogue is given a positive reception here.

1. Teaching and Learning Together

While Pope John Paul II in *Ut Unum Sint* underlines the importance of common prayer and common justice work for the church's unity, Canada adds to these the widespread experience of teaching and learning theology together. In Canada many (though not all) theological students from different Christian churches study their theology with one another in the same classrooms. In Toronto, for example, although students register in any one of eleven theological faculties that are rooted in diverse church traditions, they are able to pursue together their studies in scripture, church history, systematic theology, spirituality, ethics, preaching, and pastoral care. This common study

---

[1] First presented on April 4, 2003, at a conference on ecumenism in Canada entitled "Our Pilgrimage towards Christian Unity," Laval University, Quebec City, Canada. Previously published in *Ecumenism* 152 (December 2003): 30–32.

is a wonderful seedbed for ecumenical reception. I recall a course I taught on grace in which there were students from seven church traditions together in my classroom. Lutheran, Baptist, Presbyterian, Mennonite, Roman Catholic, Anglican, and United Church of Canada: together we studied the Bible and Augustine on grace, the Eastern fathers, Aquinas, Luther, and contemporary ecumenical efforts to overcome divisions about the doctrine of justification. By studying together these historical and contemporary positions on grace, students from different churches were able to enter into what Pope John Paul II calls the "purification of past memories," reexamining together "their painful past," acknowledging the "mistakes made," and seeking a "calm, clear-sighted and truthful vision of things."[2] This helps reproduce the experience of ongoing exchange familiar to ecumenical dialogue groups as they advance in mutual understanding. By studying their theology together, students of different churches are ready to receive the fruits of ecumenical dialogue—indeed, they may contribute to those fruits.

Of course, studying together is not always an experience of calm. Just this week, in my course on the Trinity, the Evangelical and Roman Catholic students were arguing passionately with one another about their respective positions on the salvation of non-Christians. But at least they were in dialogue, thereby overcoming as well what John Paul II calls "misunderstandings and prejudices" about each other that they may have inherited from the past.[3] When we consider that thousands of ordained and other pastoral leaders of our churches in Canada have received their theological education in this way we can see positive long-term implications for ecumenism in this country.

Many theology professors from different Christian communions also have the experience of teaching together in Canada. Teaching together as colleagues helps nurture a spontaneous mutual recognition of each other's faithfulness to Christian tradition. Such spontaneous recognition lays the foundation for a more formal mutual recognition of teachings, sacraments, and ministries in the future, such as that now enjoyed by the Anglican and Lutheran churches in Canada.

---

[2] John Paul II, encyclical, *Ut Unum Sint*, *Origins* 25 (1995–96): 49, 51–72; see n. 2. Also available at: http://www.vatican.va/holy_father/john_paul_ii/encyclicals /documents/hf_jp-ii_enc_25051995_ut-unum-sint_en.html.

[3] Ibid.

2. A Variety of Cultures

Canada is home to people of many cultures. Cherishing always its two founding cultures of French and English, Canada now also includes large numbers of immigrants from many countries. In Toronto this semester, my course of seven students studying Karl Rahner included people from three continents. In my Roman Catholic parish in Toronto the majority of my fellow parishioners are immigrants from the Philippines, Jamaica, and Sri Lanka. This means that the eucharist is celebrated in English and in Tamil, devotional practices honoring Mary play a major role in the lives of some parishioners, and liturgical music is heavily influenced by calypso. The variety of cultures is a fact of life in Canada, celebrated and encouraged by formal and informal structures and deeply affecting all the churches. This means that Christian churches in Canada are also multicultural experiences, filled with the diversity of spiritualities and practices rooted in many countries.

Jean-Marie Tillard, the Canadian theologian who played such an important role in ecumenical dialogue, has noted the relationship between ecumenism and the diversity of cultures. Both underline the diversity within the unity of the church: both point to the nature of catholicity. Besides theological pluralism, Tillard noted, "there is at a more fundamental level a pluralism of cultures, contexts and practical options in the Catholicity of the Church."[4] The variety of expressions of Christian life within one church tradition, even within one parish, helps Canadian Christians recognize that unity is not uniformity, and it prepares them to recognize the diversity of Christian expressions that come from other churches as well. Multicultural experiences within one church nurture the recognition of ecumenically diverse expressions from many churches.

Pope John Paul II discusses the richness of the many gifts the Eastern Christian traditions have offered the church. But too often, he notes, "the other's diversity was no longer perceived as a common treasure, but as incompatibility."[5] Because Canadian Christians regularly

---

[4] J.-M. R. Tillard, "Theological Pluralism and the Mystery of the Church," in *Different Theologies, Common Responsibility: Babel or Pentecost?*, ed. Claude Geffré, Gustavo Gutiérrez, and Virgil Elizondo, *Concilium* 171 (Edinburgh: T & T Clark, 1984): 62–73, at 67.

[5] John Paul II, apostolic letter *Orientale Lumen*, n. 18. See http://www.vatican.va /holy_father/john_paul_ii/apost_letters/1995/documents/hf_jp-ii_apl_19950502 _orientale-lumen_en.html.

experience the treasure of diversity they are more ready to recognize that the diversity of other Christian traditions could also be not incompatibility, but treasure to share.

3. A Collegial Conference of Bishops

Last, a word about episcopal leadership in my own church communion, the Roman Catholic Church in Canada. The Canadian Conference of Catholic Bishops (CCCB) strongly emphasizes a collaborative and collegial working style. This working style is found appealing by Christians of other church traditions in Canada, especially those with an emphasis on strong lay participation. It allows the Roman Catholic Church in Canada to model a form of leadership that is recognizably open to future forms of closer unity with other church communions.

The CCCB regularly draws on the expertise of lay leaders, members of religious orders, and theologians, many of whom are given major responsibility for leadership and decision-making in the offices of the conference. Although the Roman Catholic Church does not ordain women, its delegations and consultant groups in ecumenical and interchurch work frequently include as many women as those of most other churches, sometimes even more. Among the bishops themselves, collegial consultation is emphasized. When the CCCB sends delegates to meetings of the worldwide Synod of Bishops the delegates are asked to represent the views of the whole conference, not just to speak for themselves. Considerable time and effort are invested to ensure that the views of the synod delegates reflect the priorities of the entire conference. In fact, for the Synod of October 2001 the conference requested that the major focus of the interventions be collegiality, the episcopal conferences, and inculturation.[6] This emphasis on collaboration and collegiality by the Canadian bishops helps pave the way for a new praxis of teaching authority by churches in Canada.

---

[6] For a report on the synod to the church in Canada by the Canadian delegates, see http://www.cccb.ca/site/Files/CdnSynod.html.

Making Peace for Peacemaking[1]

Last year marked the publication of an historic agreement between two church communions that have been deeply estranged ever since the Protestant Reformation. Mennonites and Roman Catholics clashed in the sixteenth century, but 450 years later they have announced their common vocation to peacemaking.

In a surprising and carefully written report, members of the International Dialogue between the Catholic Church and the Mennonite World Conference testify that they are *Called Together to Be Peacemakers.*[2]

The writers readily acknowledge the historic significance of their statement, noting that rupture and separation began the relationship—or lack of relationship—between Roman Catholics and

---

[1] First presented in August 2004 at a meeting of Bridgefolk, a North American organization for dialogue between Mennonites and Roman Catholics, Saint John's Abbey, Collegeville, MN. Previously published in *Benedictine Bridge*, newsletter of Holy Wisdom Monastery, Middleton, WI, 17 (Ordinary Time 2005): 6–9.

[2] Willard Roth and Gerald W. Schlabach, eds., *Called Together to Be Peacemakers: Report of the International Dialogue between the Catholic Church and Mennonite World Conference, 1998–2003*, abridged ed. (Kitchener, ON: Pandora Press, 2005). Also at http://www.vatican.va/roman_curia/pontifical_councils/chrstuni/mennonite -conference-docs/rc_pc_chrstuni_doc_20110324_mennonite_en.html. Subsequent references to this document occur intratextually with the abbreviation "CTP" followed by the section number.

Mennonites in the sixteenth century. Mennonites are raised with the painful memory of many of their forebears who were martyred by Catholics in league with sixteenth-century governments. "Since then, from the sixteenth century to the present, theological polemics have persistently nourished negative images and narrow stereotypes of each other," they acknowledge (CTP 193). So the very fact of an agreement is a significant accomplishment.

The agreed statement is not grudging or minimal. On the contrary, it probes carefully into early Christian history and the Reformation era as well as discussing the church, the sacraments, and the approach of each church communion to peace and violence. The writers are frank in signaling areas of unresolved differences or disagreements, but they also indicate a striking number of agreements—many probably for the first time in a Roman Catholic–Mennonite conversation.

Four areas of convergence are especially striking.

First, the writers reread certain periods of church history together in an atmosphere of openness that participants say has been "invaluable." Openness allowed a broader view of Christian history and counteracted the loss of perspective resulting from centuries of separation. Participants write: "Our common re-reading of the history of the church will hopefully contribute to the development of a common interpretation of the past. This can lead to a shared new memory and understanding. In turn, a shared new memory can free us from the prison of the past" (CTP 27).

Participants explain that memories must be purified before they can be healed. "This involves facing those difficult events of the past that give rise to divergent interpretations of what happened and why," they explain (CTP 192). So the agreement sets out to examine the situation of Western Europe on the eve of the Reformation. Emphasizing the complexity of this period, it notes that "church life and piety were flourishing" (CTP 34), with an abundance of good preaching, vernacular translations of the Bible, lay religious movements, and movements of reform. The facts about the rupture between Anabaptists (the forebears of Mennonites) and Roman Catholics are reviewed and different images of each other are acknowledged. While "Catholics never suffered any persecution at the hands of the Mennonites" (CTP 48), they have known persecution, says the statement. But Mennonites are unique, since they were persecuted but did not persecute any group. "The danger of persecution and martyrdom became a part of the Mennonite identity," the statement recognizes (CTP 47).

The statement also studies the way Roman Catholics and Mennonites think about two earlier periods in church history: the Constantinian era and the medieval period. Because Roman Catholics and Mennonites have different views of these earlier periods, those views affect the self-understanding of each church communion and its view of the other.

A second part of the agreed statement is its discussion of ordinances and sacraments. While Mennonites speak of "ordinances" and Roman Catholics of "sacraments," the Mennonite description of the way ordinances are understood to work sounds very familiar to Roman Catholic ears accustomed to sacramental talk. In particular, the statement is creative in emphasizing that Mennonites experience ordinances not only as signs, but as effective signs. The statement observes, "Mennonite confessional statements as well as centuries of practice suggest that baptism is understood not only as a sign that points beyond the baptismal ritual to its historical and spiritual significance, but that in and through baptism the individual and the community of faith undergo effectual change" (CTP 123). Mennonite confessional documents reveal "the expectation of *transformation*" through participation in baptism (CTP 123). Again, while emphasizing that Mennonites understand their celebration of the Lord's Supper as "a memorial and a sign," the statement notes, "Mennonite confessions of faith do not dismiss the effectual power of the ordinance to bring change to the participants and to the community of faith" (CTP 126). Roman Catholics can feel quite at home with all this talk about the "effects" of baptism and eucharist, a point often emphasized in Catholic sacramental theology.

Third, I think the presentation of the Roman Catholic position on peace will find a particular welcome among Mennonites, for whom nonresistance to violence has played an identity-shaping role. The statement presents recent Roman Catholic teaching on war and peace in quite an exciting way. It uses a broad perspective to describe Catholic teaching, discussing the social vision of the church, religious freedom, peacemaking, and the call of all Christians to holiness. Within the discussion of peacemaking, the statement notes the new attitude in Catholic discussions of peace and war, arguing that the Catholic tradition "has increasingly endorsed the superiority of non-violent means and is suspect of the use of force in a culture of death" (CTP 157). Even in the Catholic teaching about just war, the "criteria have grown more stringent in recent years, insisting that the function of the Just War Tradition is to prevent and limit war, not just legitimate it" (CTP 158). It continues, "The Just War today should be understood as part of a broad Catholic theology of peace applicable only to exceptional cases" (CTP 159).

In both of these last two cases—sacraments/ordinances and the issue of peace and war—I see fruits of the dialogue. One tradition has pushed the other to recover aspects of itself that had been neglected or underdeveloped. This is truly the "exchange of gifts" that Pope John Paul II had called for in his encyclical on ecumenism, *Ut Unum Sint*.[3]

Fourth, the statement ends in a spirit of repentance where each church communion asks forgiveness for sins and failings of their community toward the other. The Roman Catholic writers made a wise choice, I think, by not speaking alone but echoing the official apologies of the whole Roman Catholic Church made on the Day of Pardon at the time of the millennium. During those prayers Pope John Paul II led Roman Catholics in confessing sins committed in the service of truth where Christians have used methods "not in keeping with the Gospel" (CTP 201) to defend the truth, and "sins which have rent the unity of the body of Christ" (CTP 200). The Roman Catholic dialogue members echo the Pope's words from that service of repentance: "Have mercy on your sinful children and accept our resolve to seek and promote truth in the gentleness of charity, in the firm knowledge that truth can prevail only in virtue of truth itself" (CTP 201). Mennonites, for their part, confess that they "have frequently failed to demonstrate love towards Catholics" and have "thoughtlessly perpetuated hostile images and false stereotypes of Catholics and of the Catholic Church" (CTP 204).

Finally, there is one area where I would suggest that the Roman Catholic writers could have gone further in probing and presenting their own position. While Roman Catholic teaching on the relationship between Scripture and tradition is correctly presented, its

---

[3] John Paul II, encyclical *Ut Unum Sint*, *Origins* 25 (1995–96): 49, 51–72; see n. 28. Also at http://www.vatican.va/holy_father/john_paul_ii/encyclicals/documents/hf_jp-ii_enc_25051995_ut-unum-sint_en.html.

implications are not fully drawn. Roman Catholics agree with Mennonites that the Scriptures are the highest authority for the faith and life of the church. But Roman Catholics add that tradition is indispensable for the interpretation of the Scriptures, while Mennonites say that the church needs "to test and correct its doctrine and practice in the light of Scripture itself." Mennonites hold that "[t]radition is valued, yet it can be altered or even reversed, since it is subject to the critique of Scripture" (CTP 103).

But the suggestion of a contrast here is somewhat misleading. In fact, there are different levels or kinds of tradition within Roman Catholic life and teaching. Roman Catholics also test their teaching by the light of Scripture. The agreement itself mentions examples in the Roman Catholic tradition where teachings are being altered or reversed. On nonviolence and the just war theory, for example, Roman Catholic tradition shows significant signs of alteration or—I would say—growth, and on religious liberty Vatican II reversed an earlier Catholic position. The apologies made by John Paul II for a variety of earlier positions and actions by Roman Catholics demonstrate the possibility of some kinds of change within the Catholic tradition.

On the other hand, Roman Catholics believe that central teachings like the divinity and humanity of Christ are not changeable, although their formulation could be altered as the church enters different times and cultures. Such central teachings are a defense and translation of the biblical faith, not really an addition to the same faith that both Catholics and Mennonites believe is tested by Scripture.

The agreed statement missed an opportunity to clarify how Roman Catholics distinguish between changeable and unchangeable teachings. Such a clarification would have actually shown the fuller implications of the agreement itself, which explores such distinctions without naming them.

This just shows that the dialogue has not ended; in fact, it has barely begun. Yet this first step shows real promise for the future. As Mennonites and Roman Catholics start to make peace between themselves, they take a step toward becoming peacemakers together.

4

Christ's Church Local and Global[1]

When I participate in a baptism in my Roman Catholic parish in Toronto I have a familiar experience of the reality we are talking about today: Christ's church local and global. As I sing and celebrate with the family and friends of the newly baptized I welcome another Christian into the local church of the Archdiocese of Toronto with which I am in communion. At the same time I feel myself linked to the whole church throughout the world. At this baptism I am now welcoming another sister or brother into this local church, and through this local church to be joined with all of the baptized in the church spread throughout the world, reaching backward to the time of Christ and forward to the final fulfillment of all things.

This example allows me to begin by noting two things. First, Roman Catholics recognize themselves to be in real though not full communion with all those sharing the same faith and baptism in the one church of Christ. Vatican II taught that the discord and disunity within this one church of Christ "openly contradicts the will of Christ, provides a stumbling block to the world, and inflicts damage on the most holy cause of proclaiming the good news to every creature."[2]

---

[1] First given on April 17, 2007, as a panel presentation at the National Workshop on Christian Unity, Chicago, IL. Not previously published.

[2] Vatican II, *Unitatis Redintegratio* (Decree on Ecumenism), n. 1. Also at http://www.vatican.va/archive/hist_councils/ii_vatican_council/documents/vat-ii_decree_19641121_unitatis-redintegratio_en.html.

While I share mutual recognition of the baptism in my home parish with all the other Christian churches, I cannot yet partake of the eucharist together with them, and so the catholicity of the whole church is damaged.

Second, what is the relationship between the local church and the global church in Catholic self-understanding? The Catholic Church understands the one church as a communion of communions. The U.S. Methodist–Roman Catholic Dialogue describes Catholic teaching in this way: "Though no one by itself exhausts the fullness of Christ's church, when understood in their interconnectedness the entire church is present in the local church."[3] The Congregation for the Doctrine of the Faith explains that the whole church is "*in and formed out of the Churches*"; the local churches are "*in and formed out of the* [whole] *Church*."[4] And neither the whole church nor the local church has a priority; neither comes first. This point emerged more clearly after the long and polite debate between Walter Kasper and Joseph Ratzinger a few years ago about whether the local or the global church has ontological priority. At the end of their debate they agreed that the local church and what they called the "universal church" are simultaneous; they are "incorporated into and interpenetrate one another," as Kasper summarizes the agreements.[5]

Now I want to explore some recent developments in Catholic thought about the relationship of the local church and the whole church. The Second Vatican Council wished to recover the patristic emphasis on the local churches that make up the one church of Christ, and so it emphasized the local churches in their diversity, pastored by bishops who together exercise their oversight of the flock in a

---

[3] United Methodist Church (U.S.) and United States Conference of Catholic Bishops, *Through Divine Love: The Church in Each Place and All Places* (S.I.: United Methodist-Catholic Dialogue, 2006), n. 60. See http://www.usccb.org/beliefs-and-teachings/ecumenical-and-interreligious/ecumenical/methodist/upload/Through-Divine-Love-the-Church-in-Each-Place-and-All-Places.pdf.

[4] Congregation for the Doctrine of the Faith, *Communionis Notio: Letter to the Bishops of the Catholic Church on Some Aspects of the Church Understood as Communion*, n. 9. See http://www.vatican.va/roman_curia/congregations/cfaith/documents/rc_con_cfaith_doc_28051992_communionis-notio_en.html.

[5] Walter Kasper, "Letter in Final Response to Cardinal Ratzinger's Position on the Relation between the Local and Universal Church, Written at Editors' Invitation," *America* 185 (November 26, 2001): 28.

collegial way together with the bishop of Rome. Of course we know that the emphasis at Vatican II on episcopal collegiality was a reforming emphasis, an emphasis intended to counter an overly centralized exercise of authority by the pope that had grown stronger since the time of the Reformation. But it is one thing to teach about collegiality; it is quite another thing to implement this teaching. Orthodox theologian John Garvey comments that "[c]ollegiality was a principle, but not really a practice"[6] in the Roman Catholic Church. At the 2001 World Synod of Bishops, where I served as one of two theological advisors to the five delegated Canadian bishops, this was the most frequently discussed issue of the entire meeting. Bishops from every continent expressed frustration and concern that collegiality was not adequately practiced. If you take collegiality as a test of the local church's health in Roman Catholic practice, you would have to conclude that Roman Catholics seriously need medical attention.

When I listened to the Canadian bishops at the synod I heard their frustration about their own local churches. When people want to know Catholic teaching about something, one bishop complained, they look it up in the Catechism or on the Vatican website: they rarely pay much attention to their bishop. Too often, they said, in practice the local bishop is still seen as a plant manager for the universal church. Others have observed that a bishop often seems more accountable to the pope than to the diocese of which he is pastor and shepherd. While Vatican II took good steps toward recovering an ecclesiology of communion and the importance of the local church, the implementation of these steps still has a long way to go.

In the work of the U.S. Lutheran–Roman Catholic Dialogue that culminated in an agreed statement entitled *The Church as Koinonia of Salvation*, we found an interesting difference of emphasis between Lutherans and Roman Catholics in our thinking and practice—and even our definition—of the local church. Lutherans tend to define the local church as the congregation where the sacraments are celebrated and the Word preached. They have a good theology to describe the reality of this "face-to-face congregation," as we called it, but their theology of the cluster of congregations shepherded by a local bishop was less strong. Of course Lutherans agree, in accord with modern

---

[6] John Garvey, "The New Pope: An Orthodox View," *Commonweal* 132 (May 20, 2005): 7.

ecumenical breakthroughs, about the need for regional *episcope*, and they have recovered the historic episcopate in full communion with the Episcopal Church. But their emphasis on the local congregation leads to an impoverished theology of regional ministry and leads as well to suspicion of Catholic structures of episcopal authority. Catholics, on the other hand, while elaborating a full theology of the local church as a cluster of congregations shepherded by a bishop, very often have no adequate theology of the parish or congregations that make up the diocese.

In our dialogue work we concluded that these two emphases—on the local congregation and on the regional cluster of congregations— should be seen as complementary, in fact as "theologically normative."[7] Indeed, the lack of full catholicity, which would include both of these emphases in a fully developed balance, means that our communities and our ministries are "wounded." The dialogue urges both Catholics and Lutherans to "pray together for the grace of repentance and conversion needed for healing the wounds of our division."[8] The text of the World Council of Churches document *Called to Be One Church* echoes this reflection on woundedness when it says: "Our continuing divisions are real wounds to the body of Christ, and God's mission in the world suffers."[9] And again it says, "apart from one another we are impoverished."[10]

Some of you may feel that the Roman Catholic Church is quick to point out the wounds of other churches—or how they are not churches in the full sense—but rather disinclined to see its own woundedness. It seems to overlook the wounds in itself, where, it continues to teach, the church of Christ subsists. Your suspicions may have been increased this past summer by the publication of a rather strange and obscure

---

[7] Randall Lee and Jeffrey Gros, eds., *The Church as Koinonia of Salvation: Its Structures and Ministries (Lutherans and Catholics in Dialogue, X)* (Washington, DC: United States Conference of Catholic Bishops, 2005), n. 91. Also at http://www.usccb.org/beliefs -and-teachings/ecumenical-and-interreligious/ecumenical/lutheran/koinonia-of -salvation.cfm.

[8] Ibid., n. 105.

[9] World Council of Churches, *Called to Be One Church (as adopted)* (February 23, 2006), n. 1. See http://www.oikoumene.org/en/resources/documents/assembly /2006-porto-alegre/1-statements-documents-adopted/christian-unity-and-message -to-the-churches/called-to-be-the-one-church-as-adopted.

[10] Ibid., n. 7.

set of Responses by the Congregation for the Doctrine of the Faith to some questions about the church. Many both inside and outside the Roman Catholic Church wondered why it had been thought necessary to reiterate some of these negative statements about how Protestant and Anglican Churches cannot be called "churches" in the proper sense, and how the church of Christ subsists in the Catholic Church. But often the discussion within a church family sounds quite different when heard from the inside rather than the outside, and this is a good example of that difference. From inside the Roman Catholic communion, I am persuaded that a major purpose of this strange document—a document obscure and difficult to interpret—was in fact to counter an anti-ecumenical group of Roman Catholic scholars from Germany who opposed dialogue with other churches. This group of scholars argued that the meaning of "subsists" at Vatican II was simply "is," so that the council taught that the Roman Catholic Church is identical with the church of Christ. Furthermore, they criticized Pope John Paul II when he said in his encyclical on ecumenism that the church of Christ is present and effective in Christian communions other than the Catholic Church. Countering this anti-ecumenical viewpoint, the Responses from the Congregation for the Doctrine of the Faith stolidly repeat Vatican II on the elements of sanctification and truth found outside the Roman Catholic Church. And then they add, "It is possible, according to Catholic doctrine, to affirm correctly that the Church of Christ is present and operative in the churches and ecclesial Communities not yet fully in communion with the Catholic Church"[11] because of these elements of sanctification and truth. So the CDF here is actually defending Vatican II and John Paul II in opening the door to a dialogue where our mutual wounds can be acknowledged more fully.

But you could be forgiven if you had not noticed that the CDF document includes a defense of ecumenism. The document is obscure, almost impenetrable in meaning—as though it is written in code. Improving its communication style is a step my church communion should pursue as a means of improving dialogue.

---

[11] Congregation for the Doctrine of the Faith, *Responses to Some Questions Regarding Certain Aspects of the Doctrine on the Church* (June 29, 2007), response to second question. See http://www.doctrinafidei.va/documents/rc_con_cfaith_doc_20070629_responsa -quaestiones_en.html.

While acknowledging our wounds, Roman Catholics also bring gifts to the table of dialogue, and one gift we keep offering to other Christians is the gift of the papacy. Of course not everyone views it this way. My friend and ecumenical colleague, George Vandervelde, who died last year during the Week of Prayer for Christian Unity, used to say that he wasn't so sure he wanted some of the gifts Catholics were offering. But the Anglican-Roman Catholic International Commission titles their last statement on this topic "The Gift of Authority"—envisioning authority as a gift. They also envision the papacy as a gift "to be shared," a gift the Anglican communion should prepare itself to receive, a gift that "could be offered and received even before our churches are in full communion."[12] But the statement also says something else, which I think is very interesting. It says that Roman Catholics should desire not only that such a gift be received, but that they should want to offer this ministry as a gift to the whole church of God.[13] This text suggests that receiving gifts is not the only difficult part of the ecumenical gift exchange. Even offering them suitably can be a challenge.

This reminds me of something that used to happen in my husband's large family. For many years my mother-in-law Kathleen used to offer my father-in-law Joe a gift. It was the same gift, offered over and over again: a sundial. She had prepared and wrapped it nicely, and the first time he opened the gift he said he liked it. But he didn't really want this gift: he never used it, and then he forgot about it. And so the next year she wrapped up the sundial again, and offered it to him, and of course everybody laughed. For at least three or four more years Kathleen would again wrap up the sundial, and Joe would open up the wrapped package, and everyone would laugh and clap.

Of course by this time it had become a joke. But it is an interesting story, I think, because it shows that sometimes a gift needs to be repaired or changed before it is offered. This is what Roman Catholics

---

[12] Anglican-Roman Catholic International Commission/Catholic Truth Society (Great Britain), *The Gift of Authority: Authority in the Church III, An Agreed Statement by the Anglican-Roman Catholic International Commission (ARCIC)* (London: Catholic Truth Society; Toronto, ON: Anglican Book Centre; New York: Church Publishing Incorporated, 1999), n. 60. Also at http://www.vatican.va/roman_curia/pontifical _councils/chrstuni/documents/rc_pc_chrstuni_doc_12051999_gift-of-autority _en.html.

[13] Ibid., n. 62.

know about the papacy: it is a gift for the whole of Christ's church, but first it needs repair. Could the bishop of Rome once more in the future exercise a ministry of unity for the whole church of Christ throughout the world? Could he serve again as shepherd and spokesperson for the whole church? Yes, I believe he could; but to do so his ministry needs repair. The papacy needs to exercise the ministry of unity in the universal church in a more pastoral way, in a less centralized way, in a way that defends the diversity of local churches and their distinctive traditions. Even Pope John Paul II recognized that the papacy needs renewal—"open to a new situation," is how he puts it[14]—and so he asked for the help of all of the churches in repairing this ancient and precious gift. "This is an immense task," he wrote, "which we cannot refuse and which I cannot carry out by myself."[15]

Of course, some Roman Catholics feel they don't want to reform the papacy so it can be shared with others: they want it all for themselves, as a source of their "identity." So we Roman Catholics must learn to want to share the gift of the papacy with others. We must become willing not just to keep wrapping it up and offering it, but first to do the hard work of reforming it. But reforming—repairing—a gift is hard work. It takes imagination, faithfulness, and perseverance. It also takes the help of all Christians, and for this we rely on all the churches.

[14] John Paul II, encyclical *Ut Unum Sint, Origins* 25 (1995–96): 49, 51–72; see n. 95. Also at http://www.vatican.va/holy_father/john_paul_ii/encyclicals/documents /hf_jp-ii_enc_25051995_ut-unum-sint_en.html.
[15] Ibid., n. 96.

5

"Pray without Ceasing"[1]

The theme of this Week of Prayer for Christian Unity is "pray without ceasing" (1 Thess 5:17). Taken from the short letter of Paul to the Thessalonians, this exhortation to pray without ceasing reminds us of the necessity of prayer for the Christian life. Paul wants the church to help the weak, to encourage the fainthearted and admonish idlers, not to repay evil for evil. And in the midst of their rejoicing always and giving thanks everywhere, he reminds his hearers that they must "pray without ceasing." But today this prayer without ceasing is set alongside the great prayer of Jesus for the unity of his followers. Jesus prayed that his followers may all be one: "As you, Father, are in me and I am in you, may they also be one in us, so that the world may believe that you have sent me" (John 17:21). When we pray without ceasing for the unity of the church, our prayer is joined to the prayer of Jesus for the unity of his followers, and we know that his prayer will be effective.

I think Christians have sensed for a long time that prayer is really at the heart of the ecumenical movement. Why is this? When we pray

[1] First presented on January 23, 2008, as the homily at the Toronto School of Theology worship service marking the Week of Prayer for Christian Unity, Toronto, Canada. Previously published with minor modifications in *Bondings*, quarterly newsletter of the Oblates of St. Francis de Sales, Toledo-Detroit Province, 21 (Spring 2008): 6–8.

together without ceasing for the unity of the church, we stop listening to ourselves and we can hear God speaking. I think this was the experience of Paul Wattson, who started the Week of Prayer for Christian Unity one hundred years ago. He prayed, and he learned that God wanted to overcome the divisions that kept Christians apart. And so he began to call members of his church community together to pray for the unity of the church. Paul Wattson heard God speaking. When we pray together without ceasing for the unity of the church, we stop listening to ourselves and we can hear God speaking. This was also the experience of Paul Couturier, who thirty years later heard the prayers of this week and said: "But these all express Roman Catholic ideas! We should find a prayer that all Christians can pray together." Paul Couturier heard God speaking. He heard the Lord say, "For my thoughts are not your thoughts, nor are your ways my ways" (Isa 55:8). And so today, following the insight of Paul Couturier, we pray for the unity of the church as Christ wills, in the time that he wills, by the means that he wills. When we pray together without ceasing for the unity of the church, we hear God speaking.

When we pray together without ceasing for the unity of the church we also hear each other praying. This is really a significant experience, isn't it? Have you ever been having an argument with someone that is interrupted by the bell signaling a scheduled worship service? You may have to stop in the midst of making a really good point, put down your books and papers, set aside your ideas, and find your way together to the chapel. Perhaps you are visiting at this chapel, or perhaps your debate partner is visiting, or perhaps both of you know very well the way to this space. Both of you must page through the hymnal, say the words of confession together, and perhaps line up together to receive the eucharist that binds us into one. Suddenly the earlier debate looks a bit different, doesn't it, as we realize that our opponent in argument is really our brother or sister in Christ and that both of us are asking God to forgive us, to heal us, and to show us the truth. When I pray with my dialogue partners in the search for Christian unity I can never treat my disagreement with them as the last word, because I discover that God has the last word, and it's directed at both of us.

When we pray together without ceasing for the unity of the church we also hear each other praying. Listening to the prayers of others is a bit like listening to other languages, and of course sometimes we begin to learn the language of our ecumenical partners as well—we learn a second language—and the ear of our heart is opened. This has certainly been my rich experience from praying with my ecumenical colleagues. From my Mennonite and Methodist colleagues I have expanded the number and kind of hymns that I love to sing. From my Orthodox colleagues I have learned to love icons and the long chants of Vespers. From my Anglican colleagues I have learned to relish the beauty and rhythm of plainsong and of the spoken word in liturgy. From my United Church of Canada and Pentecostal colleagues I have learned to relax in the tradition of more spontaneous worship. From the Lutherans and Presbyterians I have learned what a good sermon sounds like, and from my Evangelical colleagues I have even learned to give a fair testimonial of what God has been doing in my life this week. When we listen to the prayer of others it slowly becomes our prayer too; it becomes like a second language. It is not that we ever forget how to pray in our mother tongue, which is for me the prayer styles and beautiful rhythms of my own Catholic liturgical tradition. No, it is not that we forget our mother tongue. But, with Charles Wesley, we can sing within ourselves, "Oh, for a thousand tongues to sing my great Redeemer's praise," and we can rejoice in the many other tongues used by Christians all around us.

When we pray together without ceasing for the unity of the church, we get tired. It seems to demand so much perseverance. It seems to go on for so long. How long, O Lord, must we wait for the unity of the church for which you prayed? We want to work together to proclaim the Gospel, to help the weak, to encourage the fainthearted, to admonish idlers, not to repay evil for evil. Haven't we prayed long enough for the unity of the church? A hundred years? A thousand years? What's taking you so long? Can't those other churches see that the traditions of my church and its customs and insights are really the best way, the truest way, to be a Christian? When we pray together without ceasing for the unity of the church, we get tired. We realize that prayer for unity has its delights, but it also has its challenges. Prayer together without ceasing is not always fun: sometimes it is an ascetical discipline, a long Lenten fasting from a shared eucharist and from a shared pooling of all of the richness of our traditions.

When we get tired, we also get tempted. This, too, is an experience of togetherness that Christians know well. The *Princeton Proposal for Christian Unity* says that today many serious Christians are tempted to substitute identity for truth. Rightly turning from a kind of liberal indifference, some Christians are tempted to ask, says the *Princeton Proposal*, "Is it Catholic enough?" "Is it Reformed enough?" "Is it Mennonite enough?" "Does it adequately express the ethos of the United Church?" instead of asking, "Is it true?"[2] We turn our traditions into brand names. I think a focus on identity rather than truth can be a special temptation for our colleges in the Toronto School of Theology, since we are sometimes set in unhealthy competition with each other. We can be tempted to seek our identities alone instead of seeking the truth together. But Jesus reminds us that our unity is needed for the world to believe. In fact, we in the TST colleges are blood relatives of each other, made one by the blood of the cross of Christ. This is the truth to which we witness together, our deepest identity anyway. Let it refresh us when we tire even as it binds us into one.

I have said that when we pray together without ceasing for the unity of the church we hear God speaking. We hear each other praying. We sometimes get tired and even tempted. And finally, when we pray together without ceasing for the unity of the church, we can even hear each other talking when we leave the chapel. Praying together sharpens the ears to hear not just prayers but also theological and exegetical insights. From each other we learn not only styles of prayer; we also learn styles of thought, and we learn to add these different styles to our own.

This happened to George Vandervelde, our colleague and teacher from the Christian Reformed Church who died one year ago this week.[3] In his search for Christian unity George often prayed with Catholics. This led him to decide that the *Heidelberg Catechism*'s statement accusing Catholics of idolatry in their eucharistic teaching and practice was mistaken. His church used this teaching. So for ten years he argued with his church about it. He finally succeeded in persuading the Christian Reformed Church to lift its accusation of idolatry against Catholic eucharistic teaching and practice.

---

[2] See Carl Braaten and Robert W. Jenson, eds., *In One Body through the Cross: The Princeton Proposal for Christian Unity* (Grand Rapids: Eerdmans, 2003), n. 41.

[3] George Vandervelde, professor of theology at the Institute of Christian Studies, Toronto, died on January 19, 2007.

When we pray together without ceasing for the unity of the church we also learn different styles of thought. I remember one dramatic experience of this very clearly. I was drafting a statement of agreement for the international dialogue between the Roman Catholic Church and the Disciples of Christ. Our topic was complex and important. We had spent five days at an ecumenical monastery for men and women. We ate together, talked together, and, repeatedly, prayed together. But now it was late at night, the meeting would end the next day, and we had run into a roadblock. As midnight came and went, our small drafting group of three colleagues sat together in a mood of dismay. We stared at the words of the Roman Catholic position and saw no way to reach agreement or even to formulate our disagreement. My mind seemed drained of thought, numb with effort. Suddenly, gently, my two Disciples colleagues, David and Nadia, began formulating the Roman Catholic position. This was my position, but they said it for me. Accurately and sympathetically, they found for me the right words to express the position of my church communion when I myself could not find them. I remember being astonished at the time, and recognizing that we had actually achieved a common mind on the question. The next day our entire dialogue group came to a major agreement because of our late-night work. We ended our week of dialogue with a service that was filled with joyful song and prayers of praise.

Such a noncompetitive achievement is sustained and made possible when we pray together without ceasing and search for the truth. When we hear God speaking, we begin to hear each other speaking as well. In fact, we begin to hear God speaking through each other: and then we know that we're really praying.

6

Friendship in the Ecumenical Movement: Its Theological Significance[1]

George Vandervelde is a friend of mine. I met him in the same way that I have met many other friends: in an ecumenical discussion. Over many years, through our common pursuit of Christian unity we became colleagues and eventually friends.

Some friendships between ecumenists become well known: Abbé Fernand Portal and Lord Halifax, Rev. Spencer Jones and Fr. Paul Wattson, Fr. Jean-Marie Tillard and Rev. Julian Charley. But anyone involved in ecumenical work for a long time learns about and often shares other friendships that typically develop in the ecumenical context. Do such friendships have more than a sentimental or anecdotal meaning? I believe the answer is surely yes. To honor George Vandervelde on the occasion of his retirement, I want to reflect on the theological significance of friendship in the ecumenical movement.[2]

---

[1] Previously published as "The Theological Significance of Friendship in the Ecumenical Movement," 125–32, in Michael Goheen and Margaret O'Gara, eds., *That the World May Believe: Essays on Mission and Unity in Honour of George Vandervelde* (Lanham, MD: University Press of America, 2006).

[2] George Vandervelde, professor of theology at the Institute of Christian Studies, Toronto, retired in 2004.

I will argue that friendship establishes the proper context of ecumenical dialogue, enhances understanding between the dialogue partners, and nurtures the perseverance necessary for making progress.

1. Establishing the Proper Context

Ecumenical progress is far more likely to occur in an atmosphere of collaboration rather than competition. Achieving agreement on contentious and divisive topics is difficult in any case, but it becomes easier when colleagues enter discussion with a cooperative attitude. Friendship establishes that collaborative atmosphere, that cooperative attitude. Friendship establishes the proper context of ecumenical work.

Although ecumenical dialogues focus on research, the way they approach this research differs from the approach often presupposed in other scholarly undertakings. The success of dialogues depends upon teamwork and personal development. Fruitful ecumenical discussion demands the ability and willingness to listen and cooperate on the part of scholars who hold very diverse viewpoints. It demands common engagement in an intellectual search for theological advances that sometimes seem impossible.

Hence I find that, more than in many other kinds of research, ecumenical research calls into play one's willingness to enter into relationships, to risk vulnerability for the sake of the common effort, and to refuse competition as an acceptable mode of inquiry. Unlike some academic investigations where competition is nurtured and even rewarded, ecumenical investigations move ahead only when competition is eschewed. I often notice this important feature of the ecumenical style when I examine the names at the end of ecumenical agreed statements. Every member of the bilateral commission must agree with every word of a bilateral statement, and all members are listed as the signatories. By refusing to equate scholarship with its competitive forms, ecumenical study serves as a countercultural model within academic circles, recalling scholars to an earlier ideal of being truly a college together.

Ecumenical scholars must collaborate in a further way as well. They must be willing and able to speak for the whole of the communion they represent, rather than simply for themselves as individuals. As a form of intellectual communion, such representation places greater demands upon scholars than does simple advocacy for their own theological opinions. Moreover, by appointing theologians to ecumenical commissions, bishops and other church leaders are in effect asking these theologians for advice that is based upon their careful theological research. Such commissions offer an opportunity for cultivating genuine cooperation between the theological community and the ecclesial teaching authority.

On more occasions than I can remember, deeply collaborative dialogue has led to a common mind among participants who once disagreed or did not even understand each other. I clearly remember one dramatic instance. Near the end of a meeting of the Disciples of Christ–Roman Catholic International Commission for Dialogue, our group's discussions on a proposed agreed statement had run into a roadblock. Late at night the drafters sat together in a mood of dismay, staring at the words of the Roman Catholic position and seeing no way to reach agreement on a key point under discussion. My mind seemed drained of thought, numb with effort. Suddenly, gently, my two Disciples of Christ colleagues—David Thompson and Nadia Lahutsky—began formulating the Roman Catholic position. Accurately and sympathetically, they found for me the right words to express the position of my church communion when I myself could not find them. I remember being astonished at the time and recognizing that we had genuinely achieved a common understanding of the question. Such a noncompetitive achievement would have been impossible without the deep friendship we shared. The next day the entire dialogue group was able to approve the proposed agreed statement because of our late-night work.[3]

2. Enhancing Understanding

Friendship not only establishes the proper context of ecumenical dialogue. It also enhances understanding between the dialogue partners, helping them to grasp one another's positions. Because friends

---

[3] Disciples of Christ–Roman Catholic International Commission for Dialogue, "Receiving and Handing on the Faith: The Mission and Responsibility of the Church (1993–2002)," *Mid-Stream* 41/4 (2002): 51–79.

can listen to each other sympathetically, without hostility or a competitive attitude, they often learn something new from each other. They discover aspects of the other's position that previously they had neglected or distorted. Suddenly they see the other's stance in a new light.

Something similar can occur between church communions, leading them to mutual recognition of each other's Christian faith, which is the basis for reception of ecumenical agreement. For example, the *Joint Declaration on the Doctrine of Justification* speaks of the "new insights" the Lutheran Church and the Roman Catholic Church have achieved. Then it adds: "Developments have taken place which not only make possible, but also require the churches to examine the divisive questions and condemnations and see them in a new light."[4] For the *Joint Declaration*, the new light enables the two church communions to "articulate a common understanding" of justification, in which the emphases of each are recognized as complementary, not contradictory.[5]

A friendship can develop between communions once ignorant of or hostile toward each other. In the past, churches addressed each other polemically and emphasized the mistakes each had made in interpreting the Gospel. But after a "purification of past memories" between the churches, says Pope John Paul II,[6] they are able to change their "way of looking at things,"[7] gaining "a calm, clearsighted and truthful vision of things, a vision enlivened by divine mercy and capable of freeing people's minds and of inspiring in everyone a renewed willingness, precisely with a view to proclaiming the Gospel to the men and women of every people and nation."[8] Now they can discern in a new way the position each holds, seeing each other in

---

[4] The Lutheran World Federation and the Roman Catholic Church, *Joint Declaration on the Doctrine of Justification* (Grand Rapids: Eerdmans, 2000), n. 7. Also at http://www.vatican.va/roman_curia/pontifical_councils/chrstuni/documents/rc_pc_chrstuni_doc_31101999_cath-luth-joint-declaration_en.html.

[5] Ibid., n. 5.

[6] John Paul II, encyclical *Ut Unum Sint, Origins* 25 (1995–96) 49, 51–72, n. 2. Also at http://www.vatican.va/holy_father/john_paul_ii/encyclicals/documents/hf_jp-ii_enc_25051995_ut-unum-sint_en.html.

[7] Ibid., n.15.

[8] Ibid., n. 2.

a "new light."[9] In ecumenical dialogue this reevaluation of each other's position is a necessary step on the way to reception of each other's insights.

Jean-Marie Tillard emphasizes that reception is preceded by two aspects of mutual recognition. First, Christians recognize in each other the same faith given to the apostolic community and faithfully preserved over time in every generation. They must distinguish between what should be received from former generations and what is merely a contingent characteristic of a certain time in the church's history. "Tradition cannot be confused with the museum of everything concerning faith," he emphasizes.[10] Second, Christians recognize in each other the same faith given to the church at Pentecost and faithfully preserved throughout the world in every culture. "[I]n order to be universally *received*," writes Tillard, the revelation of universal salvation "had to be *recognized* as really delivered to humanity as such. This was so that the essential requirements of salvation might not depend upon the characteristics of one specific race or culture."[11] Often the formulations and liturgical celebrations of the churches differ from culture to culture. But the churches do not receive merely a copy of the gift given to the apostolic church by the Spirit, Tillard observes. They receive in fact "this very gift." He continues: "Because they *recognize* it in each other, they are one Church in the indivisible grace of Pentecost."[12] The churches recognize in each other the same Gospel faith and so they are "one Church in the indivisible grace of Pentecost."[13] Although the soils in which the Gospel has grown may be different, Tillard underlines, "the seed is the very same, fully identical."[14]

Reception then involves a recognition of the same faith in another person or community. That same faith, as Tillard underscores, may be expressed with contingent characteristics that differ from those of one's own faith expression. It may have grown in a different soil and

---

[9] *Joint Declaration on the Doctrine of Justification*, n. 7.

[10] Jean-Marie R. Tillard, "Tradition, Reception," 328–43, in Kenneth Hagen, ed., *The Quadrilog: Tradition and the Future of Ecumenism: Essays in Honor of George H. Tavard* (Collegeville, MN: Liturgical Press, 1994), at 334.

[11] Ibid., 338–39.

[12] Ibid., 341.

[13] Ibid.

[14] Ibid., 342.

hence have different liturgical, theological, and cultural features. But it is the same gift given to all Christian believers; and as Tillard says, "[b]ecause they *recognize* it in each other, they are one Church."[15] The Anglican–Roman Catholic International Commission explains reception in a similar way: "By 'reception' we mean the fact that the people of God acknowledge such a decision or statement because they recognize in it the apostolic faith."[16]

Here I can testify to the correctness of the phrase "shock of recognition." Arrogantly, when I began teaching theology I was convinced that I had little to learn about Christianity from Evangelicals. But then at the Institute for Ecumenical and Cultural Research[17] I encountered Evangelicals who became my friends in the ecumenical movement. Richard Mouw from Fuller Theological Seminary and Paul Bassett from the Nazarene Theological Seminary showed me that they confess the same apostolic faith that I confess, and that they also sought the same kinds of reforms within their own church communions that I was seeking. A similar recognition took place when I listened to George Vandervelde talking frequently about the mission of the church. Divisions between Christians about less important things, he said, keep us from the more important thing, which is preaching Christ together. Although for some people this point could imply an anti-intellectual dismissal of theology, for George it underscored the seriousness with which theological discussions should aim to resolve the differences that continue to divide the churches.

I remember the period when I was choosing a title for my book, *The Ecumenical Gift Exchange.*[18] George laughed and said that maybe he didn't want some of the gifts my church communion was offering—for example, the papacy as currently exercised. His comment reminded me that one gift ecumenical partners offer each other in the gift exchange is serious criticism. Such criticism can be heard because of the basic mutual recognition present between dialogue

---

[15] Ibid., 341.

[16] Anglican–Roman Catholic International Commission, "Authority in the Church: Elucidations (1981)," in *The Final Report* (London: SPCK & Catholic Truth Society, 1982), n. 3.

[17] Located in Collegeville, MN; now the Collegeville Institute for Ecumenical and Cultural Research.

[18] Margaret O'Gara, *The Ecumenical Gift Exchange* (Collegeville, MN: Liturgical Press, 1998).

partners. Henry Chadwick explains: "Reception arises when it is recognized that the partner in dialogue loves God and his Church and seeks to be obedient to the gospel; moreover, that this obedience transcends allegiance to anything sectarian."[19] Basil Meeking stresses the way that dialogue seeks the truth in the presence of God. "The very process of the dialogue is an opening up, one to the other, of an agreement to help each other to be ready for the grace and unifying power of Jesus Christ. . . . We have to show ourselves, our churches, to each other as we are—our gifts, for growth in understanding and mutual upbuilding in grace and love; our limitations and failures, for pardon and healing. It is a process in which the participants are called to a new faithfulness to the truth of Jesus Christ."[20]

Some might wonder whether discussion of such attitudes is really relevant to the search for deepened understanding of Christian faith. Is reception, an act of understanding, really furthered by friendship, which is a form of love? Long ago, during my first university course in theology, I enthusiastically underlined these lines from Hans Urs von Balthasar in his discussion of the relationship of truth and love: ". . . love is so convinced of the total character of truth . . . that it is prepared to give up its own partial standpoint for the sake of this totality. . . . Love's renunciation of a partial truth for the sake of love is one of the highest forms of manifesting the truth."[21] Friendship in the ecumenical movement functions in this way to bring colleagues past real but partial truths to the recognition of a larger picture.

3. Nurturing Perseverance

Finally, friendship not only establishes the proper context of ecumenical dialogue and enhances understanding between the dialogue partners. It also nurtures the perseverance that is utterly necessary if ecumenical work is to move forward.

---

[19] Henry Chadwick, "Reception," 95–107, in Gillian R. Evans and Michel Gourgues, eds., *Communion et réunion: mélanges Jean-Marie Roger Tillard* (Leuven: Leuven University Press, 1995), at 107.

[20] Basil Meeking, "Review of the Dynamics and Issues in the Previous Five-year Dialogue," *Mid-Stream* 23 (1984): 335–45, at 339.

[21] Hans Urs von Balthasar, "The Freedom of the Subject," *Cross Currents* 12 (1962): 13–30, at 29.

The titles of two popular discussions of ecumenism tell us something important about dialogue today. Robert Bilheimer's study on the role of prayerfulness in ecumenism is titled *A Spirituality for the Long Haul.*[22] Thomas Ryan's guideline for ecumenical work is called *A Survival Guide for Ecumenically Minded Christians.*[23] These books reveal something significant: ecumenical work today is a long-term enterprise and it demands survival tactics. To put it another way, ecumenical dialogue is a form of asceticism. It invites Christian scholars to enter into a process that may achieve no tangible success or rewards during their lifetime. In their labors, ecumenists are required to follow various ascetical practices. They repeatedly fast from celebrations of the eucharist when not in full communion with the presider; they spend their time and talents on lengthy studies of positions they only gradually come to understand; they endure the embarrassment and frustration that flow from the sins of their own church communion and from those of their dialogue partner's church communion as well; and frequently their efforts are feared or suspected by members of their own church.

I don't think I could have survived in this ascetical way of life without friendships within the ecumenical movement. Some of these friends are Roman Catholic colleagues from my own church communion. Jeff Gros and Donna Geernaert have shown me the unique ecumenical contributions that scholars working with episcopal conferences can make. Jean-Marie Tillard, Harry McSorley, and George Tavard have illustrated for me how to put one's whole scholarly career at the service of ecumenism. These models of ecumenical commitment in the Roman Catholic tradition help me to persevere when I see what a long way the Roman Catholic Church must go before receiving fully the commitment to ecumenism made by the Second Vatican Council.

But friendships with colleagues in other church traditions are also essential to ecumenical perseverance. Friends working in ecumenism share the same poignant experience of love for their own church traditions and restlessness within them, a cognitive and affective

---

[22] Robert S. Bilheimer, *A Spirituality for the Long Haul: Biblical Risk and Moral Stand* (Philadelphia: Fortress Press, 1984).

[23] Thomas Ryan, *A Survival Guide for Ecumenically Minded Christians* (Ottawa: Novalis Publishing; Collegeville, MN: Liturgical Press, 1989).

dissonance peculiar to ecumenists. Friends from diverse church communions offer one another intellectual and emotional hospitality on the journey toward full communion. Thomas Ryan writes explicitly about the importance of such ecumenical hospitality. He testifies: "My own faith journey has been enormously enriched by the often challenging encounters with members of other churches."[24] He notes that ecumenism provides "hospitable space" for everyone, so that ecumenists often have a "primary home" in their own church communion but a "secondary home" in their partner's communion where "they have spent enough time to feel 'at-home.'"[25] But to be guests, he continues, "we must be ready to go where the other lives, to see and understand the way things are done in the other's household, to develop an affection for that space and the things we find there."[26] Visiting takes time, and friendship with colleagues in other church communions makes a priority of reserving the time that hospitality requires.

Friends are especially important if one is to sustain perseverance in the reform of one's own church communion. One evening a few years ago I gave a public lecture to a large group on the controversial topic of reforming the papacy, and George Vandervelde was in the audience. Sitting at the side of the lecture hall, he quietly took notes, asked a helpful question, and left before I had a chance to talk with him. But I remember thinking at the time: he is one of the few people in this whole auditorium who understands what I am really saying and why. I had the same feeling when George Tavard and I met with George Vandervelde one evening to discuss Roman Catholic teaching on the eucharist and its relationship to the eucharistic teaching of the Christian Reformed Church. As we shared a meal and discussed Vandervelde's ongoing attempt to change the Christian Reformed Church's negative teaching about Roman Catholic eucharistic views, I was struck by the importance of encouraging and sustaining one another in our efforts to reform our own church communions.

Yves Congar writes that "those involved in the ecumenical movement have by virtue of that a *votum unitatis, votum catholicitatis* [desire for unity, desire for catholicity], which gives to their present belief a

---

[24] Ibid., 125.
[25] Ibid., 126.
[26] Ibid., 126–27.

dynamic dimension in which their intention of plenitude is fulfilled."[27] Ecumenical friendships provide a particularly intense experience of both the desire for unity and the foretaste of unity achieved. Perhaps this is why such friendships are so effective in nurturing ecumenical perseverance. Like the disciples on the road to Emmaus, ecumenical friends walk along the road together with Christ as he opens the meaning of the Scriptures to them. Together they are amazed at what he is saying, but they do not recognize him yet for who he is. But sometimes, at the breaking of the bread in the other's home even when they cannot yet partake, their eyes are opened and they recognize again: we indeed have a common Lord, and he is in our midst. Because they recognize a common Lord, ecumenical friends at such moments also recognize each other as his disciples and are further sustained for the long journey ahead.

Conclusion

In this essay of appreciation for George Vandervelde, I have argued that friendships in the ecumenical movement have a theological significance that goes beyond anecdote or sentiment. They establish the proper context for ecumenical work, and they help illumine our minds and strengthen our hearts to pursue it effectively.

Jesus no longer calls his disciples servants, he says, but friends (John 15:15). And if Jesus has called us his friends, then we in the many churches are also friends of each other. Ecumenists who experience this have been made ready for the demands of dialogue.

---

[27] Yves Congar, *Diversity and Communion*, trans. John Bowden (Mystic, CT: Twenty-Third Publications, 1984), 133.

Table Manners:
Jesus' Lavish Hospitality[1]

When I hear the text for the gospel today, two weeks after the celebration of Corpus Christi, I feel as though it's an extension of that feast. At Corpus Christi we focused on the continuing presence of Jesus in the eucharist. In the text of today we look at those to whom Jesus was first physically present.

The text of the gospel (Matt 9:9-13) displays a characteristic of Jesus that really got the attention of his contemporaries. He was evidently rather surprising in his choice of table companions. He seemed willing to share table fellowship with anyone, no matter what the person's reputation. This practice of Jesus is a good one for us to think about, because it scandalized a lot of people. They were people like us, religious people, people highly knowledgeable about their religious tradition and very committed to it. Quite a bit like us.

Of course Jesus was not denying the centrality of religious tradition, but he wanted people to get religion right. Like the prophet Hosea in our first reading (Hos 6:3-6), Jesus stressed mercy, not

[1] First presented on June 7, 2008, as the presidential reflection during the celebration of the eucharist at the sixty-third annual convention of the Catholic Theological Society of America, Miami, FL. Previously published with minor revisions as "Table Manners: Christ's Lavish Hospitality" in *Commonweal* 136 (February 27, 2009): 13–14.

sacrifice. When he applied this text to the people sitting around the table with him, he meant that God's outreach to sinners outweighs other considerations and is the heart of the law.

My Lutheran colleagues in ecumenical dialogue love to show the link between these stories of table fellowship and the perspective we heard from Romans (Rom 4:18-25). There Paul uses the story of Abraham and Sarah to illustrate how it is faith that saves us, not works. If we open ourselves in faith to what God is doing, we'll find ourselves—just like Sarah—amazed at the unexpected results.

For Paul, and for Luther, who read Paul, this message is really good news. It relieves us of the imagined burden of earning something that can never be earned anyway. Salvation is a gift, won by Jesus, and here in the gospel story we learn that he gives it away rather lavishly to the least likely of people. Only mercy, only faith, is required. So the picture of Jesus sitting at the table with sinners is a kind of icon for Paul's teaching that faith, not what we do, justifies.

This is a story warning against self-righteousness, then. Self-righteousness is a constant temptation for religious people, and we Catholics sometimes give in to it. We forget that Jesus is the host of the eucharistic table and instead think that we are the hosts: we are in charge of what is said and done at the table; we are in charge of who may eat there, who may speak there, and even when they may speak. We try to keep disreputable people away, at least those who do not meet our standards. But if our first priority is to regulate, we of course miss the main point.

I often think about the inclusiveness of Jesus when I attend ecumenical dialogue meetings with my partners in the Disciples of Christ Church. The Disciples in the dialogue attend Catholic eucharists every day during our meetings, but of course they do not receive communion. This is painful for everyone there, but especially for the Disciples, who broke away from the Presbyterian Church precisely because it was demanding elaborate proofs of worthiness before admitting anyone to the communion table.

Of course the tradition of restricting eucharistic practice to a closed circle is an ancient one in Christian history, and such a discipline has many good reasons to support it. From the earliest centuries the church was concerned to show the link between baptism and a way of life. Christian baptism means not just new beliefs but a transformation of life. I myself—a religious person—always follow this strict discipline of the Catholic Church in my own life, and furthermore, at times I explain and defend it.

But sometimes our Catholic concern with eucharistic discipline strikes me as painfully similar to the attitude of the religious people scandalized by Jesus' table companions. And it seems odd to me that we continue to apply these ancient disciplines so rigorously in a very different context from that of the early church. In those days the rules served to exclude the unbaptized and Gnostics from the eucharist by making its reception the last step of Christian initiation. But today these disciplines also usually exclude Protestants and Anglicans— other Christians whose baptism we recognize and whom we call our brothers and sisters in Christ. Although our ecclesiological perspective on them changed at Vatican II, our eucharistic discipline toward them still does not fully mirror these changes: though better than preconciliar practice, it still has an inner inconsistency. This is especially painful when we recognize that today Disciples of Christ, Lutherans, and most of our ecumenical partners confess the real presence of Christ in the eucharist, even if they do not use the language of "transubstantiation" to describe it. They are hardly like the Gnostics or other nonbelievers during the first centuries of the church.

Kevin Seasoltz, a Benedictine liturgical scholar, notes a certain contrast between Jesus' tables and ours. In the light of subsequent Christian tradition, he writes, "the Lord's table has often been reserved for those who think themselves worthy to approach it." But the gospels, he says, "report that the broken, the sinful, and the unrighteous were both privileged and delighted to share communion with Jesus."[2] Seasoltz's reflections should lead us to reconsider the disciplines that surround our tables and our pulpits, and to ask whether sometimes they have neglected what Jesus sought: mercy, not sacrifice.

Fortunately for us Catholics, however, it is the Jesus of the gospel stories who has invited us this evening to his banquet and who has offered us the feast of himself. We too are sinners—whose sin may be self-righteousness—and we too have been fed at this feast of mercy. At its deepest, the Catholic tradition of celebration knows that Jesus was lavish in extending his hospitality. His hospitality is the one that

---

[2] R. Kevin Seasoltz, "One House, Many Dwellings: Open and Closed Communion," *Worship* 79 (2005): 405–19, at 408.

forgives sins and heals divisions. His hospitality is the one that feeds the hungry hearts and strengthens the weary minds of theologians. Not one of us really deserves the eucharist: it is a gift given to us by our Lord Jesus Christ. Like beggars, we came with our bowls empty. But now we have been fed. Happy are we who have been called to this banquet.

Ecumenical Dialogue as a
Process of Personal Transformation[1]

1. How Ecumenical Dialogue Can Be a Process of
Personal Transformation

In this talk I will propose that participation in ecumenical dialogue is at best a process of personal transformation. And I will draw upon my own experience of bilateral ecumenical dialogues to illustrate how this is so.

In our worship service we have just celebrated how the victory won by Christ's paschal sacrifice means that everything will be changed before the coming of the kingdom of God. Paul wrote, "we will all be changed" (1 Cor 15:51) because of the victory given us by our Lord Jesus Christ. In Canada our French translation of this theme affirms that all must be "transformé" by Christ's victory. Such transformation is a common experience among those who enter into dialogue between the churches.

The Second Vatican Council also recognized that changes would be needed before the unity for which Christ prayed can be achieved. In the *Decree on Ecumenism* the Catholic Church taught that the dis-

[1] First presented on February 2, 2012, as "A Dialogue of Transformation" on the occasion of receiving the annual Ecumenism Award given by the Washington Theological Consortium, Washington, DC. Not previously published.

cord and disunity among Christians "openly contradicts the will of Christ, provides a stumbling block to the world, and inflicts damage" on the proclamation of the Gospel. The council taught that the ecumenical movement is the work of the Holy Spirit because it seeks to overcome this discord and disunity.[2] But the council recognized that "there can be no ecumenism worthy of the name without a change of heart."[3] It set the Roman Catholic Church on the path of dialogue with other churches toward the full unity for which Christ prayed, but the council also affirmed explicitly that a change of heart was needed before this goal could be attained. Dialogue between the churches must include personal transformation or it is not really ecumenical dialogue at all.

How are Christians to undergo such personal transformation in dialogue with each other? In his 1995 encyclical on ecumenism, Pope John Paul II underlined that repentance is a precondition of transformation—a repentance that leads us to "change our way of looking at things." Only then are Christians ready, he says, to "re-examine together their painful past and the hurt which that past regrettably continues to provoke even today." John Paul II believed that repentance of this kind could lead to "a calm, clearsighted and truthful vision of things, a vision enlivened by divine mercy and capable of freeing people's minds and of inspiring in everyone a renewed willingness, precisely with a view to proclaiming the Gospel to the men and women of every people and nation."[4]

But what is this "calm, clearsighted and truthful vision of things" of which John Paul II speaks, and why does it "change our way of looking at things"? A few years ago I heard a talk by Constance Fitzgerald that helped me understand this change, this transformation, more fully. In her reflection on the Dark Night of the Soul, Fitzgerald notes that the Carmelite mystic John of the Cross called this dark night "the purification of memory," which she also relates to the experience of impasse. She explains: "In the deeper reaches of

---

[2] Vatican II, *Unitatis Redintegratio* (Decree on Ecumenism), n. 1. Also at http://www.vatican.va/archive/hist_councils/ii_vatican_council/documents/vat-ii_decree_19641121_unitatis-redintegratio_en.html.

[3] Ibid., n. 7.

[4] John Paul II, encyclical *Ut Unum Sint, Origins* 25 (1995–96): 49, 51–72; see n. 15 and n. 2. Also at http://www.vatican.va/holy_father/john_paul_ii/encyclicals/documents/hf_jp-ii_enc_25051995_ut-unum-sint_en.html.

a contemplative life, a kind of unraveling or loss of memory occurs which can be more or less conscious. Then one's usual way of harboring memories is incapacitated."[5] While a person may continue to have memories from the past, they are somehow "uncoupled from the self" so that "they do not mean what one thought they did."[6] What and how one remembers are called into question in a painful experience in which one feels that one is losing one's very identity and hold on the truth. But John of the Cross believed that in the Dark Night of the Soul the "memory is being deconstructed or dispossessed in a redemptive movement whereby the incredibly slow appropriation of theological hope gradually displaces all that impedes new vision, new possibility, the evolution of a transformed self."[7]

In her application of these insights Fitzgerald argues that the Dark Night has societal, not just individual, implications. But of course I thought as well of its ecumenical implications. In dialogue, the memory of our church tradition as we have known it gives way to a kind of Dark Night in which that earlier memory is deconstructed and only very slowly replaced by a new vision. As with an individual, so also with dialogue between Christians: steps toward transformation are painful and frequently disorienting, accompanied at times by fear, denial, or anger. But gradually, when the historical memory of Christians is purified and a new vision of oneself and the other church traditions emerges, dialogue becomes an experience not just of information but of transformation, of conversion.

2. Five Examples of the Transformational Process

Now I want to share with you my experience of this process of personal transformation by talking about five bilateral dialogues in which I have participated. Each dialogue provides a different example of an obstacle to Christian unity and how the effort to address it proved to be transformational.

---

[5] Constance Fitzgerald, "From Impasse to Prophetic Hope: Crisis of Memory," *Proceedings of the Catholic Theological Society of America* 64 (2009): 21–42, at 23.
[6] Ibid.
[7] Ibid., 24.

2.1. *Rereading Our Common History*

Perhaps the most fundamental obstacle to unity between Lutheran and Roman Catholic Christians has been their centuries-old disagreement about precisely how God's grace justifies sinners. During my involvement in dialogue between Lutherans and Catholics both in the United States and at the international level, I had a modest part in the effort to address that obstacle through a joint rereading of our common history. And I experienced firsthand one of the most stunning transformational outcomes of such an approach in the Western church, the *Joint Declaration on the Doctrine of Justification.*[8] When I was a member of the U.S. Lutheran–Catholic Dialogue's Continuation Committee we helped to ratify and receive this important breakthrough document, signed by the Roman Catholic Church and the Lutheran World Federation in 1999. Because of new developments, the *Joint Declaration* explains, both Lutherans and Roman Catholics are now obligated to see divisive questions and historic condemnations "in a new light." To see "in a new light" is almost a summary of ecumenical work, and the *Joint Declaration* is quite precise about what this new light reveals. Although the sixteenth-century doctrinal condemnations regarding justification appear in this "new light," the signers declare, nothing is "taken away" from their "seriousness." Some of these condemnations were not "simply pointless" and "[t]hey remain for us 'salutary warnings' to which we must attend in our teaching and practice."[9] While the *Joint Declaration* is able to overcome earlier controversial questions and condemnations, this does not mean that the churches involved "take the condemnations lightly" or that they "disavow their own past."

It seems that the *Joint Declaration* is referring to that "necessary purification of past memories" of which John Paul II had spoken and to which John of the Cross also referred, a reorientation that allows the two churches to recognize that past positions once thought to be contradictory can now be seen as complementary. And this is just how the *Joint Declaration* is able to understand the different emphases

---

[8] The Lutheran World Federation and the Roman Catholic Church, *Joint Declaration on the Doctrine of Justification* (Grand Rapids: Eerdmans, 2000). Also at http://www.vatican.va/roman_curia/pontifical_councils/chrstuni/documents/rc_pc_chrstuni_doc_31101999_cath-luth-joint-declaration_en.html.

[9] Ibid., n. 42.

of Roman Catholics and Lutherans. For example, God's forgiveness of sins and the imparting of new life in Christ, once seen as contradictory points, are now presented as simultaneous acts of God in justifying.[10] Or again: to recognize that we depend completely on God for our justification and salvation—as Lutherans emphasize—is not to deny that believers are fully involved in their faith and, moved by grace, give their consent—as Roman Catholics emphasize.[11]

In a similar way, the *Joint Declaration* shows how complementary understandings of faith and works, the *simul iustus et peccator*, and the five other areas of dispute between Lutherans and Roman Catholics need no longer divide the partners today because they now see these historic positions "in a new light."

While the *Joint Declaration* is the best known example of rethinking history together by Lutherans and Roman Catholics, it is by no means the only one. In *The Hope of Eternal Life*, completed in 2010, careful historical work on the teachings of each church by the U.S. Lutheran–Roman Catholic Dialogue led us to recognize a common belief in the possible need for purgation of the justified after death, giving a new slant to the arguments about purgatory and indulgences that had helped to set off the Reformation in the sixteenth century.[12] And similarly careful historical work led the Lutheran–Roman Catholic International Commission on Unity in 2006 to find parallel descriptions of a cluster of instruments for God's revelation in both Luther's thought on Gospel practices and in the work of Vatican II on tradition, each with the recognition of Scripture's primacy in matters of faith.[13]

I remember very clearly when members of the International Commission recognized the importance of showing readers *how* we had reread our history together. We decided that earlier dialogues had

[10] Ibid., n. 23.

[11] Ibid., nn. 19–21.

[12] *The Hope of Eternal Life: Common Statement of the Eleventh Round of the U.S. Lutheran–Catholic Dialogue*, ed. Lowell G. Alman and Richard J. Sklba (Minneapolis: Lutheran University Press, 2011). Also at http://www.usccb.org/beliefs-and-teachings/ecumenical-and-interreligious/ecumenical/lutheran/upload/The-Hope-of-Eternal-Life1.pdf.

[13] Lutheran–Roman Catholic Commission on Unity, and Pontifical Council for Promoting Christian Unity, *The Apostolicity of the Church: Study Document of the Lutheran–Roman Catholic Commission on Unity [of] The Lutheran World Federation [and] Pontifical Council for Promoting Christian Unity* (Minneapolis: Lutheran University Press, 2006). Also at http://www.vatican.va/roman_curia/pontifical_councils/chrstuni/information_service/pdf/information_service_128_en.pdf.

sometimes given readers only the *results* of their study, without walking with them through the steps that led toward a changed perspective. By rereading history together we were led to a transformation, seeing each other in a new light, and we wanted to share this experience with our readers.

2.2. *Analyzing Our Teachings*

A different kind of impediment to Christian unity is presented by church communions' mutual misunderstanding of one another's teachings. Though such misunderstanding of course has its history, that history is not always so distant, complicated, and relatively inaccessible as the sixteenth-century difference between Lutherans and Catholics about justification. Consequently, it may be susceptible of correction by careful and sustained joint analysis. My exchanges with colleagues in the Disciples of Christ–Roman Catholic International Commission for Dialogue have given me a vivid experience of this type of impediment, its correction, and the correction's transformational result.

Because the Disciples of Christ began as a free church movement that broke away from the Presbyterian tradition in the nineteenth century they had little direct knowledge of Catholic teaching on the eucharist and little experience of Catholic devotional practice. But Disciples place the eucharist at the center of their self-understanding, and so they already shared something important with Roman Catholics when we entered into our dialogue.

Our shared commitment to the eucharist allowed us to unearth a set of misunderstandings about the eucharist. The first concerned the attitude of Disciples toward the word "transubstantiation." Studying Thomas Aquinas together for the first time, the dialogue members saw that Aquinas had "used transubstantiation both as a means to counter materialist views of the eucharist, and to affirm the real change of bread and wine . . ." Aquinas intended "not a local or material change, but a supernatural change."[14] But by the sixteenth

---

[14] Disciples of Christ–Roman Catholic International Commission for Dialogue, *The Presence of Christ in the Church, with Special Reference to the Eucharist: Fourth Agreed Statement of the Disciples of Christ–Roman Catholic International Commission for Dialogue, 2003–2009*, n. 33. See http://www.vatican.va/roman_curia/pontifical_councils/chrstuni/information_service/pdf/information_service_141_en.pdf.

century "substance" was taken to mean "materially present," which was just the opposite of what Aquinas had intended when he used the term "transubstantiation" to oppose materialist understandings of the eucharist.[15]

When the Disciples of Christ came into existence in the nineteenth century they understood their celebration of the Lord's Supper to be "more than a recollection" of the Last Supper, but they found the term "transubstantiation" to be "unnecessarily metaphysical."[16] In addition, Disciples had been shaped by another philosophical tradition in which what Aquinas described as "accidents" and the Council of Trent as "species" were understood to constitute the real, and what Aquinas and Trent called "substance" was seen as an unnecessary abstraction. The use of Aristotle's philosophical perspective by Aquinas had been an effective apologetic strategy in the thirteenth century, but that perspective no longer had the same meaning in the sixteenth century. And by the nineteenth century, within the very different philosophical framework in which the Disciples were formed, it was simply incomprehensible. I will never forget the moment of realization we all experienced together when this misunderstanding was discovered. It was a moment of breakthrough when the blinders fell from our eyes. Within the Disciples' philosophical framework, "transubstantiation" was taken to mean "almost the opposite of what Aquinas had intended."[17] Thinking that "transubstantiation" meant the material, spatial presence of Christ in the eucharist, the Disciples rejected this term precisely in order to preserve the mystery of the real presence, which they affirm. While Disciples would hardly choose to begin using the word "transubstantiation," the dialogue helped them recognize their misunderstanding of it and to underline their agreement with Roman Catholics both in affirming the mystery of Christ's real presence in the eucharist and in opposing "reductionist understandings that see Christ's presence as simply materialist or figurative."[18]

Of course, misunderstandings held by Roman Catholics also helped to shape this conclusion. We Catholics had allowed ourselves to focus

---

[15] Ibid., n. 34.
[16] Ibid., n. 37.
[17] Ibid.
[18] Ibid., n. 45.

too narrowly on the presence of Christ in the elements of consecrated bread and wine and to ignore his presence in the proclaimed word of God and in the gathered assembly celebrating the memorial of his once-for-all sacrifice on the cross. In our dialogue with Disciples, the Catholic members came to recognize the distinctive ways that Disciples recognize Christ's real presence: as host at the eucharistic feast, as present at communion, as present in the bread and wine, which "by the power of the Holy Spirit . . . become for us, through faith, the Body and Blood of Christ," as the Disciples affirmed to us.[19] Hence the Commission concluded that both churches "affirm the mystery of Christ's real presence in the eucharist, especially in the bread and wine," an agreement they could reach only, they explained, "through the elimination of mutual misunderstandings."[20]

2.3. *Aiming to Exchange Our Ecclesial Gifts*

A third type of barrier to Christian unity is some longstanding mutual alienation that prevents appreciation of both another communion's gifts and the needs of one's own communion. Becoming able both to accept the other's gifts and to offer one's own gifts overcomes this barrier and is a form of transformation. I have experienced this transformational process in my dialogue with Mennonites in a Catholic–Mennonite movement for dialogue called Bridgefolk.

Bridgefolk is a North American movement, but its work has been assisted by the significant forward steps taken by the International Dialogue between the Catholic Church and the Mennonite World Conference, the first undertaking of its kind since the Reformation. This was a very painful effort, especially for the Mennonite members, because of the painful history of martyrdom that lies in the memory and indeed the identity of the Mennonite community. I remember one of the first times that I attended a dialogue meeting with Mennonites, a meeting whose topic was the Anabaptist martyrs of the sixteenth century. I met a colleague who said bluntly to me and the other Catholics at the meeting: "Your forefathers and foremothers killed my forefathers and foremothers. You are in the church that made my ancestors into martyrs." This was such a deep memory for

---

[19] Ibid., n. 43.
[20] Ibid., n. 45.

this Mennonite that it shaped his entire identity and his perspective on my identity as well, whereas that history was something I knew almost nothing about. In its agreed statement the International Dialogue noted that "the danger of persecution for martyrdom became a part of the Mennonite identity."[21] This perspective also led Mennonites and Roman Catholics to remember only negative things about each other: as the statement observed, "[w]e sometimes restricted our views of the history of Christianity to those aspects that seemed most in agreement with the self-definition of our respective ecclesial communities."[22]

But members of the International Dialogue found that rereading their common history together, though painful, was also "invaluable."[23] They thought it allowed a new interpretation of the past that they would hold in common, a shared new memory "that can free us from the prison of the past."[24] Together they also found a way to ask forgiveness from each other for the sins of their past.

This work of the International Dialogue affected the atmosphere of the discussions in North America taking place at Bridgefolk. In an atmosphere of partial reconciliation, Mennonites and Roman Catholics were drawn to Bridgefolk with different desires. Each wanted to receive a particular gift from the other. The Mennonites came to Bridgefolk because they wanted to retrieve the rich liturgical heritage largely lost to them at the time of the Reformation. Roman Catholics came to Bridgefolk in order to deepen their commitment to peacemaking.

At Bridgefolk I met Mennonites who for years had been attracted to the monastic practice of morning and evening prayer, and they also were moved by the richness of the eucharistic liturgy they found in Catholic churches. Some of these Mennonites had developed a prayer book for saying morning and evening prayer in the Anabaptist

---

[21] Willard Roth and Gerald W. Schlabach, eds., *Called Together to Be Peacemakers: Report of the International Dialogue between the Catholic Church and Mennonite World Conference, 1998–2003*, abridged ed. (Kitchener, ON: Pandora Press, 2005), n. 47. For the unabridged text, see http://www.vatican.va/roman_curia/pontifical_councils /chrstuni/mennonite-conference-docs/rc_pc_chrstuni_doc_20110324_mennonite _en.html.

[22] Ibid., n. 25.

[23] Ibid., n. 26.

[24] Ibid., n. 27.

tradition,[25] and they longed to enrich their own tradition of eucharistic celebration. When Bridgefolk Mennonites and Catholics were unable to celebrate eucharist together because we are not in full communion, we began more frequent and longer celebrations of the footwashing that is deep in the Anabaptist tradition and remains a part of the Holy Thursday liturgy for Roman Catholics. Mennonites were eager to receive liturgical gifts from their Roman Catholic partners and even to rediscover their own liturgical heritage.

For their part, Roman Catholics came to Bridgefolk because they found an authentic witness to peacemaking in the long Anabaptist tradition of nonviolence. When Mennonites heard from Roman Catholics how much the Just War Tradition is being reinterpreted in papal teaching, they were very excited. Learning that Pope John Paul II applied the criteria for a just war very strictly, Mennonites found that they often were in de facto agreement with the position of their Roman Catholic partners on questions of peace and of the justice required for peace. I myself found Mennonite perseverance in peacemaking to be an inspiring witness, and it was this witness that drew me to my first Bridgefolk meeting just as the United States undertook war in Iraq. I thought that perseverance in peacemaking was an important gift that Roman Catholics could receive from Mennonite partners.

In my book on the ecumenical gift exchange[26] I reflect on this idea: that ecumenical dialogue can be understood as an exchange of gifts. But unlike a family gift exchange, where we give up the gift we bring while also receiving one, the ecumenical gift exchange allows each group to keep its gifts while also receiving others from its partners in dialogue. George Tavard notes that these gifts are really the gifts given by the Holy Spirit for the whole of the church: in dialogue, we receive back some of the gifts we have been missing since our separation. And, speaking personally, I must say that I find Mennonite–Roman Catholic dialogue especially interesting because the gifts are not the usual doctrinal gifts that one associates with ecumenical work; rather, they are gifts of prayer and of discipleship.

---

[25] Arthur Paul Boers, et al., eds., *Take Our Moments and Our Days: An Anabaptist Prayer Book* (Scottdale, PA/Waterloo, Ontario: Herald Press, 2007).

[26] Margaret O'Gara, *The Ecumenical Gift Exchange* (Collegeville, MN: Liturgical Press, 1998).

2.4. *Resolving to Improve Our Structures of Ecclesial Authority*

A fourth kind of obstacle to Christian unity is created by differences between communions' structures of authority, especially of teaching authority. Typically the differing structures all are deficient, but in different ways. Consequently, more than one type of improvement is required if the obstacle is to be removed. Dialogues between Anglicans and Roman Catholics, for example, have recognized and attempted to address this type of obstacle.

In its work on teaching authority the Anglican–Roman Catholic International Commission amply documents its members' recognition of dissimilar strengths and weaknesses in Anglican and Roman Catholic structures. The Roman Catholic members recognized their church's need for a greater exercise of collegiality among bishops and of conciliarity within the whole church, exercises that should be maintained in balance with the primacy given to the bishop of Rome. At the same time, Anglican members joined the Roman Catholics in acknowledging that "the primacy of the bishop of Rome can be affirmed as part of God's design for the universal *koinonia*."[27] In their third agreed statement on teaching authority Anglicans can even speak of the papacy as a "gift" God wants to give the church, while Roman Catholics can affirm their need to incorporate a genuine practice of synodality into their structures.[28] And since both Anglicans and Roman Catholics recognize the need for a balance between papacy and conciliarity, the International Commission also crafted a carefully articulated theology of infallibility that affirms both the authority of conciliar or papal teaching and the need for that teaching to be received by the whole church.[29]

---

[27] Anglican–Roman Catholic International Commission, "Authority in the Church II," in *The Final Report* (London: SPCK & Catholic Truth Society, 1982), n. 15. Also at http://www.vatican.va/roman_curia/pontifical_councils/chrstuni/angl-comm -docs/rc_pc_chrstuni_doc_1981_authority-church-ii_en.html.

[28] Anglican–Roman Catholic International Commission/Catholic Truth Society (Great Britain), *The Gift of Authority: Authority in the Church III, An Agreed Statement by the Anglican–Roman Catholic International Commission (ARCIC)* (London: Catholic Truth Society; New York: Church Publishing, 1999), n. 60. Also at http://www.vatican .va/roman_curia/pontifical_councils/chrstuni/documents/rc_pc_chrstuni_doc _12051999_gift-of-autority_en.html.

[29] Ibid., nn. 41–44.

During my eighteen years as a member, the Anglican–Roman Catholic Dialogue of Canada was often called to assist the International Commission in its work. We clarified the nature of infallibility in a 1982 agreed statement, and we commented on the "legitimate" range of "theological opinion that exists within the Roman Catholic Church," which we thought the Vatican's 1991 *Observations* on ARCIC's work had often overlooked.[30] At the same time, we noted that Anglicans and Roman Catholics in Canada had many experiences of widespread collaboration in their pastoral care for interchurch marriages, seminary education, and social ministries. I notice that this experience continues. No matter how acerbic or remote the official relations between our two churches appear at times, the relationships of colleagues and students in ecumenical consortia such as the Toronto School of Theology remain warm and interdependent. In Toronto we could not carry out adequate theological education without each other, and we all know it.

The dialogue between Anglicans and Roman Catholics shows something important about ecumenism today, however, because it illustrates that structural changes may be more difficult than changes in our ideas or even in our liturgical and ethical practices. For example, it was not easy for Lutherans and Catholics to see justification in a new way, or for Disciples of Christ and Catholics to rectify their misunderstanding about the eucharist, or for Mennonites and Catholics to become able to exchange gifts of prayer and discipleship. But perhaps it is even more challenging for us to admit deficiencies in our structures of teaching—or, indeed, of decision-making—in our respective churches and to draw on the partner church in order to correct them.

At present this difficulty is illustrated more sharply in dialogue between the two communions. Debates on the exercise of authority characterize current internal tensions within both communions. The Anglican communion debates authority issues surrounding same-sex marriage, while the Roman Catholic communion discusses the proper

---

[30] Anglican–Roman Catholic Dialogue of Canada, "Reply to the Vatican Response to the Final Report of the Anglican–Roman Catholic International Commission (1993)," in *Common Witness to the Gospel: Documents on Anglican–Roman Catholic Relations 1983–1995*, ed. Jeffrey Gros et al. (Washington, DC: United States Catholic Conference, 1997), 78–104, nn. 54–69. See also Anglican–Roman Catholic Dialogue of Canada, "A Response to *The Gift of Authority*" (2008), available at http://gs2004.anglican.ca /atsynod/reports/006-8.htm.

exercise of papal ministry in relationship to collegiality—for example, in the translation of liturgical texts or the role of episcopal conferences. The establishment of an Anglican ordinariate to welcome disaffected Anglicans into full communion with the bishop of Rome adds new structural problems to the discussion. In my judgment, difficulties over the exercise of ecclesial authority are the most difficult ones in ecumenical dialogue today, not because we lack understanding of what structural changes are needed but because we do not yet have the will to make them.

Members of the Anglican–Roman Catholic Dialogue of Canada always experienced a strong sense of trust and a mutual recognition of each other's faith and ministries. This trust extended far beyond the formality of the scheduled discussions. During my time in this dialogue I observed it in laughter over meals, in sincere shared prayer, and in frank conversations late into the night over a beer or two. I remember the drama of one late-night conversation when our two bishop cochairs, Anglican and Roman Catholic, confessed to one another the serious problems with authority that their own church communions were experiencing and wondered aloud how they would ever be resolved. It is this experience of personal transformation that the entirety of both Anglican and Roman Catholic Churches must have if we are to overcome the differences in structures of ecclesial governance that divide us.

2.5. *Learning to Collaborate for the Sake of Evangelization*

The fifth barrier to Christian unity I will discuss in this talk is the one generated by different styles of evangelization. I have learned a lot about this barrier from dialoguing with Evangelicals. I first underwent a shock of recognition in my initial meeting with Evangelicals and Pentecostals at the Collegeville Institute for Ecumenical and Cultural Research in 1982. Arrogantly, I thought I had nothing to learn from these groups. But I was brought up short by the unequivocal discovery that we shared both the same fundamentals of Christian faith and the same restlessness about our church homes, homes we all recognized were in need of reform.

Evangelicals and Roman Catholics today are recognizing their common commitment to the doctrinal and moral core of the Gospel, and this has received a lot of media attention. But in the newly formed Evangelical–Roman Catholic Dialogue of Canada I have learned to recognize at least two other shared areas that are prone to be over-looked. One is the rich variety in interpreting Scripture. At our meetings we have spent hours together in spontaneous prayer and *lectio divina*, and we have developed a comfortable familiarity with each other's prayer styles. But perhaps more distinctive is the sense of shared mission. Catholics and Evangelicals share a commitment to evangelization that transforms their experience of each other. In an increasingly secular culture the two groups discover each other more often as allies than as competitors. While this can become a shallow instrument for simple political goals, at its deepest level I believe it indicates the continuing sense in each tradition that the unity of the church is meant to serve its mission to the world.

Sometimes we Catholics and Evangelicals have mutual criticisms to offer each other on our styles of evangelization. This mutual criticism is also a part of dialogue. Last year one of my Pentecostal colleagues said he saw no point in continuing the dialogue with Catholics if they did not believe that only Christians could be saved. So I gently explained to him the teaching of the Catholic Church: that Jesus Christ is the only savior, but that some can be saved without explicit faith in Christ if they follow their conscience where God is speaking to them. I said to him: "Isn't the fact that we disagree about this a good reason for continuing the dialogue?" He was persuaded, and he continued to participate in the prayers and discussions of our group. But long after our discussion had ended I found myself humbled by his zeal for the Gospel. I think often of the balanced words of the Second Vatican Council in its *Decree on Non-Christian Religions* when it first speaks of other religions throughout the world: "The Catholic Church rejects nothing which is true and holy in these religions. She looks with sincere respect upon those ways of conduct and of life, those rules and teachings which, though differing in many particulars from what she holds and set forth, nevertheless often reflect a ray of that Truth which enlightens all men. Indeed, she proclaims and must ever proclaim Christ, 'the way, the truth, and the life' (John 14:6), in whom men find the fullness of religious life, and in whom God has reconciled all things to Himself (cf. 2 Cor 5:18-19)."[31]

---

[31] Vatican II, *Nostra Aetate* (Declaration on the Relationship of the Church to Non-Christian Religions), in *The Documents of Vatican II*, ed. Walter M. Abbott (New York: America Press, 1966), n. 2. Also at http://www.vatican.va/archive/hist_councils/ii
_vatican_council/documents/vat-ii_decl_19651028_nostra-aetate_en.html.

Conclusion

In this talk I have maintained that ecumenical dialoguing is at best a process of personal transformation. And I have used my own experience of five bilateral ecumenical dialogues to illustrate how this is so. The different dialogues focused on somewhat different obstacles to the unity of Christ's church, and the diversity of those obstacles led the dialogues to adopt somewhat different approaches in their efforts to address them. In one case our approach could be aptly described as jointly rereading our common history, in another as jointly analyzing our teachings, in a third as jointly seeking to exchange our ecclesial gifts, and in a fourth as jointly resolving to improve our structures of ecclesial authority. In all of these cases, however, the degree of our success in addressing the obstacles corresponded closely to the degree of our personal transformation. While the obstacle to unity was the occasion of our efforts, and some progress toward overcoming it was the fruit, the degree of success of the efforts matched the extent of the change, transformation, conversion experienced by each of us as participants in the dialogue.

Let me conclude by suggesting that the major purpose of the first four ecumenical efforts and corresponding personal transformations of which I spoke is the fifth and last one. It is our learning to collaborate for the sake of evangelization; it is the great transformation that would allow us to announce the Gospel to a world that longs to hear this good news. In our present discord and division, Vatican II said rightly, "we openly contradict the will of Christ, provide a stumbling block to the world, and inflict damage on the proclamation of the Gospel."[32] In our present sorry state of internal division we don't make a very effective argument for the unity God seeks with humankind." As one of my colleagues on the Evangelical–Roman Catholic Dialogue of Canada put it recently, the poor and weak of the world *need* the churches to be unified; in our present state of division we are of little help to those who depend on our concerted response to the impoverishment of their bodies, minds, and spirits.

Fortunately, as Vatican II teaches, the dialogue among Christians is the work of the Holy Spirit. When Paul writes of the ultimate transformation at the world's end he assures his readers that God

---

[32] See above, n. 2.

"gives us the victory through our Lord Jesus Christ" (1 Cor 15:57). But, he exhorts those readers, "be steadfast, immovable . . . because you know that in the Lord your labor is not in vain" (1 Cor 15:58). Perhaps this can be a source of hope for us in the continuing challenges we face in ecumenical work. Our labor is not in vain because victory is given to us through our Lord Jesus Christ. May we know the sweetness of this word from the Lord.

Part Two

Deepening
the
Ecumenical Perspective

Understanding Vatican I
on Papal Primacy[1]

Introduction

When considering the relationship between the collegiality of the bishops and the primacy of the bishop of Rome, two mistakes are frequently made. The first envisions collegiality and primacy as two fundamentally opposed factors that must be periodically "recalibrated" for the proper equilibrium between them to be maintained.[2] But this view tends to quantify collegiality and primacy, as though just the right amount of each is specified by a recipe that will yield a tasty and nutritious dish. A second mistake envisions the primacy of the bishop of Rome as linked with the past and the collegiality of the bishops as linked with the present. Although this view usefully connects the contrast to the history of church councils, it also gives a premature evaluation of the two factors, as though papal primacy is the theme of an outdated book about authority, a book now replaced by Vatican II's publication on episcopal collegiality.

[1] Previously published as "Three Successive Steps to Understanding Vatican I's Teaching on Papal Primacy," *The Jurist* 64 (2004): 208–23.

[2] I am grateful to Gilles Routhier for this insight, which we first discussed during our work together for the Canadian Conference of Catholic Bishops' delegation to the worldwide Synod of bishops in Rome, September 30–October 27, 2001.

Both mistakes lead to neglecting the importance of carefully investigating Vatican I's teachings on primacy, leaving them instead to be regarded as an inflexible bloc of thoughts and conclusions with little relevance for collegiality. But this will not do. Unless the teachings on primacy are understood adequately, their meaning cannot be properly retrieved, evaluated, transposed, and employed in current discussions of collegiality.

Modern scholarship recognizes that adequately grasping the meaning of a text may require attending not just to the text itself but also to the extra-textual comments of its author or authors and its interpreters and even to the underlying worldviews. In briefly exploring the teaching of *Pastor Aeternus* on papal primacy, I will take small versions of all three steps, devoting most of my time to the third.

1. Focusing on the Text of *Pastor Aeternus* on Papal Primacy

A first step in studying Vatican I on papal primacy is to focus simply on the *text* of *Pastor Aeternus*. Whenever I return to this text, I am always astonished to remember what a short time the council participants actually devoted to discussing its treatment of primacy. The long schema on the church was circulated to the bishops on January 21, 1870. On May 9, a schema treating just the papacy was distributed. Beginning with the words "Pastor aeternus," it had been prepared by the Deputation on the Faith in light of bishops' written comments.[3] Although this text as a whole was discussed from May 13 through June 3, most of the attention was given to the proposed definition of infallibility. Discussion of the three chapters on primacy lasted little more than a week, beginning on June 6 and ending on June 14. Following the subsequent debate on infallibility, voting on amendments to the text began on July 2 and continued on July 9, July 11, and July 16. The final vote on the text as a whole occurred on July 18, 1870.

---

[3] An English translation of this second draft of the proposed schema, as well as the final form of *Pastor Aeternus*, can be found in the appendix of my book: Margaret O'Gara, *Triumph in Defeat: Infallibility, Vatican I, and the French Minority Bishops* (Washington, DC: Catholic University of America Press, 1988), 257–69.

When they look at this text today, many theologians emphasize that it is not as bad as it could have been. Hermann Pottmeyer writes, "The text of the council is undoubtedly marked by the atmosphere of its time, but it does *not* define the primacy of jurisdiction as an absolute, monarchical sovereignty as understood by Capellari and de Maistre. . . . [I]f we look at the definition against the background of the original, extreme ultramontanist proposal, we are struck by its relative moderation."[4] Jean-Marie Tillard takes this approach as well. Calling *Pastor Aeternus* "a subtle document interpreted by an ultra-montane outlook,"[5] he concludes, "When all its words are weighed in the light of the discussions which took place, the constitution emerges as the charter of a firmly ultramontane view of the Church, but one more moderate than many had hoped for and one which, through its silence on certain issues and its occasional imprecision, is not without openings for further discussion."[6]

Within the text itself, then, theologians find many examples of a wording more moderate than some interpretations recognize. Pottmeyer, for example, notes that the council locates its definition within the ancient and universal tradition of the church, mentioning explicitly the tradition of the first millennium.[7] Bishops are described as "true shepherds," and the words of St. Gregory the Great are used to show commitment to the honor of his brothers.[8]

Tillard notes that *Pastor Aeternus* at certain points shows that the primacy of the bishop of Rome depends upon the fact that his see is located in Rome. Although the importance of this point in the document should not be exaggerated, says Tillard, still its presence "bears witness to roots which go down deep into the tradition of the undivided Church. For there at least the primacy which Rome was recognized to hold was tied in the first place not to the person of the bishop but to the particular significance which the local church at Rome had among the local churches."[9] Similarly, Tillard emphasizes

---

[4] Hermann J. Pottmeyer, *Towards a Papacy in Communion: Perspectives from Vatican Councils I & II*, trans. Matthew J. O'Connell (New York: Crossroad, 1998), 61.

[5] Jean-Marie R. Tillard, *The Bishop of Rome*, trans. John de Satgé (Wilmington, DE: Michael Glazier, 1983), 25.

[6] Ibid., 26.

[7] Pottmeyer, *Towards a Papacy in Communion*, 71.

[8] Ibid., 72.

[9] Tillard, *The Bishop of Rome*, 69.

the limits on papal primacy contained in the phrase "truly episcopal" of *Pastor Aeternus*: "far from exalting the bishop of Rome unduly, as the Minority feared, by placing his power above the general run of bishops or outside the normal episcopal condition," this approach "sets him fair and square in his proper place within the company of bishops."[10]

The Anglican–Roman Catholic International Commission has also emphasized a strict reading of the text of *Pastor Aeternus*. Noting the "misunderstanding" of the text's terms of "universal, ordinary and immediate" jurisdiction of the bishop of Rome, ARCIC explains, "The jurisdiction of the bishop of Rome as universal primate is called ordinary and immediate (i.e., not mediated) because it is inherent in his office; it is called universal simply because it must enable him to serve the unity and harmony of the *koinonia* as a whole and in each of its parts."[11] The service of the bishop of Rome to the unity of the church, according to Vatican I, was "explicitly intended" to support the ministry of the brother bishops "in their ministry of oversight."[12]

Summing up his reading of the text of Vatican I, Pottmeyer concludes, "Vatican centralization cannot appeal to Vatican I for its theological justification. That council taught the proper origin and particular authority of papal primacy of jurisdiction by invoking the special mission of Peter, but it did not deny the proper origin, and equally supreme authority, of the college of bishops. More than that, Vatican I declared that primacy is obliged to assert, confirm, and vindicate the authority of the bishops in their dioceses." Pottmeyer continues: "The council did not determine the scope of the primatial right of the pope . . . did not make its own the claim that the jurisdiction of the bishops comes directly from the pope. . . . Finally, the council let it be understood that it did not intend any break with the tradition of the first millennium and the tradition of the churches of

---

[10] Ibid., 143.

[11] Anglican–Roman Catholic International Commission, "Authority in the Church II," in *The Final Report* (London: SPCK & Catholic Truth Society, 1982), n. 18. Also at http://www.vatican.va/roman_curia/pontifical_councils/chrstuni/angl-comm -docs/rc_pc_chrstuni_doc_1981_authority-church-ii_en.html.

[12] Anglican–Roman Catholic International Commission, "Authority in the Church I," in *The Final Report*, n. 12. Also at http://www.vatican.va/roman_curia/pontifical _councils/chrstuni/angl-comm-docs/rc_pc_chrstuni_doc_197609_authority-church -i_en.html.

the East."[13] All of these points show the possibility of interpreting *Pastor Aeternus* in a way sympathetic to episcopal collegiality.

2. Focusing on the Discussions about the Text of *Pastor Aeternus* on Papal Primacy

A second step in studying the teaching of *Pastor Aeternus* on papal primacy is to focus on *discussions* of its text before, during, and after the council. Pottmeyer, for example, notes that the text itself fails to make clear that "the council did not intend to define primacy as absolute sovereignty of the pope."[14] To make the council's intention clear, "it takes an examination of the other records of the council."[15]

Especially important are the minority bishops, those 73 bishops from many countries who opposed the definition of papal infallibility. Because of their opposition, most of these bishops left before the final vote on July 18, 1870, when 533 bishops voted *placet* for *Pastor Aeternus* and 2 voted *non placet*.

Because the minority bishops succeeded in influencing the final form of *Pastor Aeternus* and introduced many changes into its formulation, understanding their views is an important key to understanding the text itself. Some of this interest is sparked by the assessment expressed by Charles-Henri Maret: "The minority has triumphed in its defeat."[16] Gustave Thils asks, "But without this minority, to what extremes would the fathers have gone?"[17] And Yves Congar notes that contemporary interpretations see the minority bishops as prophetic, "like the vanguard of Vatican II."[18]

---

[13] Pottmeyer, *Towards a Papacy in Communion*, 74–75.

[14] Ibid., 72.

[15] Ibid.

[16] Charles-Henri Maret, in personal notes written to himself, cited by Gustave Bazin, *Vie de Mgr Maret, évêque de Sura, archevêque de Lépante, primicier de l'insigne chapitre de Saint-Denys, doyen et professeur de la Faculté de Théologie en Sorbonne*, 3 vols. (Paris: Berche et Tralin, 1891), 3: 218. Also see http://gallica.bnf.fr/ark:/12148/bpt6k134549b/f5.image.

[17] Gustave Thils, *L'infaillibilité pontificale: source, conditions, limites* (Gembloux: J. Duculot, 1969), 176.

[18] Yves Congar, "Bulletin d'ecclésiologie: conciles et papauté," *Revue des Sciences philosophiques et théologiques* 60 (1976): 281–308, at 288.

My own work on the French minority bishops focused on their arguments against the definition of papal infallibility, not papal primacy. But some of their arguments throw light on the issue of primacy as well. For example, Guillaume Meignan, bishop of Châlons, argues that the definition of papal infallibility is inopportune because unnecessary. He continues: "now, why would that of infallibility be timely now when faithful, priests, and bishops all obey with so great unanimity the orders, even the desires of the sovereign pontiff?"[19] Georges Darboy, archbishop of Paris, contends that "the unity of doctrine and also of communion, and the central authority of the supreme pontiff . . . blossomed and flourish quite apart from any dogmatic definition of infallibility." In fact, he argues, unity would not become stronger with a stronger central authority; on the contrary, a tightening can cause things to perish, to be stopped up. Thus the central authority as instituted by Christ, which does not separate bishops from pope nor pope from bishops, should be kept lest the actual unity in the church which it has furthered be destroyed. [20]

Félix Dupanloup, bishop of Orléans, maintains that a definition of papal infallibility would seem opposed to the faithful's belief that the bishops, with the pope, constitute the teaching church. It would seem to make the bishops not voices but simply "echoes." The church's teaching is a witness to Revelation, he continues, and Catholics have always understood it to be "a testimony by all who are witnesses." The faithful will not easily understand a teaching that makes it unnecessary for bishops to give testimony to the faith of all their churches, that makes of the pope "the sole witness."[21] Jean-Baptiste Callot, bishop of Oran, requests a clarification of the definition of papal infallibility that would show the duty of a pope to consult with a council in making doctrinal decisions, rather than exercising infallibility alone or expecting a divine revelation.[22] Henri Maret, titular bishop of Sura and dean of the theological faculty at the Sorbonne, also argued that infallibility in an absolutely certain

---

[19] Henri Boissonnot, *Le Cardinal Meignan* (Paris: Victor Lecoffre, 1899), 298–99.

[20] Mansi 52: 160A-C.

[21] Félix Dupanloup, *Lettre de Mgr l'évêque d'Orléans au clergé de son diocèse: observations sur la controverse soulevée relativement à la définition de l'infaillibilité au prochain concile* (Paris: Charles Douniol, 1869), 48–49.

[22] Mansi 52: 1045C-1046A.

fashion is "only in the agreement and the concerted action of the pope with the bishops, the bishops with the pope."[23] Augustin David, bishop of Saint-Brieuc, regards that view as the correct one. "In proclaiming definitions of faith, the supreme pontiff is never even to be thought of as endowed with infallibility separately from the teaching church, by himself alone, even [when] speaking as supreme pastor," he argues.[24]

These views of the French minority reveal their interpretation that the conciliar schema proposed to define as *de fide* the separate, personal, absolute infallibility of the pope. Proceeding on this interpretation, they formed their case against the schema, and they succeeded in influencing the final form of the text sufficiently that they were able to accept its teaching after it was approved by the council. Their viewpoint is important, therefore, for grasping the intended meaning of *Pastor Aeternus*.

In the preceding paragraphs I have relied on my own study of the French minority bishops, but a parallel study of the German-speaking bishops highlights similar positions.[25] Recent scholarship continues to show an interest in correctly understanding the conciliar discussions and views of both minority bishops and also bishops who voted in favor of the final text. Pottmeyer draws on the conciliar debates in his study of Vatican I, noting that many bishops objected to describing papal authority as "ordinary and immediate" because it seemed to supersede the ordinary and immediate authority of the bishops in their dioceses. Pottmeyer notes that "the bishops made it unambiguously clear that in their view not only the primacy of the pope, but also the authority of the bishops, belongs to the God-given constitution of the church."[26] He cites the German bishop Wilhelm Emmanuel Ketteler, bishop of Mainz, who complains that the proposed text tends to define the pope's authority in extreme terms, giving the impression that the rights of the bishops are being denied.[27] Other bishops as well

---

[23] Henri Maret, *Du concile général et de la paix religieuse*, 2 vols. (Paris: Henri Plon, 1869), 1: xx–xxi. See also https://archive.org/stream/a592229901mareuoft#page/20/mode/2up.

[24] Mansi 52: 988B-C.

[25] Klaus Schatz, *Kirchenbild und päpstliche Unfehlbarkeit bei den deutschsprachigen Minoritätsbischöfen auf dem I. Vatikanum* (Rome: Gregorian University Press, 1975).

[26] Pottmeyer, *Towards a Papacy in Communion*, 63.

[27] Mansi 52: 208D-209A, cited by Pottmeyer, *Towards a Papacy in Communion*, 64.

noted that their rights are affirmed but nowhere listed in the proposed schema.[28] Pottmeyer underlines the importance of the Deputation on the Faith's response to such objections from the bishops, acknowledging that "no mention at all was made of the collegial collaboration of the bishops" but that, "on the other hand . . . the deputation asserted the authority of the college of bishops."[29] He explains that the deputation regarded "the doctrine of the supreme and full authority of the college of bishops as a perfectly obvious integral part of the ecclesiastical and theological tradition," and adds: "The truth that was controversial, and therefore needed to be defined, was the likewise supreme and full jurisdictional authority which the pope possesses independently of the active collaboration of the bishops."[30]

Tillard as well argues that *"Pastor Aeternus . . .* lends itself to a moderate interpretation when the finer points in the discussions surrounding it are taken into account, marginally though these are represented in the text itself."[31] He also studies the interventions of the minority bishops, who protested that the proposed schema pictured bishops as no more than shadows of the bishop of Rome.[32] "[O]n this matter they all agree in insisting that the 'primacy' of the bishop of Rome is not such as to conflict with what the Tradition holds to be of *divine right* for the episcopate."[33] Tillard draws on the clarifications of the Deputation on the Faith during the council to bring out "the key insight . . . present at Vatican I even if little developed. The power, *potestas*, exists in relation to the charge (*officium, munus*). It exists only in order to make it possible to carry out that responsibility. Because the power of the bishop of Rome is essentially fulfilled in the unity of the Church, it should obviously be articulated with the power of the other bishops who are also charged with building the Church."[34] Hence, Tillard argues, the minority bishops left a "watermark" on the final version of the text of *Pastor Aeternus* such that a modern reform of the exercise of primacy would not be in contradiction to its teaching.

---

[28] Pottmeyer, *Towards a Papacy in Communion,* 64–65.
[29] Ibid., 67–68.
[30] Ibid., 69.
[31] Tillard, *The Bishop of Rome,* 28.
[32] Ibid., 130.
[33] Ibid., 131.
[34] Ibid., 147.

Attention to the discussions surrounding the conciliar sessions allows current interpreters of Vatican I to exegete the final text in light of the intention of its authors. Hence it is an important part of the effort that seeks a correct interpretation of the council's teaching on papal primacy and its relationship to collegiality.

3. Focusing on the Worldviews behind the Discussions about the Text of *Pastor Aeternus* on Papal Primacy

For years I myself have followed both successive steps mentioned above in my effort to grasp the teaching of Vatican I on papal primacy, interpreting it in a moderate way that is sympathetic to the emphasis on collegiality in Vatican II texts and in ecumenical dialogue. But I have found myself increasingly dissatisfied with limiting myself just to these two steps. I now realize that attending only to the text or even including the discussions surrounding it can lead too quickly to a defense of—even an apologetic for—*Pastor Aeternus*.

Of course, I agree entirely that *Pastor Aeternus* is a complex, nuanced document that demands interpretation. Its meaning is not the unilateral one claimed by August Hasler in his controversial scholarly study[35] or its short popularized version.[36] But while aiming to highlight the complexity of the text, scholars who spend all their time making the careful nuances and distinctions I have been considering easily open themselves to the charge that they "do protest too much." Hence I think it is important to add an analysis of *worldviews* to the preceding steps in order to adequately interpret this conciliar document. Only in this way will we come to see the overall framework within which we can relate Vatican I's teaching on primacy to Vatican II's teaching on collegiality, and place both in relationship to recent ecumenical and theological discussion about finding an exercise of primacy that is "open to a new situation."[37]

---

[35] August Bernhard Hasler, *Pius IX (1846–1878), päpstliche Unfehlbarkeit und 1. Vatikanisches Konzil: Dogmatisierung und Durchsetzung einer Ideologie*, 2 vols. (Stuttgart: Anton Hiersemann, 1977).

[36] August Bernhard Hasler, *How the Pope Became Infallible: Pius IX and the Politics of Persuasion*, trans. Peter Heinegg (Garden City, NY: Doubleday, 1981).

[37] John Paul II, encyclical *Ut Unum Sint*, *Origins* 25 (1995–96): 49, 51–72; see n. 95. Also at http://www.vatican.va/holy_father/john_paul_ii/encyclicals/documents/hf_jp-ii_enc_25051995_ut-unum-sint_en.html.

Therefore I find myself enthusiastic about scholarly approaches that attend to the worldview of participants in Vatican I, a worldview presupposed but perhaps not explicitly recognized by them. Tillard, for example, follows Congar[38] in arguing that Vatican II moved away from a pyramidal conception of the church toward an ecclesiology of communion.[39] This means that Vatican I's teaching on the primacy must first be understood as a highpoint in such a pyramidal ecclesiology. But then its meaning must be transposed into or reconceptualized as an ecclesiology of communion, in order to take into account more recent developments in ecclesial self-understanding. Similarly, Bernard Lonergan notes the shift from classicism to historical-mindedness. While a classicist perspective emphasizes permanence of meaning and the fixity of human nature, historical-mindedness recognizes that "intentionality, meaning, is a constitutive component of human living . . . not fixed, static, immutable, but shifting, developing, going astray, capable of redemption."[40] Vatican I can be better understood as illustrating the classicist mind-set, which had little room for the realities of reception, collegiality, and the diversity of local churches that are emphasized in the ecclesiology of communion undergirding Vatican II. Such an analysis of worldview can be combined with Karl Rahner's interpretation of Vatican II as the first official manifestation of the Roman Catholic Church as world-church, with all the diversity that implies.[41] Rahner notes the significance of this development for the exercise of governing authority by the college of bishops with the pope, since "a world-Church simply cannot be ruled by that Roman centralism which was usual in the time of Pius XII."[42] He too calls for a major transition, which he compares to the epochal transition from Judaeo-Christianity to Gentile Christianity. All of these analyses underline the large changes in worldview

---

[38] Yves Congar, "La 'réception' comme réalité ecclésiologique," *Revue des Sciences philosophiques et théologiques* 56 (1972): 369–403, at 392–93.

[39] Jean-Marie Tillard, "The Roman Catholic Church: Growing Towards Unity," *One in Christ* 14 (1978): 217–30.

[40] Bernard Lonergan, "The Transition from a Classicist World-View to Historical-Mindedness," in *A Second Collection: Papers by Bernard J. F. Lonergan, SJ*, ed. William Ryan and Bernard Tyrrell (Philadelphia: Westminster, 1974), 1–9, at 5–6.

[41] Karl Rahner, "Basic Theological Interpretation of the Second Vatican Council," in *Theological Investigations*, Vol. 20, *Concern for the Church*, trans. Edward Quinn (New York: Crossroad, 1981), 77–89, at 79–80.

[42] Ibid., 89.

that we should take into account when interpreting the teaching of Vatican I on papal primacy.

While the authors I have just cited are making general points about ecclesiology or epistemology, others compare worldviews more specifically as they study Vatican I. Such comparisons enrich the framework within which Vatican I can be interpreted.

Pottmeyer, for example, argues that Vatican I does not represent continuity with the first millennium in its teaching on papal primacy, but instead is a change of paradigm.[43] In the first millennium the church regarded the bishop of Rome as the "witness to, and protector of, the tradition of the Apostles Peter and Paul, which possessed a special authority for the entire church."[44] In the second millennium the church "became aware that the preservation of tradition called for action to redefine the tradition as the circumstances may require." It discovered itself "as an active subject shaping itself, its tradition, and its life," and it began to define the papacy in terms of monarchy.[45] While the discovery of the pope's active role was valuable, less valuable was the church's tendency to define that active role in terms of monarchy. In fact, Pottmeyer contends, "the conception of papal primacy as sovereignty became one of the central ideas of the ultramontanist movement."[46] At Vatican I, "those who appealed to the tradition in behalf of greater episcopal collaboration with the pope were implicitly appealing to the paradigm of the first millennium, that is, to the church as a community of witnesses. The defenders of absolute sovereignty, however, were arguing one-sidedly within the context of the paradigm of the second millennium."[47]

While Vatican I does not define papal primacy as absolute monarchical sovereignty, Pottmeyer states,[48] its conception of primacy is one-sided, centralized, and defensive.[49] But Vatican I and its decrees "leave open the possibility that the Petrine office may take various forms and that primacy may be exercised in a variety of ways. . . . The council simply asserted that primacy, as the pope was exercising it at that time and as, in the council's judgment, he was bound to

---

[43] Pottmeyer, *Towards a Papacy in Communion*, 24.
[44] Ibid., 25.
[45] Ibid., 27.
[46] Ibid., 53.
[47] Ibid., 56.
[48] Ibid., 61.
[49] Ibid., 73–74.

exercise it in the current situation for the greatest good of the church, is a legitimate concrete form of that Petrine office which goes back to Peter and his mission."[50]

Ghislain Lafont likewise imagines a different exercise of primacy from the one presented by Vatican I. He too sees a big shift afoot. He claims that Christianity has been influenced by a preference for Plato and an acceptance of a hierarchical worldview.[51] When faced with modernity and its emphasis on autonomy of judgment and rationality, the church failed to relate this insight to creation and instead reacted by defensively rejecting modernity. Linked to this rejection, says Lafont, is the continuing Gregorian "form" of the church, in which truth and the struggles against heresy become increasingly important. "This way of reflection opens up for us the second element in the Gregorian form of the Church: a precise theology of the primacy of the pope, the successor of the apostle Peter who received from Christ the mission to strengthen his brothers," he explains.[52] The nineteenth century, then, "can be considered the century in which the Church understood itself as a 'perfect society,' possessing all the structures necessary to constitute a sociopolitical body but with the added fact that it also understood itself as based on a divine institution where the primacy of the pope enjoyed considerable extension and where it penetrated the understanding of the faithful."[53] This happened through the liturgy, missionary congregations, and the personality of the popes, says Lafont, and all of these led to *Pastor Aeternus,* "with its double proclamation of a universal primacy of jurisdiction of the Roman pontiff and the infallibility of his doctrinal definitions."[54] To correct the imbalances that come from the church's continuing in the Gregorian form, Lafont calls for a replacement, not a reform. He views the church as "structured communion" and seeks to discover "new operational structures, less top-heavy, more supple, of service to the various charisms and their respective institutions."[55]

---

[50] Ibid., 75.

[51] Ghislain Lafont, *Imagining the Catholic Church: Structured Communion in the Spirit,* trans. John J. Burkhard (Collegeville, MN: Liturgical Press, 2000), 14–21.

[52] Ibid., 46.

[53] Ibid., 54–55.

[54] Ibid., 55.

[55] Ibid., 202.

Klaus Schatz also emphasizes the contrast between two views of history, but he relates them differently than Pottmeyer. Already in the seventeenth and eighteenth centuries, he notes, "the Febronians took the first centuries of the Church as their only yardstick" while "their opponents proceeded from the actual present situation as their norm and unhistorically transposed it to the past."[56] These two positions "reappear in similar form at Vatican I," he contends.[57] When the minority bishops argued that lengthy consensus-building and reception were the ways by which doctrine was discerned in the church's history, the majority responded that papal infallibility had been secure until the conciliarist movement.[58]

However, while the first position emphasized ecclesial consensus and reception, the second provided a way of reaching binding decisions. Hence this second, papalist position provided the church with a more effective means for surviving the catastrophes that would shake the church in the eighteenth and nineteenth centuries.[59] In fact, Schatz argues, ultramontanism began to seem like a movement promising the church freedom from state control. Writing his 1819 book on the pope, Joseph de Maistre believed that "the papacy and papal infallibility were the only guarantees of social order and stability."[60]

Hence it is not surprising that the majority of council bishops in 1870 thought that the church offered the world a principle of authority lacking in the world, "and without which it will end in chaos and destruction."[61] Where the debates two centuries earlier had focused on the primacy of the pope, that primacy was presupposed at Vatican I: instead, the debate focused on infallibility. Schatz observes that the majority bishops "wanted the definition of infallibility to be as efficient an instrument as possible for making swift decisions and preventing future conflicts."[62] Hence, for example, they refused to set conditions on how the pope would consult with the church.

---

[56] Klaus Schatz, *Papal Primacy: From Its Origins to the Present*, trans. John A. Otto and Linda M. Maloney (Collegeville, MN: Liturgical Press, 1996), 142.

[57] Ibid.

[58] Ibid., 159.

[59] Ibid., 143.

[60] Ibid., 148.

[61] Ibid., 158.

[62] Ibid., 161.

In retrospect, says Schatz, the definitions in *Pastor Aeternus* "must be seen essentially as an attempt by the Catholic Church to maintain its place within a world and a society that were becoming increasingly secularized."[63] The church focused on its own institutional center, emancipating its governance from the state and its teaching from secular ideas. But after 1870, Schatz points out, developments occurred that show "that the dogma of infallibility has not had the significance attributed to it in 1870 by its supporters or by its opponents. Instead," he continues, "the papal primacy of jurisdiction has acquired a greater scope than it actually had in 1870."[64] This presents special problems, since Vatican I laid down some conditions for the exercise of papal infallibility, but almost none for the exercise of papal primacy.

In fact, Schatz notes, popes in the succeeding 125 years have tried to answer questions about doctrine and morals through new forms of papal teaching, not through infallibly taught definitions. Leo XIII initiated a style of papal teaching that did not limit itself to condemnations but also offered constructive theological analysis.[65] Until 1968 and the negative response to *Humanae Vitae*, Schatz observes, this "'merely' authentic papal magisterium fulfilled the function of the unused infallibility."[66] This was in itself an expansion of the authority of the papal magisterium in the exercise of primacy, and it was combined with more papal interventions throughout the world, especially in the nomination of bishops, and with the missionary travels of Pope John Paul II.[67]

On the eve of Vatican II, Rome ruled more strongly and intervened more often than it had in 1870, Schatz observes, in part because of new means of communication and of church-state separation.[68] In this situation Vatican II set the ecclesiology of communion with its contribution of collegiality alongside Vatican I's ecclesiology of jurisdiction. But it did not really integrate them well, and it does leave the pope able to exercise his authority alone.

---

[63] Ibid., 165.
[64] Ibid., 166.
[65] Ibid., 167–68.
[66] Ibid., 168.
[67] Ibid.
[68] Ibid.

The discussion by Schatz makes clear just how incomplete the reconsideration of papal primacy actually is. Not really the focus of Vatican I's debates, papal primacy emerged as a kind of alternative infallibility after that council and continues to function without many restrictions on its exercise either in theory or in practice. Rather than being reexamined, papal primacy was presupposed at Vatican II and its definitions simply repeated along with affirmations about collegiality. In other words, rather than being a carefully considered and defined teaching, papal primacy received little careful theological reflection at either council. On the one hand, this shows how much further theological work on and practical reform of papal primacy lie ahead. On the other hand, it tends to downplay the authority of the teaching about primacy from both councils. Papal primacy was not really the focus of either council, and it did not receive much theological analysis at either event. Like some other ideas that were presupposed without being carefully examined—apostolic succession, women's ordination, or the positive providential purpose of other religions, for example—papal primacy has remained relatively unexamined since the Reformation. Hence it presents a fairly open theological project.

In pursuing the next steps in this theological project, Schatz underlines the historical reality of consensus and reception in the way that primacy has actually operated. "Roman dogmatic definitions . . . have never been able to put a swift end to a disputed question unless the time for it was ripe for other reasons," he notes.[69] He also emphasizes the significance of strengthening intermediate structures, such as regional synods and provincial councils, which give "independent expression of episcopal collegiality."[70] Both of these are elaborations of Vatican II's ecclesiology of communion.

In an article on Vatican II's reception of Vatican I's teaching on primacy, Alfonso Carrasco Rouco makes a similar point. He too notes that Vatican I put little emphasis on its teaching about papal primacy. Relating Vatican I's two dogmatic constitutions to each other, he argues that the council's main emphasis was on the supernatural origins of the Christian economy, the "otherness of Revelation" as

[69] Ibid., 180.
[70] Ibid., 181.

contrasted with contemporaneous claims for autonomous reason.[71] In its teachings on both Revelation and papal infallibility, he argues, Vatican I expressed its dominant concern: "the affirmation of authority and its foundation."[72] By defining both Revelation and papal infallibility the council affirmed its conviction that Revelation is present in history as a supernatural gift and is reliably preserved and defended by the bishop of Rome.

Vatican II also focuses on Revelation, he asserts, but more on its transmission in the church. In its teaching on the sacramentality of the episcopal office, the council maintained this focus[73] by teaching that the bishop's jurisdiction is given by the sacrament itself, not the pope, and that every bishop is a vicar of Christ. Within this discussion the primacy is linked to Christ's will. The pope cannot place himself above the word of God; he does not institute the episcopal college or give the bishops jurisdiction. Rouco concludes: "The [Second Vatican] Council opened perspectives in which the ministry does not appear as a power over the Church, but as structurally a service of Christ and of his work of communion in the Spirit. These perspectives offer a solid basis for a process of reception of the definitions of *Pastor aeternus* concerning the nature of the ministry of the bishop of Rome."[74] Vatican II thus provides a decisive moment in the process of reception of the meaning of the "primacy of jurisdiction" affirmed by Vatican I.

Finally, Richard Gaillardetz joins the group of analysts who underline a similarity between Vatican I and Vatican II.[75] Vatican I offered an ecclesiology reduced to its juridical form, he asserts; Vatican II lays an ecclesiology of communion next to this earlier inheritance. But neither actually elaborates a full theology of papal primacy. Gaillardetz finds that teachings on primacy are being developed in both the teaching and the practice of John Paul II. In *Ut Unum Sint*, Gaillardetz finds ideas about the primacy that go beyond both councils. In this encyclical the bishop of Rome is head of the college only

[71] Alfonso Carrasco Rouco, "Vatican II's Reception of the Dogmatic Teaching on the Roman Primacy," *Communio: International Catholic Review* 25 (1998): 576–603.

[72] Ibid., 589.

[73] Ibid., 598.

[74] Ibid., 602.

[75] Richard R. Gaillardetz, "Reflections on the Future of Papal Primacy," *New Theology Review* 13 (November 2000): 52–66.

because he is first a member. As his service of the church, he keeps watch in order to ensure communion. His is "a service of unity . . . entrusted within the College of Bishops to one among those who have received from the Spirit the task, not of exercising power over the people . . . but of leading them toward peaceful pastures."[76] Gaillardetz also points to elements of recent papal practice. He is pleased with the exercise of primacy represented by the symbolic papal actions in the visits to many countries.[77] The prayer with other Christian leaders and with representatives of other religions, along with the millennium prayer for forgiveness for past sins, are other symbolic actions giving a new definition to the exercise of papal primacy. He is less happy with the tendency of John Paul II to serve as chief theologian of the church or to intervene in the affairs of local churches in opposition to their decisions rather than confirming or supporting them. If we followed Gaillardetz in his line of thought we would see a rich theology of papal primacy just beginning to emerge, with only a few guidelines from the two councils. To Gaillardetz's sources from John Paul II, I would add the corpus of ecumenical dialogue agreements on the petrine ministry that call for "the ecumenical conversion, or reconversion, of the papacy" so that it "freely decides to place itself at the service of Christian unity."[78]

The goal in this section of my paper has been to illustrate how a comparison of underlying worldviews can enhance our understanding of Vatican I's teaching on papal primacy and thus help us clarify its relationship with Vatican II's teaching on episcopal collegiality. Lonergan, Rahner, Congar, Tillard, Pottmeyer, and Lafont enable us to see the contrast between the two councils. This gives us a way to distinguish between their teaching on papal primacy and the particular perspective or worldview within which they present it. Schatz, Rouco, and Gaillardetz offer us a perhaps more surprising finding: the similarity of the two councils. Although each council taught about the primacy of the pope, neither made it a major focus of discussion or elaboration. This suggests that many aspects of papal primacy are in fact open or disputed questions. It leaves us free to

---

[76] Ibid., 54 (quoting *Ut Unum Sint*, n. 94).

[77] Ibid., 56.

[78] Paolo Ricca, "The Papacy in Discussion: Expectations and Perspectives for the Third Millennium," *One in Christ* 33 (1997): 283–89, at 288.

treat the promising developments from the present pontificate and from ecumenical dialogue as resources for a future enriched understanding and practice of papal primacy.

Conclusion

In this brief paper I have argued that a careful study of Vatican I's teaching on papal primacy is a necessary part of reaching a proper understanding of collegiality. Such a study must include analysis of the text of *Pastor Aeternus*, of course, as well as attention to the discussions surrounding its passage. However, detailed attention to the worldviews shaping Vatican I will also be required if the full transposition of its meaning is to be successfully achieved.

Having given some attention here to those worldviews, I suggest that the issue of papal primacy at Vatican I may be more open than is commonly thought.

Anglican Orders and Ecumenical Dialogue on Ordained Ministry[1]

Ecumenical dialogue and its implications for canon law is a fitting topic for this convention, with its focus on "The Church and the Churches: Fostering *Communio*." Archbishop Rembert Weakland suggested to you earlier how the Catholic Church could be restructured to more effectively accommodate the many cultures it includes. Alongside this matter of cultural pluralism, Jean-Marie Tillard considers a distinct matter that also is related to the issue of ecclesial unity: theological pluralism. Within the one church of Christ, a legitimate pluralism exists—in fact, such pluralism is inherent to the church. "The essential question is whether this doctrinal pluralism constitutes a breach in communion in faith," he maintains.[2]

---

[1] First presented on October 15, 1998, as *"Apostolicae Curae* after a Century: Anglican Orders in Light of Recent Ecumenical Dialogue on Ordained Ministry in the Church," in a plenary session at the sixtieth annual convention of the Canon Law Society of America, Orlando, FL. Previously published in *Canon Law Society of America Proceedings* 60 (1998): 1–18.

[2] Jean-Marie R. Tillard, "Theological Pluralism and the Mystery of the Church," in *Different Theologies, Common Responsibility: Babel or Pentecost?*, ed. Claude Geffré et al., *Concilium* 171 (1984): 62–73, at 70.

Today we seek deeper understanding of the communion that should exist within the Roman Catholic Church as it pursues its mission of genuinely proclaiming the Gospel in every culture. The same mission also impels us to seek healing of the divisions between Christian communions that may have arisen over differences once thought to be contradictory but now recognized as complementary.

In his apostolic letter on the riches of the Eastern churches, *Orientale Lumen*, Pope John Paul II refers to such a recognition: "We have increasingly learned that it was not so much a historical episode or a mere question of pre-eminence that tore the fabric of unity as it was a progressive estrangement, so that the other's diversity was no longer perceived as a common treasure, but as incompatibility."[3] I find this a very illuminating idea: "the other's diversity was no longer perceived as a common treasure, but as incompatibility." The pope wants us to recognize that some types of pluralism are a richness, a common treasure, rather than divisive differences.

In *Unitatis Redintegratio*, the Second Vatican Council taught that the divisions between Christians make it "more difficult" for the church "to express" its catholicity,[4] and that "a change of heart" is required for these divisions to be overcome. "There can be no ecumenism worthy of the name without a change of heart," the council taught.[5] I share with that council the conviction that the discord and disunity among Christians "openly contradicts the will of Christ, provides a stumbling block to the world, and inflicts damage" on the proclamation of the Gospel.[6]

With a change of heart comes a change of mind that clarifies the theoretical basis of ecumenical dialogue. In its use of the word *subsistit*,[7] *Lumen Gentium* recognized that the one church of Christ

[3] John Paul II, apostolic letter *Orientale Lumen*, *Origins* 25 (1995–96): 3–13; see n. 18. Also at http://www.vatican.va/holy_father/john_paul_ii/apost_letters/1995/documents/hf_jp-ii_apl_19950502_orientale-lumen_en.html.

[4] Vatican II, *Unitatis Redintegratio* (Decree on Ecumenism), n. 4. Also at http://www.vatican.va/archive/hist_councils/ii_vatican_council/documents/vat-ii_decree_19641121_unitatis-redintegratio_en.html.

[5] Ibid., n. 7.

[6] Ibid., n. 1.

[7] Vatican II, *Lumen Gentium* (Dogmatic Constitution on the Church), in *The Documents of Vatican II*, n. 8. Also at http://www.vatican.va/archive/hist_councils/ii_vatican_council/documents/vat-ii_const_19641121_lumen-gentium_en.html.

extends "beyond the visible limits" of the Roman Catholic Church.[8] In *Unitatis Redintegratio* we see the implications of this shift in the recognition of the real though imperfect communion that Roman Catholics already share with other baptized Christians.[9] Hence ecumenical dialogue is founded on the presupposition that dialogue partners are already in real though imperfect communion; our task is to seek full communion for the sake of the church's mission of proclaiming the Gospel.

My part of this task today is to explore the light that ecumenical dialogue can shed on our reevaluation of *Apostolicae Curae*, in which Pope Leo XIII in 1896 declared Anglican orders to be "completely null and void." According to the document this negative judgment was made because of an Anglican liturgical form insufficient for the valid consecration of bishops and a sixteenth-century intention on the part of the consecrators that was not the proper intention to do what the church does.[10] Over a century after its promulgation in 1896, *Apostolicae Curae* still stands as a canonical and emotional obstacle in the path toward full communion between the Roman Catholic Church and the Anglican Church. A change of heart invites us to see whether we Roman Catholics might now come to a change of mind regarding the earlier judgment.

Before turning to this question, let me note the recent publicity given to *Apostolicae Curae* when it was named by Joseph Ratzinger and Tarcisio Bertone in their commentary on the three concluding paragraphs of the Profession of Faith that had been officially inserted into the Code of Canon Law by Pope John Paul II in *Ad Tuendam Fidem*.[11]

---

[8] Johannes Willebrands, "Vatican II's Ecclesiology of Communion," *Origins* 17 (1987–88): 27–33, at 32.

[9] Vatican II, *Unitatis Redintegratio*, n. 3.

[10] An English translation of *Apostolicae Curae* is available in Christopher Hill and Edward Yarnold, eds., *Anglican Orders: The Documents in the Debate* (Norwich: Canterbury Press, 1997), 265–79; and in R. William Franklin, ed., *Anglican Orders: Essays on the Centenary of "Apostolicae Curae," 1896–1996* (Harrisburg, PA: Morehouse Publishing, 1996), 127–37. Also at http://www.newadvent.org/library/docs_le13ac.htm.

[11] *Ad Tuendam Fidem* is dated May 18, 1998. See John Paul II, motu proprio *Ad Tuendam Fidem, Origins* 28 (1998–99): 113, 115–16. Also at http://www.vatican.va/holy _father/john_paul_ii/motu_proprio/documents/hf_jp-ii_motu-proprio_30061998 _ad-tuendam-fidem_en.html. The commentary by Ratzinger and Bertone is dated June 29, 1998. See Joseph Ratzinger and Tarcisio Bertone, "Commentary on Profession of Faith's Concluding Paragraphs," *Origins* 28 (1998–99): 116–19. Also at http://www

Ratzinger and Bertone provide a rather disparate list of teachings to illustrate objects of the Profession of Faith's second proposition ("I also firmly accept and hold each and every thing definitively proposed by the Church regarding teaching on faith and morals"), the kind of teachings to be held definitively. *Apostolicae Curae* appears on that list.[12] Leaving aside the question of the commentary's authority,[13] I note the observation of Avery Dulles about its mention of *Apostolicae Curae*. Dulles says: "According to the commentary this decision, published in 1896, was definitive. But the commentary says nothing about the validity of Anglican orders today. In view of the participation of bishops from other churches in Anglican ordinations, new developments in Anglican sacramental theology, and some modifications in the Anglican ordinals, the shape of the question has somewhat changed." He continues: "I am not saying, of course, that Anglican orders are now valid. I am simply pointing out the limits of what is affirmed in the commentary."[14] I think Dulles's observation is correct. Whether or not they agree with Ratzinger and Bertone's opinion about *Apostolicae Curae*, Roman Catholics remain free to explore whether today's situation should lead the Roman Catholic Church to a conclusion about Anglican orders now and in the future that differs from the one reached about them in 1896.

In 1982 the Anglican–Roman Catholic International Commission said that its agreements on the eucharist and ordained ministry in *The Final Report* set a new context for evaluating a mutual recognition of ministry. Within the new context, the verdict of *Apostolicae Curae* should be reappraised, they conclude.[15] I agree that today our evalu-

---

.vatican.va/roman_curia/congregations/cfaith/documents/rc_con_cfaith_doc_1998_professio-fidei_en.html.

[12] Ratzinger and Bertone, "Commentary on Profession of Faith's Concluding Paragraphs," 119 n. 11.

[13] Ladislas Örsy suggests that the "Commentary" by Ratzinger and Bertone has the authority only of a "personal statement" by its high-ranking authors, since it gives no evidence that it received approval for its publication from the whole Congregation for the Doctrine of the Faith or from the pope (Ladislas Örsy, "Intelligent Fidelity: The Apostolic Letter *Ad tuendam fidem* and Its Roman Commentary Revisited," *Céide: A Review from the Margins* 2 [1998]: 29–31, at 30).

[14] Avery Dulles, "How to Read the Pope," *The Tablet* 252 (1998): 967–68, at 968.

[15] Anglican–Roman Catholic International Commission, "Ministry and Ordination: Elucidation (1979)," in *The Final Report* (London: SPCK & Catholic Truth Society, 1982), n. 6. Also at http://www.anglicancommunion.org/ministry/ecumenical/dialogues/catholic/arcic/.

ation of the 1896 judgment takes place in a new context, and I would add some other factors to ARCIC's list. The new context is shaped by three developments: (1) a reevaluation of the historical data surrounding the judgment made by *Apostolicae Curae*; (2) evolution in both the Roman Catholic theology of ordained ministry and the liturgy of the sacrament of orders; and (3) ecumenical agreements on the ordained ministry. In what follows I will say something on each of those three developments. I will conclude with some thoughts on how the developments give us new insights about intention.

1. Reevaluation of the Historical Data Surrounding *Apostolicae Curae*

In his encyclical on commitment to ecumenism, *Ut Unum Sint,* Pope John Paul II places a strong emphasis on the power of memory. He believes that the ecumenical journey includes what he calls "the necessary purification of past memories."[16] He observes that Christians have harbored misunderstandings and prejudices[17] about each other inherited from the past that lead to misgivings in the present. Sometimes these bad memories about the past are true, sometimes they are distorted—a kind of false-memory syndrome. But not all of these bad memories, John Paul II believes, should be ignored; they should be faced and purified.

The first step in the purification of memories is repentance, he says, repentance for "exclusions which seriously harm fraternal charity," for certain refusals to forgive, for a certain pride, for "unevangelical insistence on condemning 'the other side.'" Repentance is accompanied by the vision of new horizons, as we discover ways the Holy Spirit is at work in other churches and learn of the holiness and Christian commitment present among members of those churches.[18] After such repentance we are ready for a new look at the past. Inspired by a sincere desire for mutual forgiveness and reconciliation, the pope affirms, the disciples of the Lord "are called to re-examine together

---

[16] John Paul II, encyclical *Ut Unum Sint, Origins* 25 (1995–96): 49, 51–72; see n. 2. Also at http://www.vatican.va/holy_father/john_paul_ii/encyclicals/documents/hf_jp-ii_enc_25051995_ut-unum-sint_en.html.

[17] Ibid.

[18] Ibid., n. 15.

their painful past and the hurt which that past regrettably continues to provoke even today."[19] He continues: "What is needed is a calm, clearsighted and truthful vision of things, a vision enlivened by divine mercy and capable of freeing people's minds and of inspiring in everyone a renewed willingness, precisely with a view to proclaiming the Gospel to the men and women of every people and nation."[20]

When ecumenists have sought such a clearsighted and truthful vision of past things surrounding the judgment made by *Apostolicae Curae*, some important points have emerged. George Tavard's book, *A Review of Anglican Orders*, constitutes a good example of reevaluating the historical evidence.[21] A common argument against the validity of Anglican orders is based in a criticism of the Anglican Ordinals of 1550 and 1552 and the *Book of Common Prayer* of 1549 and of 1552. These ritual books, explains Tavard, "were designed to exclude the sacrificial dimension of the eucharist and the correlative notion that priests are ordained to offer the sacrifice of the mass for the quick and the dead."[22] Thomas Cranmer, the composer of the Ordinal and the *Book of Common Prayer*, is certainly criticized by Pope Paul IV for his teachings on the eucharist and the ordained ministry, and for the changes introduced into the church's ordination rite. However, Tavard notes, "the Ordinal was in question insofar as it was not a rite approved by Rome or in use in the universal Church. But it was not in question as to its capacity, when used by the right persons, to make authentic priests."[23]

Similarly, Tavard continues, Paul IV does not ask questions about matter and form when he looks at the rites used to make a bishop: these questions are irrelevant for him. "What is relevant is that some bishops, because they denied the papal primacy at their ordination, have functioned as false bishops."[24] This negative judgment says nothing about the Ordinal the bishops used.[25] The clue to their intention, for Paul IV and the medieval frame of reference he inherited, was not the words and gestures the bishops used, but rather "their

---

[19] Ibid., n. 2.

[20] Ibid.

[21] George H. Tavard, *A Review of Anglican Orders: The Problem and the Solution* (Collegeville, MN: Liturgical Press, 1990).

[22] Ibid., 14.

[23] Ibid., 28.

[24] Ibid., 54.

[25] Ibid.

fidelity to the Church as the universal Communion of the faithful."[26] When English bishops under King Edward affirmed the religious supremacy of the British monarchy and denied papal authority, Paul IV refused to recognize their acts.

By the end of the sixteenth century the popes had still not condemned Anglican orders or the ordination rite in the Ordinal used by Anglicans. Instead, they rejected the religious supremacy of the British monarchy and those made bishops under its authority. This was because the theology of the episcopate throughout the medieval period, and really until Vatican II, understood episcopal power to be conveyed by papal confirmation. While the bishop's sacramental powers came from his ordination as a priest, his jurisdictional power as bishop came from the papal confirmation. "Accordingly," explains Tavard, "when they substituted the royal supremacy for the papal primacy, Henry VIII, Edward VI, and Elizabeth removed the effective source of episcopal authority."[27]

But by the seventeenth century the theological picture had shifted.[28] Scholasticism as it was conceived during the Counter-Reformation was the dominant theological school in the Roman Catholic Church, and debates between Jansenists, Dominicans, Jesuits, and Molinists about grace fostered intense speculation about the essence of the grace of the sacraments, as well as their matter and form. It was in this changed theological atmosphere that Leo XIII was asked in a hopeful spirit by the former French Roman Catholic missionary Fernand Portal and Anglican Charles Linsley Wood, Second Viscount Halifax, to render a judgment about the validity of Anglican orders. The commission chosen by the pope to study this issue was a balanced one: three members opposed validity of Anglican orders and three regarded them as possibly or definitely valid. Two more members were added during the deliberations, one pro and one con.

What was the atmosphere in which the commission pursued its work? Tavard lists a number of factors. The growing centralization of the Roman Catholic Church was accompanied by a distrust of diversity in worship forms.[29] The English Roman Catholic archbishop

[26] Ibid., 82.
[27] Ibid., 69.
[28] Ibid., 82.
[29] Ibid., 85.

of Westminster, Cardinal Herbert Vaughan, wrote to Leo XIII, arguing that English Roman Catholic bishops opposed the recognition of Anglican orders by the Roman Catholic Church: such recognition would "keep Anglicans in their heresy."[30] On the other hand, the condemnation of Anglican orders would bring an influx of Anglo-Catholic converts into communion with Rome. The Roman Catholic bishops in England also believed and argued that Leo's predecessors had condemned Anglican orders, and that respect for the papacy would diminish if Leo now declared them valid.[31] Leo XIII was also influenced in his thinking by the neoscholastic emphasis on form and matter in sacramental theology. Moreover, he was affected by an understanding of tradition in which "novelty is a mark of error."[32] Leo believed that "Protestantism had inaugurated the deleterious reign of the new," leading eventually to the French Revolution and liberalism.[33] Therefore, "to Leo XIII," Tavard concludes, "the Reformation was totally repulsive."[34]

The views of two members of the pope's commission who argued for the validity of Anglican orders can illuminate us. Monsignor Louis Duchesne, church historian from France, said that the Anglican Ordinal is sufficient for ordaining; and he noted that many Oriental liturgical rites are no more explicit about the sacrificial aspect of the priesthood than is the Anglican Ordinal.[35] He cautiously suggested conditional ordination of converted Anglican clergy. Emilio De Augustinis, SJ, dogmatic theologian from Italy, argued that the heresies of Cranmer about the eucharist and the identity of the true church are irrelevant, since those ordaining intended to do what the church does.[36] Two other commission members also felt inclined to support the validity of Anglican orders. But the other half of the Commission opposed their validity, and Leo XIII finally relied on the opinion of Cardinal Raffaele Pierotti, OP, Master of the Sacred Palace

[30] Ibid., 95.

[31] Edward J. Yarnold, *"Apostolicae Curae:* Past and Future Processes," *The Month* 257 (1996): 430–34, at 431.

[32] George H. Tavard, *"Apostolicae Curae* and the Snares of Tradition," *Anglican Theological Review* 78 (1996): 30–47, at 43.

[33] Ibid., 44.

[34] Ibid., 43.

[35] Tavard, *A Review of Anglican Orders,* 93–94.

[36] Ibid., 94–95.

and the pope's theological adviser. Pierotti argued that "the form [of the sacrament] must clearly identify the sacrament in question."[37] He also argued that a condemnation of Anglican orders was opportune, because it would lead to a large number of Anglican conversions.

Leo XIII formally concluded that Anglican orders were null and void. The Anglican Ordinal's form for the ordination of presbyters, he taught, does not indicate the essence of the priesthood, which is to offer the eucharist as the sacrifice of Christ on Calvary made sacramentally present. Moreover, he taught that the intention to do what the church does must be present in the form of the sacrament of orders, but in the Anglican case it was not; hence the intention too was defective. In the Roman Pontifical, the Roman Catholic book of episcopal rituals, the texts used for ordaining bishops made very little reference to the sacrificial aspect of the eucharist, but the texts used for ordaining presbyters gave slightly more emphasis to it. Cranmer, however, removed the latter references in his ordination liturgy for presbyters, and Leo XIII interpreted that change as indicating a defect in intention and also as manifesting what he called a fundamental deficiency in Anglicans' "native character and spirit."[38]

Why did Leo XIII argue to the defect of intention based on the defect in form, and to the defect in form for the consecration of a bishop based on the defect in form for the ordination of a presbyter?[39] Why did he follow this neoscholastic view rather than the historical studies of Duchesne and the theological arguments of De Augustinis on intention that emerged more from the tradition of Augustine during the Donatist controversy? Tavard argues that ultimately the pope hoped for a flood of conversions by Anglo-Catholics following the condemnation of orders in the Anglican Church.[40] In this, of course, he was badly mistaken.

Today we know something that Leo XIII did not know. His predecessors had not condemned the validity of Anglican orders; rather, they had rejected the religious supremacy of the British monarchy and those made bishops who affirmed this supremacy instead of papal primacy. Furthermore, we are aware of the pressures he was

---

[37] Ibid., 97.
[38] The translation is from Hill and Yarnold, eds., *Anglican Orders*, 275.
[39] Tavard, *A Review of Anglican Orders*, 104.
[40] Ibid., 112.

under from his study commission, from the English Roman Catholic episcopate, and from his own taste for neoscholastic sacramental theology and the avoidance of all novelty. And today we also know that in fact some changes were coming to Roman Catholic theology itself in its understanding of ordination. Let me turn briefly to those changes.

2. Evolution in the Roman Catholic Theology of Ordained Ministry and the Liturgy of the Sacrament of Orders

In its teaching on the sacramentality of episcopal ordination, Vatican II asserts that "by episcopal consecration is conferred the fullness of the sacrament of orders . . . But episcopal consecration, together with the office of sanctifying, also confers the office of teaching and governing."[41] That is to say, unlike Aquinas and the sixteenth-century popes who followed his theology of orders when they judged Anglican bishops, the council teaches that the sacrament of orders itself gives the bishop jurisdiction. This also means that Vatican II makes the episcopacy, not the presbyterate, "the fundamental category for understanding ordained ministry," as Daniel Donovan explains.[42] Further, the council emphasizes the collegial character of the episcopacy: to be a bishop is to be received into the college of bishops and to share in the responsibility for *episcope* [oversight] of the whole church.[43] The bishop is the link between Christ and the local church that—gathered around the eucharist—is filled with the many charisms given to the ordained, the religious, and the laity.[44] Everyone shares the priesthood of the faithful, although the latter and the ministerial priesthood differ "in essence and not only in degree."[45]

What of the presbyter according to Vatican II? Besides taking the bishop as its starting point for understanding the sacrament of orders, the council shifts its theology of the presbyter, mainly by expanding

[41] Vatican II, *Lumen Gentium*, n. 21.
[42] Daniel Donovan, *What Are They Saying about the Ministerial Priesthood?* (New York: Paulist Press, 1992), 10.
[43] Vatican II, *Lumen Gentium*, n. 22.
[44] Ibid., n. 26.
[45] Ibid., n. 10.

it. It underlines the ministry of the word as a crucial complement to the presbyter's eucharistic ministry. For preaching holds an eminent place among the functions of bishops;[46] and this eminence extends as well to the preaching of presbyters.[47] Donovan notes that in *Presbyterorum Ordinis* the council also argues that a proper understanding of Christian cult envisions it as including a ministry of the word.[48] Indeed, the document relates the work of evangelization and other pastoral work of the presbyter to the self-giving love of Christ's sacrifice, expanding the meaning of sacerdotal language to include all aspects of the presbyter's life.[49]

How are the foregoing changes pertinent to a reevaluation of *Apostolicae Curae*? Rather than the narrow understanding of the eucharist's sacrificial aspect that Cranmer seems to have rejected without adequately understanding it, Vatican II takes an expanded view of sacrifice and relates it to the preaching and pastoral work of the presbyter as well as to his eucharistic role. Moreover, in its teaching on the sacramentality of episcopal ordination the council shifted the Roman Catholic understanding of the sacrament of orders and how episcopal jurisdiction is given. Finally, by emphasizing the collegiality of the bishops, the significance of the local church, and the priesthood of the faithful shared by the whole people of God, the council accepted as its own several teachings of the English and continental Reformers that motivated their call for reformation in the first place.

This evolution in the Roman Catholic stance regarding the sacrament of orders was not left to theologians. The liturgy also changed. Well before Vatican II, Pius XII had determined that the matter of the sacrament was the laying on of hands, not the "porrection" of liturgical instruments (the holding out of a chalice, etc., to be touched by the ordinand), as Aquinas had taught. Paul VI continued this reform by eliminating the porrection in the ordination of the presbyter, by establishing the permanent diaconate, and by changing the Pontifical so that the rite was simplified and clarified and the ordination of

---

[46] Ibid., n. 25.

[47] Vatican II, *Presbyterorum Ordinis* (Decree on the Ministry and Life of Priests), in *The Documents of Vatican II*, n. 4. Also at http://www.vatican.va/archive/hist_councils /ii_vatican_council/documents/vat-ii_decree_19651207_presbyterorum-ordinis_en .html.

[48] Donovan, *What Are They Saying about the Ministerial Priesthood?*, 14.

[49] Ibid.

bishops was brought closer to the Eastern tradition. In fact, the latter reform narrowed the gap between the Roman Pontifical and the Anglican Ordinal that had been the liturgical basis for the condemnation of Anglican orders by Leo XIII.

3. Ecumenical Agreements on the Ordained Ministry

While Roman Catholic theology shows changes in its understanding of ordained ministry, changes that are then received into Roman Catholic liturgical practice, ecumenical dialogue also shows significant developments of understanding in its recent agreements on ordained ministry. In this section I want to highlight some of those developments—widespread throughout ecumenical dialogue—that relate to the reevaluation of *Apostolicae Curae*.

First, ecumenical dialogue has made real breakthroughs in its discussion of the eucharist by recalling a richer biblical meaning of memorial. The biblical sense of remembering is a dynamic one in which an event of the past is recalled so that its benefits may be made effective in the present. Ecumenical statements on the eucharist have recovered this biblical sense of remembering and have therefore broken past older disagreements based on more partial emphases. The *Baptism, Eucharist and Ministry* statement of the World Council of Churches [WCC], for example, explains: "The eucharist is the memorial of the crucified and risen Christ, i.e., the living and effective sign of his sacrifice, accomplished once and for all on the cross and still operative on behalf of all humankind."[50] Accomplished once and for all *and* still operative: with these two emphases the statement holds together the Protestant and Roman Catholic concerns but has gone beyond them by recovering an original biblical sense of remembering. The statement is then able to recover as well the dynamic sense of *anamnesis* and attribute to the Holy Spirit the making of "the crucified and risen Christ really present to us in the eucharistic

---

[50] World Council of Churches, "Eucharist," in *Baptism, Eucharist and Ministry* (Geneva: World Council of Churches, 1982), n. 5. Also at http://www.oikoumene.org /en/resources/documents/wcc-commissions/faith-and-order-commission/i-unity -the-church-and-its-mission/baptism-eucharist-and-ministry-faith-and-order-paper -no-111-the-lima-text?set_language=en.

meal."[51] This presence in the eucharist, it teaches, is "unique," and it continues: "The Church confesses Christ's real, living and active presence in the eucharist."[52]

While *Baptism, Eucharist and Ministry* of the WCC reflects a multilateral agreement (with the participation of the Roman Catholic Church through the Joint Working Group), the agreement on the eucharist in *The Final Report* of the Anglican–Roman Catholic International Commission [ARCIC] shows an even deeper integration of the sacrificial interpretation of the eucharist into the renewed sense of sacramental realism. ARCIC emphasizes that there is "no repetition of or addition" to the once-for-all sacrifice of Christ, but it also adds: "The eucharistic memorial is no mere calling to mind of a past event or of its significance, but the Church's effectual proclamation of God's mighty acts."[53] "In the eucharistic prayer," it asserts, "the Church continues to make a perpetual memorial of Christ's death, and his members, united with God and one another, give thanks for all his mercies, entreat the benefits of his passion on behalf of the whole Church, participate in these benefits and enter into the movement of his self-offering."[54] Hence Roman Catholic and Anglican members can affirm the real presence of Christ in the eucharist, in which "the bread and wine . . . become his body and blood"[55] in a self-giving of Christ. This becoming is not a material or local change, they maintain, but is "given through the action of the Holy Spirit, appropriating bread and wine so that they become the food of the new creation."[56]

Against the background of agreement on the eucharist, the two ecumenical statements I am examining proceed next to the difficult question of the ordained minister of the eucharist. Both statements situate the minister firmly in the midst of the church. The WCC affirms that the Holy Spirit bestows on the community diverse and complementary gifts,[57] but within that multiplicity of gifts the ordained

[51] Ibid., n. 14.

[52] Ibid., n. 13.

[53] Anglican–Roman Catholic International Commission, "Eucharistic Doctrine," in *The Final Report*, n. 5.

[54] Ibid.

[55] Ibid., n. 6.

[56] Anglican–Roman Catholic International Commission, "Eucharistic Doctrine: Elucidation (1979)," in *The Final Report*, n. 6.

[57] World Council of Churches, "Ministry," in *Baptism, Eucharist and Ministry*, n. 5.

provide "a focus of its unity."[58] Indeed, "the ordained ministry has no existence apart from the community."[59] ARCIC also speaks of the many gifts of the Holy Spirit, among which is *episcope* by the ordained ministry, given for the edification of the church.[60]

At the same time, both statements emphasize the difference between the ordained ministry and other ministries in the church. The WCC argues: "In order to fulfill its mission, the Church needs persons who are publicly and continually responsible for pointing to its fundamental dependence on Jesus Christ, and thereby provide, within a multiplicity of gifts, a focus of its unity."[61] Far from seeing the ordained simply as representatives of the community, "Ministry" explains that they are "representatives of Jesus Christ to the community," chosen and called by Christ, sent as "heralds and ambassadors" to "proclaim his message of reconciliation."[62] The presence of the ordained "reminds the community of the divine initiative, and of the dependence of the Church on Jesus Christ," the statement emphasizes.[63] Such persons may be called "priests" because of their priestly service of the royal and prophetic priesthood of the faithful "through word and sacraments, through their prayers of intercession, and through their pastoral guidance of the community."[64]

The ARCIC discussion of ordained ministry also brings out the uniqueness of the ordained ministry. While ordained ministers share through baptism in the priesthood of the people of God and represent the church in its priestly vocation of self-offering, the ministry of the ordained "is not an extension of the common Christian priesthood but belongs to another realm of the gifts of the Spirit."[65] At the eucharist, "[b]ecause the eucharist is the memorial of the sacrifice of Christ," declares ARCIC, "the action of the presiding minister in reciting again the words of Christ at the last supper and distributing to the assembly the holy gifts is seen to stand in a sacramental relation

[58] Ibid., n. 8.

[59] Ibid., n. 12.

[60] Anglican–Roman Catholic International Commission, "Authority in the Church I," in *The Final Report*, n. 5.

[61] World Council of Churches, "Ministry," in *Baptism, Eucharist and Ministry*, n. 8.

[62] Ibid., n. 11.

[63] Ibid., n. 12.

[64] Ibid., n. 17.

[65] Anglican–Roman Catholic International Commission, "Ministry and Ordination," in *The Final Report*, n. 13.

to what Christ himself did in offering his own sacrifice. So our two traditions commonly use priestly terms in speaking about the ordained ministry."[66] Along with this clear statement of a sacrificial aspect in its interpretation of ordained ministry, however, the ARCIC statement also gives a full job description for the ordained: minister of the word, teacher, servant, shepherd, called to holiness and compassion.[67] The WCC statement also provides a long job description.[68]

Perhaps most surprising is the nuanced description that both groups provide in relating the ordained ministry to its function of *episcope*. For the WCC, every church needs a ministry of unity, of *episcope*, "in order to be the Church of God."[69] "Ministry" teaches that the Holy Spirit keeps the church in the apostolic tradition, and it lists a variety of characteristics through which continuity with the church of the apostles is maintained. Such characteristics include witness, proclamation and fresh interpretation of the Gospel, celebration of the sacraments, service to the sick and needy, and the transmission of ministerial responsibilities.[70] Succession of bishops became one of the ways in which the church's apostolic tradition is expressed, the statement notes.[71] It recommends that churches without episcopal succession recover it "as a sign, though not a guarantee, of the continuity and unity of the Church," yet as "part of a wider process by which the episcopal churches themselves also regain their lost unity."[72] In fact, the statement contends, the threefold pattern itself stands in need of "reform."[73]

Not surprisingly, the ARCIC statement recognizes that *episcope* is part of ordained ministry. And of course Anglicans join Roman Catholics in expecting such oversight to be the work of the bishop, who symbolizes and maintains "[t]he communion of the churches in mission, faith, and holiness, through time and space."[74] Perhaps more surprising is ARCIC's lengthy discussion of the teaching authority

---

[66] Ibid.

[67] Ibid., nn. 7–11.

[68] World Council of Churches, "Ministry," in *Baptism, Eucharist and Ministry*, n. 11.

[69] Ibid., n. 23.

[70] Ibid., n. 34.

[71] Ibid., n. 36.

[72] Ibid., n. 38.

[73] Ibid., n. 24.

[74] Anglican–Roman Catholic International Commission, "Ministry and Ordination," in *The Final Report*, n. 16.

exercised by the bishops acting in conciliar or primatial ways,[75] its affirmation that the primacy of the bishop of Rome is part of "God's design for the universal *koinonia*,"[76] and its conviction that sometimes "[m]aintenance in the truth requires . . . a decisive judgment" on doctrine that becomes part of the church's "permanent witness,"[77] a judgment that can be made by council or "universal primate."[78] This recognition of the role of teaching authority as part of the doctrine of ordained ministry has brought the ecumenical discussion to a new level of depth.

We know, of course, that the discussion of *episcope* has not remained merely theoretical. In *The Porvoo Common Statement*, the British and Irish Anglican Churches and the Nordic and Baltic Lutheran Churches affirmed and then voted to receive a shared life of worship, mission, and service, including mutual participation of the member churches in future episcopal ordinations. *The Porvoo Common Statement* sees the primary manifestation of apostolic succession "in the apostolic tradition of the Church as a whole";[79] succession is an expression of "permanence" and "continuity of Christ's own mission in which the Church participates" (PCS 39). But the apostolic succession of the ministry is a focus for the church's continuity and faithfulness, the statement continues (PCS 40). Then it makes an interesting argument. Noting that apostolic succession is signified in the ordination or consecration of a bishop (PCS 47, 49), it observes that this continuity cannot be divorced from the continuity of the life and witness of the whole diocese. At the time of the Reformation "all our churches ordained bishops (sometimes the term superintendent was used as a synonym for bishop) to the existing sees of the Catholic Church,

---

[75] Anglican–Roman Catholic International Commission, "Authority in the Church I," in *The Final Report*, nn. 19–22.

[76] Anglican–Roman Catholic International Commission, "Authority in the Church II," in *The Final Report*, n. 15.

[77] Ibid., n. 24.

[78] Ibid., n. 26.

[79] Conversations between the British and Irish Anglican Churches and the Nordic and Baltic Lutheran Churches, *The Porvoo Common Statement* (1992) (London: Council for Christian Unity of the General Synod of the Church of England, 1993), n. 39. Also at http://www.porvoochurches.org/whatis/resources-0201-english.php. Subsequent references to this document occur intratextually with the abbreviation "PCS," followed by the section number.

indicating their intention to continue the life and ministry of the One, Holy, Catholic and Apostolic Church" (PCS 33). So the continuity "represented by the occupation of the historic sees" is more than personal, and the care for maintaining the church's pattern of life there "reflects an intention of the churches to continue to exercise the apostolic ministry of word and sacrament of the universal Church" (PCS 49). Hence the ordination of a bishop in historic succession, the statement argues, both signifies and reinforces the church's continuity in the apostolic faith (PCS 50). While not a guarantee of all the aspects of apostolicity, such ordination is a challenge to fidelity and unity, a summons and commission to realize more fully the characteristics of the church of the apostles (PCS 51). The *Porvoo* statement "can affirm . . . the value and use of the sign of the historic episcopal succession" (PCS 57) without implying "an adverse judgment on the ministries of those churches which did not previously make use of the sign" (PCS 53). In fact, the statement notes, "[t]o the degree to which our ministries have been separated, all our churches have lacked something of that fullness which God desires for his people" (PCS 54).

In this remarkable agreement we are a long way from the conceptual worldview of the English Reformation in the sixteenth century or Leo XIII's theology of ordination in the nineteenth century. Within an ecclesiology of communion, the *Porvoo* statement affirms the ministries given to the whole church, with apostolic succession of bishops at the service of the church's unity and faithfulness. *Episcope* is seen as an essential part of ministry, and its rethinking has allowed the Lutheran churches that formerly lacked episcopal succession to affirm and recover it.

The decision to accept *The Porvoo Common Statement* is an example of concrete reception of the recent ecumenical developments on ordained ministry. And what about the agreements on eucharist and ministry reached by the Anglican–Roman Catholic International Commission? After a further set of clarifications about Anglican and Roman Catholic teaching on the eucharist and ministry,[80] ARCIC received a letter from Cardinal Edward Cassidy confirming that, for

---

[80] Anglican–Roman Catholic International Commission, "The Clarifications: ARICIC II," *Origins* 24 (1994–95): 300–4. Also at http://www.anglicancommunion.org/ministry/ecumenical/dialogues/catholic/arcic/.

both the Pontifical Council for Promoting Christian Unity and the Congregation for the Doctrine of the Faith, "no further study would seem to be required."[81] Today theologians and canon lawyers are challenged to explore further how such agreements can be translated into the actual life and practice of the church.

Conclusion

I began this paper by stating that a new context has emerged in which to reevaluate *Apostolicae Curae*. This new context is shaped by three developments, and I have said something about each of them: (1) a reevaluation of the historical data surrounding the judgment made by *Apostolicae Curae*, (2) evolution in both the Roman Catholic theology of ordained ministry and the liturgy of the sacrament of orders, and (3) ecumenical agreements on the ordained ministry. These three developments offer us a wealth of new opportunities as we reconsider Anglican orders, but I want to lift out one theme that recurs frequently: it is the theme of *intention*. I think that intention offers many intriguing possibilities for canon lawyers to consider. Let me mention three.

First, Tavard's study of Anglican orders contends that the popes of the sixteenth and seventeenth centuries did not really question or condemn the validity of Anglican orders. Rather, they attacked the Anglican Church for calling to ordination men they judged to be wrong-minded. It was eventually a different approach that Leo XIII took when he focused on the form and the intention of the Anglican Ordinal used for the consecration of bishops and ordination of priests. But in fact the Reformers of the sixteenth century called for changes because they believed the church needed reform. Their intention was the reform of the church, and their theology and liturgical changes— even if faulty—were guided by that intention. In that sense it is hard to see how they did not intend to do what the church does. But whatever we think of past Anglican understanding and practice and of Leo XIII's negative judgment on it, today's discussions help to clarify today's intention on the part of Anglicans. The ecumenical

---

[81] Edward Cassidy, "Vatican Says Clarifications Strengthen Agreement," *Origins* 24 (1994–95): 299–304, at 299.

studies I have cited show agreements on a nuanced, elaborate theology of the eucharist, of ordained ministry, and of apostolic *succession* that includes teaching office. Furthermore, Vatican II brings shifts in the Roman Catholic theology of ordained ministry itself, shifts that are reflected in our Roman Catholic liturgical texts. These theological shifts show a convergence of understanding between Roman Catholics and Anglicans. But they also demonstrate the point that emerged from the Donatist controversy about intention: it is Christ who acts in the sacraments, regardless of the faith or the theology of the minister. Even if Cranmer's understanding of the eucharist and of ordained ministry was faulty, we can see more clearly today that he did his work so that the ordained might more faithfully do what the church does. Is it not time to reconsider whether it would be better to conclude that today, at least, Anglicans certainly have the intention to do what the church does? If we Roman Catholics cannot conclude this—if we place too much emphasis on correct theological understanding and liturgical form—then we also have an awkward question from our own Roman Catholic history to answer: how can we explain that the intention is the same for the theologies and liturgies of ordination in the Roman Catholic Church itself in the nineteenth century and today?

Second, whose intention should be evaluated? While an earlier approach to unity of the church emphasized the recognition of ministries and from there the reconciliation of church communions, today the reverse is the order of preference. This change in starting point echoes the shift from what Yves Congar called a pyramidal ecclesiology to an ecclesiology of communion.[82] When we think about intention, then, we might see a parallel shift: from the intention of the ordaining bishop, or the intention revealed by the liturgical form that he used, to the intention of the whole community in which he ministers. Tillard emphasizes this in an article called "Recognition of Ministries: What Is the Real Question?"[83] The real question, he says, is not the intention of the ordained minister but that of the community the minister serves. Tillard argues that "the intention of causing a

---

[82] Yves Congar, "La 'réception' comme réalité ecclésiologique," *Revue des Sciences philosophiques et théologiques* 56 (1972): 369–403, at 392–93.

[83] Jean-Marie R. Tillard, "Recognition of Ministries: What Is the Real Question?" *One in Christ* 21 (1985): 31–39.

breach cannot be deduced simply on the basis of the ministers' doctrinal position."[84] It is right to ask "to what extent the people *as such* really did change their outlook at that point" in the sixteenth century "and opt for a break with what is essential to the Tradition handed down and lived until that point."[85] With the Anglican communion, he notes, it is not so clear that there was an obstinate rejection of the traditional vision and ministry "which intended to set up another Church," all the more so since such a vision would have required its accompanying doctrine to be set out "with all the clarity needed to convince an ordinary parishioner."[86] So, Tillard says, "if today, after a history during which the most traditional vision has ceaselessly resurfaced, the Anglican communion 'recognises' in this vision its own faith, then it seems to me that it must be concluded that, in its case, the apostolic ministry has probably never been interrupted."[87]

This stress on the intention of the community as a whole, rather than that of just the ordained ministers, is also suggested by *The Porvoo Common Statement* with its emphasis on historic sees. It takes the continuing use of historic sees as a sign of the intention of those local churches to remain in faithful continuity with the one, holy, catholic, and apostolic church.

Indeed, taking seriously the intention of the whole community might be a way to explore more deeply your present convention's theme: "The Church and the Churches: Fostering *Communio.*"

Third and finally, there is a set of events I have failed to list when discussing ecumenical developments. Those are the remarkable events in which the bishop of Rome and the archbishop of Canterbury have signified the intention that the dialogue between their two communions achieve full, visible unity. The use of the expression "sister churches" by Pope Paul VI, the establishment of the Preparatory Commission by Pope Paul VI and Archbishop Michael Ramsey, the 1982 visit together to the tomb of Thomas à Becket at Canterbury by Pope John Paul II and Archbishop Robert Runcie, the return visit in 1989 by Archbishop Runcie to Rome and common prayer at the Church of St. Gregory—all these indicate, in words and symbolic

---

[84] Ibid., 37.
[85] Ibid.
[86] Ibid., 37–38.
[87] Ibid., 38.

gestures, the common intention of the two communions through their leaders. I could report details from many of these meetings to illustrate my point, but let me use one that is for me the most dramatic. When John Paul II and Archbishop Runcie met in Rome in 1989 they compared the dialogue between their two communions to a journey. "The arduous journey to Christian unity must be pursued with determination and vigor," they said.[88] But, facing difficulties with realism, they cited the admission of women to the priesthood in some Anglican provinces as a question and practice that prevents reconciliation between the Anglican and Roman Catholic communions. However, "no pilgrim knows in advance all the steps along the path," they continued. "While we ourselves do not see a solution to this obstacle, we are confident that through our engagement with this matter our conversations will in fact help to deepen and enlarge our understanding."[89] Then, in a striking statement, they declared, "We here solemnly recommit ourselves and those we represent to the restoration of visible unity and full ecclesial communion in the confidence that to seek anything less would be to betray our Lord's intention for the unity of his people."[90]

I think that events such as this one, with their reconciling gestures and statements, also show that our current context is shaped by the persistent intention for the restoration of full communion between these two church communities. We have become even more aware of our own limitations, and we seek to be corrected and converted by the other. Congar writes of this desire for unity: "Those involved in the ecumenical movement have by virtue of that a *votum unitatis, votum catholicitatis* [desire for unity, desire for catholicity], which gives to their present belief a dynamic dimension in which their intention of plenitude is fulfilled," he says.[91] Is not this growing *votum unitatis* with its accompanying openness to one another's theology and practice a significant fact on which we should reflect more deeply? If our

[88] John Paul II and Robert Runcie, "Common Declaration [2 October 1989]," *Origins* 19 (1989–90): 316–17, at 316. Also at http://www.vatican.va/holy_father/john_paul _ii/speeches/1989/october/documents/hf_jp-ii_spe_19891002_dichiaraz-comune _en.html.

[89] Ibid., 317.

[90] Ibid., 316–17.

[91] Yves Congar, *Diversity and Communion*, trans. John Bowden (Mystic, CT: Twenty-Third Publications, 1984), 133.

two communions were to be moving slowly into a new relationship with each other, would not their movement be characterized by this desire? I think it may be time to recognize this new relationship and implement it in the life of our two communions. Much of the historical, liturgical, and theological work is done. It will soon be the canon lawyers' turn.

The Holy Spirit's Assistance to the Magisterium in Teaching[1]

Introduction[2]

Roman Catholic theology asserts that the magisterium is assisted by the Holy Spirit in its teaching. But this claim rarely receives much direct attention. What kind of help does the Holy Spirit give the magisterium? On what kinds of teaching? In what circumstances? And how does this help differ from the assistance the Holy Spirit gives to Christian believers who are not part of the magisterium?

While much discussion has occurred in this century regarding the inspiration of the Scriptures, comparatively little has gone forward regarding this other important dimension of the Holy Spirit's guidance, namely, assistance to the magisterium in teaching. And yet this claim is a very important one, often used to stop further discussion

[1] First presented (with Michael Vertin) on June 7, 1996, as "The Holy Spirit's Assistance to the Magisterium in Teaching: Theological and Philosophical Issues," in a workshop session at the fifty-first annual convention of the Catholic Theological Society of America, San Diego, CA. Previously published in *Catholic Theological Society of America Proceedings* 51 (1996): 125–42.

[2] Although the authors collaborated on everything in this paper, O'Gara is the principal writer of the introduction and sections 1, 2, and 6; Vertin is the principal writer of sections 3, 4, and 5, and the conclusion.

of disputed questions as well as to explain the normative basis of earlier teaching by the councils or popes. Just what does it mean?

We have been thinking about this claim for a long time. Margaret's interest in it started during her master's studies in theology when she tried to explain to her fellow students in Protestant churches how the Holy Spirit was assisting the magisterium. Later she began to study the question in earnest by focusing on the understanding of infallibility. Meanwhile, Michael has spent his past three decades considering epistemological issues from the standpoint of philosophy. And our topic is certainly related to epistemology, since it touches on the way that the magisterium can know the faith, especially when a question is disputed. So when the topic of this year's convention was announced, we thought we might be able to offer some useful reflections on theological and philosophical aspects of it.

In fact, it is precisely the relationship of the theological and philosophical aspects of the topic that we find especially interesting. Sometimes a debate about a particular theological issue is also—or even primarily—a debate about a philosophical issue that lies beneath the theological issue but is unnoticed or unacknowledged. In the case of our topic, this certainly seems to be a fair suspicion. Roman Catholics make a certain kind of truth claim about the magisterium because they assert that the Holy Spirit assists the magisterium in its teaching, and hence first with its knowing of the truth so that it knows what to teach. But a claim to know the truth is always accompanied by philosophical presuppositions about what knowing the truth means, and about whether such knowing ever actually occurs. Even when one claims with Vatican I that the truth of revelation cannot be known by unassisted human reason but only by reason that is illumined by faith, that claim itself bespeaks presuppositions about the cognitional process through which faith-assisted human minds achieve their grasp of revealed truth. These presuppositions are what we want to examine today.

Before we start, however, let us emphasize two presuppositions that we maintain, presuppositions not generally open to dispute in Roman Catholic theology. The first is the one just indicated. God's revelation cannot be discovered by human reason alone: faith is necessary to grasp it. The second presupposition regards the magisterium. We assume that the magisterium's unique role of *episcope* within the church includes a unique role in teaching God's revelation.

Our aim, then, is to probe just *how* the Holy Spirit assists the magisterium in its teaching of revelation and of other matters related to revelation.

A final preliminary comment may be useful. We will be considering three interrelated levels that are involved in theological discussion. A first level is that of particular doctrinal problems and various proposed solutions. The second level is that of general theological accounts of how a doctrine emerges as normative within the church. The third level is that of philosophical presuppositions underlying the general theological accounts. We will suggest that there are three different general theological accounts of how a doctrine emerges as normative within the church, each with its own conception of the Holy Spirit's assistance; and that these different general theological accounts are crucially influenced by different philosophical presuppositions about how objective knowledge arises.

1. Three Particular Doctrinal Problems, and the Normativity of Some Proposed Solutions

Let us begin by recounting three particular doctrinal problems and a proposed solution to each. The degree of ecclesial consensus that the proposed solution is normative, that it constitutes a definitive standard for Christian thought and practice, differs from one example to the next.

The first doctrinal problem arose around the year AD 150, and it constituted a special challenge to harmony among Christians for the next three hundred years. Is Jesus both divine and human—and, if so, precisely how? Such names as Arius, Nestorius, Cyril, and Athanasius will remind you of the long and arduous process that culminated in 451, with the decree by the Council of Chalcedon that in Jesus there are two natures, one divine and one human, united in the divine person of the Logos. The normativity of that decree is a matter of *virtually universal* ecclesial consensus except for those once called "Monophysites."

The second doctrinal problem has been with us at least since the Reformation. Just what is the nature of justification? Luther, condemning what he took to be the Roman position, argued with some passion that faith alone, not works, is what justifies. The Council of

Trent, responding that faith without good works is dead, condemned what it took to be Luther's position. In recent decades, however, careful study by theologians on all sides of this issue has come to suggest that, whatever the precise character of the sixteenth-century differences, at least the present-day Lutheran and Roman Catholic understandings of justification are not radically opposed. Indeed, there seems to be some prospect that in 1997, the four-hundred-fiftieth anniversary of Trent's decree, Lutheran and Roman Catholic authorities will declare that these condemnations no longer apply to their dialogue partner today.[3] In light of these developments, we suggest that the normativity of the present-day Lutheran–Roman Catholic account of justification is a matter of *growing* ecclesial consensus.

The third doctrinal problem is the possibility of ordaining women to the priesthood. Lutheran, Anglican/Episcopal, and many other Protestant communions in fact do ordain women, and they offer doctrinal arguments in favor of the practice. By contrast, Orthodox and Roman Catholic communions do not ordain women; and in *Ordinatio Sacerdotalis*, Pope John Paul II declared that the church has no authority to ordain women, and that this judgment is to be held definitively by the faithful.[4] After this declaration the Congregation for the Doctrine of the Faith gave its judgment that this teaching about women's exclusion from priestly ordination pertains to the deposit of the faith and that it has been taught infallibly by the ordinary and universal magisterium.[5] This judgment by the Congregation is presently a source of controversy, such that it seems accurate to say that at least thus far its normativity is *not* a matter of widespread ecclesial consensus.

---

[3] What was anticipated in 1996 when this paper was presented became a reality on October 31, 1999, when the Lutheran World Federation and the Roman Catholic Church issued a Joint Declaration on the Doctrine of Justification. See http://www.vatican.va/roman_curia/pontifical_councils/chrstuni/documents/rc_pc_chrstuni_doc_31101999_cath-luth-joint-declaration_en.html.

[4] John Paul II, *Ordinatio Sacerdotalis*, *Origins* 24 (1994–95): 49, 51–52. Also at http://www.vatican.va/holy_father/john_paul_ii/apost_letters/1994/documents/hf_jp-ii_apl_19940522_ordinatio-sacerdotalis_en.html.

[5] Congregation for the Doctrine of the Faith, "Reply to the *dubium* concerning the Teaching Contained in the Apostolic Letter *Ordinatio Sacerdotalis*," *Origins* 25 (1995–96): 401, 403. Also at http://www.vatican.va/roman_curia/congregations/cfaith/documents/rc_con_cfaith_doc_19951028_dubium-ordinatio-sac_en.html.

2. A Classical Cognitivist View of the Holy Spirit's Assistance: Normative Doctrine as Authoritatively Taught to the Church

Bernard Lonergan contrasts classicism with historical-mindedness,[6] and his category of classicism corresponds at least roughly to what (for purposes of later comparison) we are labeling the "classical cognitivist" account of how normative Christian doctrines emerge. A hallmark of classicism is its view that doctrines are normative only insofar as they are authoritatively taught to the church. Primarily, the authoritative teacher is God. Secondarily, the authoritative teacher is the magisterium, itself divinely instituted to interpret and transmit God's revelation. This view itself rests on two prior (if usually unspoken) convictions, namely, that (a) the basic reason a religious doctrine is normative is that it is true, expressive of reality, epistemically objective, and (b) a religious doctrine is manifest as true only insofar as it is authoritatively taught.

After introducing the issue of the relative priority of teaching and learning in the church, Frederick Crowe goes on to indicate something of the classicist approach. "Suppose we put our original question to the sources themselves, and ask in that context whether teaching or learning has the priority. Some will answer, teaching, and they will do so with unshakeable certitude." On this view, Crowe continues,

> [T]here is an original teaching, and it has absolute priority. In that case, for the Church as a whole, it is not learning but teaching that has the priority. It may well be that for individual members of the Church learning always comes first, but that is only a limited and relative priority: limited to us, or some of us, and relative to an original situation where things are different. In that original situation, and therefore for the Church as a whole, teaching has a priority, a priority attached primarily to sources given us by God, and secondarily to the magisterium also given us by God to interpret the sources.[7]

---

[6] Bernard Lonergan, "The Transition from a Classicist World-View to Historical-Mindedness," in *A Second Collection: Papers by Bernard J. F. Lonergan, SJ*, ed. William Ryan and Bernard Tyrrell (Philadelphia: Westminster Press, 1974), 1–9; and "Philosophy and Theology," ibid., 193–208.

[7] Frederick E. Crowe, "The Church as Learner: Two Crises, One *Kairos*," in idem, *Appropriating the Lonergan Idea*, ed. Michael Vertin (Washington, DC: Catholic University of America Press, 1989), 370–84, at 370–71.

Crowe mentions an aspect of the classical cognitivist view that is characteristic of its approach: an emphasis on the magisterium's unique access to truth. This access is often described in terms of illumination and sometimes understood as an effect of the sacrament of orders for those called to the episcopate. On this view the priority goes to teaching, which is given by God to the church; and priority secondarily therefore goes to the magisterium, given by God to interpret the teaching correctly within the church.

Last January the national Canadian newspaper *The Catholic New Times* carried many letters to the editor that discussed the Congregation for the Doctrine of the Faith's judgment about the teaching on women's ordination. An extract from one of them provides a popular summary of the position we have been elaborating. John D'Asti of LaSalle, Ontario, writes, "Catholics interpret the passage (Matt 16:13-19) to mean that Peter was the first pope of an unbroken line of popes to whom Christ gave authority over His church to 'bind and loose' on earth and in heaven. This authority now rests in John Paul II and will rest in each of his successors, guided by God 'until the end of the world' (Matt 28:20)." He continues, "Christ's words to St. Peter tell us that His Vicar on earth has a special relationship with His Father. If and when God wants married priests or female priests, the pope will know."[8]

"If and when God wants married priests or female priests, the pope will know": in this comment, the writer puts a great emphasis on the pope as a source of knowledge because, he explains, of the pope's "special relationship" to the Father.

Vatican I was more sophisticated than this letter writer, but its teachings on the normativity of doctrine also are embedded in a largely classical cognitivist worldview. The council emphasized that "the meaning of the sacred dogmas is perpetually to be retained which our Holy Mother Church has once declared; nor is that meaning ever to be departed from under the pretense or pretext of a deeper comprehension of them."[9] Vatican I defined as dogma the unique way that, under certain circumstances and because of his office, the bishop of Rome "is possessed of that infallibility with which the

---

[8] John D'Asti, Letter to the Editor, *Catholic New Times* 20 (January 21, 1996): 12.

[9] First Vatican Council, *Dei Filius*, in DS 3020; English translation in *The Teaching of the Catholic Church as Contained in her Documents*, ed. Karl Rahner, trans. Geoffrey Stevens (Staten Island, NY: Alba House, 1967), 38.

divine redeemer willed that his Church should be endowed in defining doctrine regarding faith or morals."[10]

The emphasis of Vatican I on a classicist approach to doctrinal normativity was reflected, not surprisingly, in the emphases of the majority bishops at Vatican I. It is reflected as well in the interpretations of Vatican I after its close, which generally presented the council as having taught what Peter Chirico, citing Hans Küng, calls "*a priori* infallibility."[11] *A priori* infallibility saw little role for a process of reception after an authoritative teaching had been given. Furthermore, it regarded the magisterium as the guardian and expounder of the unchanging deposit of faith. Classicist ideas of assistance distinguish sharply between the magisterium and the rest of the church, since members of the magisterium are the ones who are assisted in knowing what the teaching is; they expound this to the rest of the church. Yves Congar has called the ecclesiology linked to this view of the Holy Spirit's assistance a "pyramidal ecclesiology."[12]

Classicist views of the Holy Spirit's assistance do not mix easily with discussions of reception. The Vatican slips into a classicist position in one sentence of its 1991 response to *The Final Report* of the Anglican–Roman Catholic International Commission, prepared jointly by the Congregation for the Doctrine of the Faith and the Pontifical Council for Promoting Christian Unity. Commenting on ARCIC's view of reception, the Vatican statement says: "For the Catholic Church, the certain knowledge of any defined truth is not guaranteed by the reception of the faithful that such is in conformity with Scripture and tradition, but by the authoritative definition itself on the part of the authentic teachers."[13] The second part of this sentence summarizes the classicist position.

---

[10] First Vatican Council, *Pastor Aeternus*; English translation in Margaret O'Gara, *Triumph in Defeat: Infallibility, Vatican I, and the French Minority Bishops* (Washington, DC: Catholic University of America Press, 1988), 269.

[11] Peter Chirico, "Papal Infallibility since Vatican I," *Chicago Studies* 22 (1983): 163–79, at 168–69, citing Hans Küng, *Infallibility? An Inquiry* (Garden City, NY: Doubleday, 1971).

[12] Yves Congar, "La 'réception' comme réalité ecclésiologique," *Revue des Sciences philosophiques et théologiques*, 56 (1972): 369–403, at 392–93.

[13] "Vatican Response to *The Final Report* of the Anglican–Roman Catholic International Commission," *Origins* 21 (1991–92): 444; cf. 446. Also at http://www.vatican.va/roman_curia/pontifical_councils/chrstuni/angl-comm-docs/rc_pc_chrstuni_doc_1991_catholic-response-arcici_en.html.

To sum up: classical cognitivists give primacy of place to authoritative teaching, and they conceive the assistance of the Holy Spirit as helping the magisterium to teach and the rest of the church to learn. Concretely, classicists explain that the decree of Chalcedon is normative because it issued from an ecumenical council. Discussions on justification are interesting to Roman Catholic classicists; but since they regard Trent as an ecumenical council, and therefore authoritative, they view its teaching as the unchanging standard in this matter: contemporary Lutheran views on justification must be judged in its light. Finally, Roman Catholic classicists feel confident that the question of women's ordination is closed. The magisterial position is clear, claiming a heritage from the practice of Jesus and the history of the church, and standing as a teaching of the ordinary and universal magisterium. Hence the question is only improperly labeled "disputed."

3. A Noncognitivist View of the Holy Spirit's Assistance: Normative Doctrine as Authentically Constructed by the Church

We are labeling "noncognitivist" the second general account of how normative Christian doctrines emerge. This account's most distinctive claim is that doctrines are normative only insofar as they are authentically constructed by the church. As we interpret this account, it is the conclusion of two prior lines of argumentation, one negative and the other positive.

The first prior line of argumentation is the following: If a doctrine ever were authoritatively taught—in the limit, by God—then that doctrine would indeed be manifest as true, expressive of reality, epistemically objective; and in that case the doctrine would be normative precisely because of its epistemic objectivity. As it turns out, however, no doctrine ever is authoritatively taught. The very idea of God's transmitting a divine message to humankind reflects an outmoded, premodern notion of the genesis and function of religious meanings. Consequently, no doctrine is ever normative by virtue of being epistemically objective.

Nonetheless—and this is the second prior line of argumentation—there are such things as normative doctrines, doctrines that quite properly serve as a standard for testing whether given words, attitudes, and actions rightly merit the label "Christian." How do such doctrines arise, and what is the basis of their normativity? The noncognitivist contention is that religious doctrines are the result of a community's effort to express its religious experiences, feelings, emotions; and normative doctrines are none other than the expressions that are recognized as successful in this regard. That is to say, normative doctrines are the consequences of authentic ecclesial constructivity, the products of authentic communal self-expression. And in this context the Holy Spirit's assistance is conceived as fostering the authentically ecclesial character of this creative process within the church, and *thereby* fostering the normativity of the doctrines resulting from that process.

The noncognitivist account of how normative Christian doctrines emerge is not usually asserted by Roman Catholics. Roman Catholic and Orthodox Christians, most Anglicans/Episcopalians, and many Protestants are resolutely cognitivist in this regard. The most prominent proponents of doctrinal noncognitivism are other Protestant Christians who envision certain distinctive features of modernity as definitive and therefore meriting incorporation by a Christian theology come of age. In this connection, a book that we have found both lucid and helpful is George Lindbeck's *The Nature of Doctrine: Religion and Theology in a Postliberal Age*.[14] Lindbeck labels the two main versions of doctrinal noncognitivism the "experiential-expressivist" explanation and the "cultural-linguistic" explanation. Experiential-expressivism envisions doctrines as simply *expressive*, at best reflecting changing Christian experience from one age to the next, and therefore needful of refinement and even modification as history unfolds. Christian experience produces Christian doctrines.[15] The cultural-linguistic explanation, by contrast, gives a privileged role to the doctrines emergent from earlier ages. For latter-day Christians the function of doctrines is *regulative*, constituting a standard

---

[14] George A. Lindbeck: *The Nature of Doctrine: Religion and Theology in a Postliberal Age* (Philadelphia: Westminster Press, 1984). Our comments on this book involve interpretations, some of which are influenced by a review article of Charles C. Hefling, "Turning Liberalism Inside Out," *Method: Journal of Lonergan Studies* 3 (October 1985): 51–69.

[15] Lindbeck, *The Nature of Doctrine*, 30.

according to which we are challenged to shape our attitudes, words, and actions. Christian doctrines produce Christian experience.[16] On both of these explanations, however, doctrines are misinterpreted if one takes them to be functioning cognitively, expressing objective reality, epistemically objective. On the contrary, they are simply the subjective products of ecclesial artistry—normative insofar as that artistry is authentic.

To sum up: doctrinal noncognitivists give primacy of place to authentic construction in the church, and they conceive the assistance of the Holy Spirit as the fostering of an authentic creative process in every ecclesial quarter. Concretely, noncognitivists explain as follows the normativity of the three proposed doctrines with which we began: The reason the normativity of the Chalcedonian decree on the divinity and humanity of Jesus is a matter of virtually universal ecclesial consensus is that it manifestly satisfies the criteria of authentically ecclesial construction. The reason the normativity of the recent Lutheran–Catholic statements on justification is a matter of growing ecclesial consensus is that those statements more and more seem to satisfy the criteria of authentically ecclesial construction. Finally, the reason the normativity of the 1995 declaration by the Congregation for the Doctrine of the Faith regarding women's ordination is a matter of currently absent ecclesial consensus is that it manifestly does not (at least yet) satisfy the criteria of authentically ecclesial construction.

4. Epistemically Objective Knowledge as the Result of Non-Subjective Knowing

Now, in the next two main steps of our presentation we carry our analysis beyond the level of general theological accounts to the level of underlying philosophical presuppositions. In this section and the next we will be focusing not on the question of how a doctrine emerges as normative within the church, but rather on the broader and more basic question of how there is genuine human knowledge of anything at all.

But why, after all, should we even bother talking about philosophical issues in the context of a theological discussion? For the very good

16 Ibid., 35.

reason that they are there already! Sometimes theologians—and sociologists and historians and physicists and others—are inclined to think that philosophical issues are fine to ponder, if that's your bag, but that such pondering is certainly not essential to the proper work of theology—or sociology or historiography or physics. In our judgment, this view is radically mistaken. Anytime you make a claim about anything at all, you are functioning at least implicitly as a philosopher. Whether in theology, sociology, historiography, physics, or any other enterprise, whenever you say *such and such is the case* you are doing at least two things. First, you are affirming something of what you mean by *is*. Second, you are treating your affirmation itself as valid, correct, true. In other words, you are proceeding at least operationally as both a metaphysician and an epistemologist. You are free to deny this, of course, but such a denial only ensures that your inevitable philosophizing remains merely operational, simply implicit, and thus unable to benefit from the refinements and corrections that can follow from addressing the philosophical issues explicitly. And that unrefined and uncorrected philosophizing will continue exerting its profound but unrecognized influence on all the questions you ask and all the answers you offer in your proper work as a theologian, sociologist, historiographer, or physicist.

Our goal here is briefly to address those philosophical issues explicitly. More exactly, we will be making four suggestions. First, in the history of explicit philosophy one can discern two very different basic conceptions of valid or epistemically objective human knowledge. Second, *one* of those conceptions is a crucial (though often unnoticed) component of *both* the classical cognitivist and the noncognitivist accounts of how normative doctrines emerge in the church. Third, *the other* main conception of epistemically objective human knowledge is a crucial (though often unnoticed) component of the historical cognitivist theological account, shortly to be presented. Fourth, since we judge that the second main philosophical conception subsumes the strengths of the first while avoiding its weaknesses, we are inclined on these philosophical grounds to favor the historical cognitivist theological account over the other two.

The distinguishing claim of the first basic philosophical conception is that epistemically objective human knowledge results from a cognitional process that is non-subjective. In other words, one's basic challenge as a would-be knower is to get beyond oneself, to transcend the limitations of one's subjectivity, to get hold of the real—envisioned as what is "out there," "over there," "up there." Insofar as one succeeds in thus proceeding non-subjectively, the result is true, valid, epistemically objective knowledge, envisioned as actual access to the realm of objects.

Historically, there are two important versions of this first basic conception. Let us label them "intuitional realism" and "intuitional agnosticism," with Plato as an example of the first and Kant as an example of the second. The intuitional realist claims that the requisite cognitional passage from subject to object at least sometimes actually occurs, and therefore that true knowledge at least sometimes actually arises. On the Platonic variation of this position, genuinely to know is intellectually to intuit the really real, identified as the set of subsistent otherworldly intelligible forms. But, in Plato's view, such intellectual intuiting sometimes does take place, and therefore genuine knowledge sometimes actually emerges. For the intuitional agnostic, by contrast, the requisite cognitional passage from subject to object never comes about, and therefore genuine knowledge never transpires. On the Kantian variation of this position, genuinely to know is intellectually to intuit noumenal reality, things-in-themselves. But, in Kant's view, such intellectual intuiting is beyond the capability of the human subject. Consequently, genuine knowledge—in the strict sense of theoretical reason—is an impossibility.

Without intending to overdraw the point, we suggest that there is something of intuitional realism behind the classical cognitivist's claim that Christian doctrines are normative insofar as they are authoritatively taught—primarily by God, and secondarily by the magisterium. For the classical cognitivist conceives doctrinal normativity in terms of epistemic objectivity, epistemic objectivity in terms of authoritative teaching, and authoritative teaching in terms of non-subjectivity. Recall what is perhaps the most prominent classical cognitivist reason why authoritative teaching is needed: at least in religious matters it is the unique way of overcoming the limitations of human subjectivity—and *thereby* achieving epistemic objectivity, and *thereby* in turn having doctrinal normativity. But the conception of epistemic objectivity as an actual attainment that arises in function of cognitional non-subjectivity is precisely what distinguishes the intuitional realist perspective.

Again, without intending to overdraw the point, we suggest that there is something of intuitional agnosticism behind the doctrinal noncognitivist's claim that Christian doctrines are normative insofar as they are authentically ecclesial constructs. Recall the reason why the noncognitivist conceives doctrinal normativity in terms of communal processes deemed epistemically just subjective. No other alternative remains. If doctrines were authoritatively taught, their non-subjectivity, thus their epistemic objectivity, and thus their normativity would be manifest; but no such authoritative teaching ever occurs. Now, the conception of epistemic objectivity as an attainment that would come about in function of cognitional non-subjectivity, but in fact never actually does—this is exactly the intuitional agnostic view.

5. Epistemically Objective Knowledge as the Result of Authentically Subjective Knowing

The distinguishing claim of the second basic philosophical conception is that epistemically objective human knowledge results from a cognitional process that is authentically subjective. In other words, one's basic challenge as a would-be knower is to proceed in fidelity to the best of one's self. The fundamental distinction is not between being a subject and somehow not being a subject (whatever the latter could mean), but rather between inauthenticity and authenticity in one's cognitional operations.

Let us label this position "intentional realism," and let us illustrate it with the updated presentation of Aquinas provided by Bernard Lonergan.[17] Lonergan begins with a careful description of the actual operations that supposedly we experience ourselves performing whenever we are knowing. Our concrete cognitional processes invariably include operations of experiencing data of sense and/or consciousness, forming hypotheses about intelligible relationships in those data, verifying those hypotheses, and evaluating what we have verified. At best, our performance of those operations is *authentic*, faithful to the imperatives to self-transcendence that pre-decisionally

---

[17] While the following account of human knowledge permeates all of Lonergan's works, for two brief and accessible summaries see his two articles, "Cognitional Structure," in *Collection*, vol. 4, in *Collected Works of Bernard Lonergan*, ed. Frederick E. Crowe and Robert M. Doran (Toronto: University of Toronto Press, 1988), 205–21, 300–303, and "The Subject," in *A Second Collection*, 69–86.

constitute the very dynamism of our concrete intentional consciousness. That is to say, at best our experiencing is *attentive*—attuned to all of the available data. At best our understanding is *intelligent*—entertaining every conceivable understanding of the data. At best our verifying is *reasonable*—working toward the correct judgment by comparing alternative fact-hypotheses in terms of all the evidence for and against them. At best our evaluating is *responsible*—working toward the correct evaluation by comparing alternative value-hypotheses in terms of all the evidence pro and con.

Next, Lonergan argues that insofar as we perform our cognitional operations authentically, the consequence is knowledge that is genuine, true, cognitionally normative, epistemically objective. In other words, epistemic objectivity is not fundamentally a matter of successfully suppressing one's own selfhood so that nothing impedes a direct grasp or encounter or intuition of objects "out there," "over there," "up there." Common though it is, such a conception is at odds with the concrete operational facts that emerge through careful appropriation of oneself as a knower. Concretely, *epistemic objectivity* is nothing other than what results from our *authentic cognitional subjectivity*. (Moreover, any effort to reject this conclusion self-destructs, for in the very act of rejecting the conclusion verbally one inevitably invokes it operationally.)[18]

Intentional realism commends intuitional realism for recognizing that we are indeed capable of epistemic objectivity, but it also criticizes it for incorrectly conceiving that achievement as resulting from cognitional intuition, immediacy, passivity. Again, intentional realism commends intuitional agnosticism for recognizing that our cognitional process is essentially discursive, mediated, self-constituting;

---

[18] A detailed discussion of religious experience is beyond the scope of the present paper. Nonetheless, it is worth mentioning that some intentional realists envision religious experience as both providing us with an enhanced criterion of cognitional self-transcendence and disposing us to operate in fidelity to it. That is to say, religious experience fosters our cognitional authenticity—our attentiveness in experiencing, our intelligence in understanding, our reasonableness in verifying, and our responsibility in evaluating. And it thereby promotes the consequence of cognitional authenticity, namely, epistemic objectivity. (See, e.g., Bernard Lonergan, *Method in Theology* [New York: Herder & Herder, 1972], 238–44, 265, 268, 292, 338.) Such religious experience may be interpreted theologically as the presence of the Holy Spirit. (See, e.g., Frederick E. Crowe, "Son of God, Holy Spirit, and World Religions," in *Appropriating the Lonergan Idea*, 324–43.)

but it also criticizes it for incorrectly concluding that we are therefore incapable of epistemic objectivity.[19]

We reiterate our earlier suggestion that intentional realism constitutes a crucial (though not always recognized) component of the third general theological account of how normative doctrines emerge in the church, an account to which we now turn.

6. A Historical Cognitivist View of the Holy Spirit's Assistance: Normative Doctrine as Authentically Discovered by the Church

Lonergan's category of historical-mindedness[20] corresponds at least roughly to what we are labeling the "historical cognitivist" account of how normative Christian doctrines emerge. On this account doctrines are normative only insofar as they are authentically discovered by the church. This view itself rests on two prior (though often just implicit) convictions, namely, that (a) the basic reason a religious doctrine is normative is that it is true, expressive of reality, epistemically objective; and (b) a religious doctrine is manifest as true only insofar as it is authentically discovered by the church.

In the process by which normative doctrines emerge within the church, the fundamental step is authentic learning by the church. Authoritative magisterial teaching, though surely a crucial contribution to the total process, is a step that is methodologically subsequent and derivative. What is obvious in the case of a human individual is no less true in the case of a human community: the activity of learning is absolutely prior to the activity of teaching. One must learn before one can teach.[21]

---

[19] In the view of those intentional realists who take account of it, religious experience tends to reinforce intuitional realism's correct conviction that we are indeed capable of epistemic objectivity in our cognitional process, and to counter intuitional agnosticism's opposite conviction on this point. Correlatively, it tends to reinforce intuitional agnosticism's correct conviction that our cognitional process is essentially discursive, mediated, self-constituting, and to counter intuitional realism's opposite conviction on this point. (See, e.g., Lonergan, *Method in Theology*, 238–44.)

[20] See above, n. 6.

[21] See Crowe, "The Church as Learner," and cf. John T. Ford, "Infallibility," in Joseph A. Komonchak et al., eds., *The New Dictionary of Theology* (Wilmington, DE: Michael Glazier, 1987), 517–21.

On this view the emergence of explicitly articulated normative doctrines within the church is a two-dimensional development. The first and more basic dimension of the development transpires on the level of concrete communal living. In response to some particular question, challenge, or crisis, the church as a whole gradually works toward the lived recognition of an answer, a reply, a response that exploits the resources embodied in its communal living from the beginning down through the present age. Moreover, this instance of concrete collective cognitional process is at best authentic. That is to say, it is a process in which all the available *data* are taken into account, every possible way of *understanding* those data is explored, and one of those hypotheses eventually comes to be affirmed as true and good only insofar as *evidence* for it is grasped as sufficient. Furthermore, the normativity of the emergent answer is a function of the authenticity of the learning process. As a particular case of epistemic objectivity, doctrinal normativity is what follows from authentic ecclesial cognitional subjectivity.

The second dimension of the development is from lived recognition to explicit articulation. What has been grasped concretely comes to be expressed thematically. What has been learned performatively comes to be formulated and taught explicitly. Moreover, the normativity of an explicitly articulated doctrine is a function of ecclesial authenticity in two ways. Primarily, it depends upon the authenticity of the concrete ecclesial learning process whose result it aspires to express. Secondarily, it depends upon the authenticity of that very process of expressing.

Crowe presents this position as envisioning "an absolute priority of learning over teaching in the Church, even with regard to the sources, divinely created and divinely given, of our faith. The sources are sources that have learned."[22] He emphasizes that this means that the church must follow the ordinary cognitional processes, "whether in the realm of nature or the realm of grace." He continues, "It means asking questions on matters of which we are ignorant; forming an idea of a possible answer, indeed forming several ideas of different possible answers; weighing the pros and cons of the several alternative ideas; finally, coming to a judgment, and being able to say 'I've learned something.'"[23]

---

[22] Crowe, "The Church as Learner," 371.
[23] Ibid.

On the historical cognitivist account the ecclesial community's attending to data, discovering alternative ways of understanding the data, weighing the evidence for the various alternatives, and making its judgments in light of that evidence are key elements of the process by which the Holy Spirit assists the church to learn and to teach. The whole church participates in the process of learning that eventually finds expression in magisterial teaching.

The Final Report of the Anglican–Roman Catholic International Commission has described well this process of interplay between ordained ministers and the whole community. "Ordained ministers," it says, are "commissioned to discern" and to "give authoritative expression" to insights that are a deeper understanding of the Gospel and its implications. Yet these ministers, it explains, "are part of the community, sharing its quest for understanding the Gospel in obedience to Christ and receptive to the needs and concerns of all."[24] This means that "the community, for its part, must respond to and assess the insights and teaching of the ordained ministers." *The Final Report* continues, "Through this continuing process of discernment and response, in which the faith is expressed and the Gospel is pastorally applied, the Holy Spirit declares the authority of the Lord Jesus Christ, and the faithful may live freely under the discipline of the Gospel."[25]

Richard McCormick provides a helpful discussion of the assistance of the Holy Spirit to the magisterium regarding the process of discovery. He focuses on the Holy Spirit's assistance to the "noninfallible magisterium" [sic] in moral questions. Two extremes must be avoided, he maintains. The first would explain assistance in a way that "dispenses with human processes," presenting a kind of fideism in which the assistance is "a new source of hierarchical knowledge, arcane and impervious to any criticism developed out of Christian experience, evidence, and reasoning." This notion of assistance envisions no need for the scholarly efforts of theologians. The other extreme, he continues, would "reduce this assistance to human processes" in a form of "neorationalism" where "the action of the Spirit is simply identified with the shrewdest thinkers in the community and ultimately im-

---

[24] Anglican–Roman Catholic International Commission, "Authority in the Church I," in *The Final Report* (London: SPCK & Catholic Truth Society, 1982), n. 6. Also at http://www.anglicancommunion.org/ministry/ecumenical/dialogues/catholic/arcic/.
[25] Ibid.

prisoned in the best reasons they can unravel." This tends to ignore the nature of moral cognition and the significance of the *sensus fidelium*.[26]

If we avoid these two extremes, McCormick continues, then we are in a good position to follow a middle course of associating the activity of the Holy Spirit with human processes without identifying it with them. For the magisterium this means avoiding error in the gathering and assessing of evidence as a judgment is made. "Now the magisterium of the Church has special advantages to overcome these handicaps in arriving at moral truth," McCormick points out.

> First of all, bishops as *pastors* are in a unique position to be in contact with the convictions, problems, beliefs, joys, sufferings, and reflections of all groups in the local Church. That is, they are positioned to consult the experience and convictions (the wisdom) of their flock. As *collegial pastors* they are in a position to pool this wisdom and weigh it through a process of dialogue and debate. In this sense the episcopal and papal magisterium have sources of information which exceed those available to anyone else.

In short, he continues,

> though we cannot capture in human categories the operations and assistance of the Holy Spirit, can we not identify the human processes within which the Spirit must be supposed to operate? And since the hierarchy is uniquely situated to implement these processes, is it not open to the assistance of the Spirit in a special way when it does so? That is, the ability of bishop-pastors (and through them to the pope) to range beyond the isolation of their own reflections or those of restricted groups is the foundation for the confidence that in doing so they will be specially open to the Spirit, and that their authentic pronouncements will show this.[27]

McCormick is discussing the assistance of the Holy Spirit to the magisterium in teachings that are not exercises of infallibility, but we propose that his insights should be applied as well to teachings that exercise infallibility. Indeed, sometimes Roman Catholic theology is inconsistent on this point, employing a historical cognitivist view of

---

[26] Richard A. McCormick, *Corrective Vision: Explorations in Moral Theology* (Kansas City, MO: Sheed & Ward, 1994), 91.

[27] Ibid., 92–93.

assistance when thinking of noninfallible teaching but switching abruptly into a classical cognitivist explanation when describing assistance in teaching infallibly. Obviously there is a difference between teachings that exercise infallibility and teachings that do not. But we contend that these two kinds of teachings are distinguished by the relationship of their content to the Gospel's central saving message, not by differing modes of the Holy Spirit's assistance. Crowe's reflections help us to see this. The French minority bishops at Vatican I also had something of this insight. The Holy Spirit does not operate according to the classical cognitivist account when assisting infallible teaching but then suddenly begin operating according to the historical cognitivist account of assistance when noninfallible matters arise—like a teacher who uses lecture style for more important topics but then switches into discussion mode for less important ones. The historical cognitivist account proposes that the Holy Spirit always assists the church precisely through its cognitional processes of communal questioning and discovery rather than replacing them with some type of privileged intuition.

The historical cognitivist stance on assistance is part of an ecclesiology of communion, and that includes an account of reception. *The Final Report* is very clear that reception is not the creation of truth or the legitimation of a magisterial decision.[28] Rather, "the assent of the faithful is the ultimate indication that the Church's authoritative decision in a matter of faith has been truly preserved from error by the Holy Spirit."[29] Reception is part of the process of interplay between magisterial teaching and evaluation by the whole church, and it is attributed by ARCIC to the Holy Spirit.

It follows that the historical cognitivist stance on assistance also leaves room for the possibility of dissenting from magisterial teachings that are not exercises of infallibility. While such magisterial teachings deserve a presumption in their favor, writes McCormick,[30] dissent is also a possible outcome "of a respectful and docile personal reflection on noninfallible teaching. Such reflection," he explains, "is the very

---

[28] Anglican–Roman Catholic International Commission, "Authority in the Church: Elucidations (1981)," in *The Final Report*, n. 3.

[29] Anglican–Roman Catholic International Commission, "Authority in the Church II (1981)," in *The Final Report*, n. 25.

[30] Richard A. McCormick, "Loyalty and Dissent: The Magisterium—A New Model," *America* 122 (June 1970): 674–76, at 675.

condition of progress in understanding in the Church. Dissent, therefore, must be viewed and respected as a part of that total approach through which we learn."[31] If dissent is part of the process of learning that precedes teaching in the church, then it too must be related in some way to the assistance of the Holy Spirit.

We suggest that magisterial teaching at Vatican II began to make a shift from classical to historical cognitivism. In *Dei Verbum* the council taught that the tradition that comes from the apostles "develops in the Church with the help of the Holy Spirit. For there is a growth in the understanding . . . of the realities and the words which have been handed down."[32] As the centuries succeed one another, it continues, "the Church constantly moves forward toward the fullness of divine truth." God, "who spoke of old, uninterruptedly converses with the Bride of His beloved Son; and the Holy Spirit, through whom the living voice of the gospel resounds in the Church, and through her, in the world, leads unto all truth those who believe and makes the word of Christ dwell abundantly in them (cf. Col. 3:16)."[33] The picture presented by Vatican II emphasizes a process of growth in which the whole church deepens its understanding, led by the Holy Spirit in a conversation that is still unfinished.

This perspective was continued in *Mysterium Ecclesiae*, which acknowledged that dogmatic truth taught infallibly is sometimes "first expressed incompletely (but not falsely), and at a later date . . . it receives a fuller and more perfect expression." It emphasized the importance of the context for understanding a teaching, and it explained that sometimes dogmatic formulations "gave way to new expressions which, proposed and approved by the sacred Magisterium, presented more clearly or completely the same meaning." For *Mysterium Ecclesiae* the assistance of the Holy Spirit enables the magisterium to maintain an "ever true and constant" meaning to the dogmatic formulas even while new expressions of this meaning are found.[34]

---

[31] Ibid., 676.

[32] Vatican II, *Dei Verbum* (Dogmatic Constitution on Divine Revelation), n. 8. Also at http://www.vatican.va/archive/hist_councils/ii_vatican_council/documents/vat-ii_const_19651118_dei-verbum_en.html.

[33] Ibid.

[34] Congregation for the Doctrine of the Faith, *Mysterium Ecclesiae*, *The Tablet* 227 (14 July 1973) 668–69. Also at http://www.vatican.va/roman_curia/congregations/cfaith/documents/rc_con_cfaith_doc_19730705_mysterium-ecclesiae_en.html.

To sum up: historical cognitivists give primacy of place to authentic learning in the church. Like classical cognitivists, they affirm that Christian doctrines are normative because they are true. But, unlike classical cognitivists, they argue that in the church (as everywhere else) true teaching follows true learning, and true learning is a process that takes time. Moreover, like noncognitivists, historical cognitivists affirm that normative Christian doctrines emerge through a process that includes the whole church. But, unlike noncognitivists, they argue that this process is not a matter of ecclesial constructing but rather of ecclesial discovering, and its results are not just Christian products but rather Christian truths. Historical cognitivists thus build on the strengths of the other two groups but correct them as well.

Regarding the assistance of the Holy Spirit, historical cognitivists agree with classical cognitivists that the Holy Spirit fosters sound Christian doctrine by fostering spiritual discernment on the part of authoritative teachers and spiritual docility on the part of ordinary hearers within the church. But they contend that the *fundamental* way the Holy Spirit fosters the emergence of normative Christian doctrine is by fostering the authentically ecclesial character of the learning process at every level within the church. The result of this process comes to expression in magisterial teaching.

Finally, historical cognitivists explain as follows the normativity of the three proposed doctrines we noted at the start. The reason the normativity of the Chalcedonian decree on the divinity and humanity of Jesus is a matter of virtually universal ecclesial consensus is that it manifestly satisfies the criteria of authentically ecclesial learning. (Indeed, the recent agreement between the Roman Catholic Church and the Assyrian Church of the East shows that they have learned that the meanings intended by each other's christological teaching are not contradictory.)[35] The reason the normativity of the recent Lutheran–Catholic statements on justification is a matter of growing ecclesial consensus is that those statements more and more seem to satisfy the criteria of authentically ecclesial learning. Finally, the reason the normativity of the 1995 declaration by the Congregation for the Doctrine of the Faith regarding women's ordination is a matter of currently absent ecclesial consensus is that it manifestly does not

[35] See http://www.vatican.va/roman_curia/pontifical_councils/chrstuni /documents/rc_pc_chrstuni_doc_11111994_assyrian-church_en.html

(at least yet) satisfy the criteria of authentically ecclesial learning. For it is only very recently that the question of women's ordination has arisen in its modern form. Furthermore, the fact that the Anglican communion and many Protestant communions presently ordain women, while the Orthodox do not, has new significance since *Lumen Gentium*'s affirmation that the one church of Christ extends "beyond the visible limits" of the Roman Catholic Church. Hence a historical-minded position on the Holy Spirit's assistance would conclude that an ecclesial consensus on this issue has not yet been reached and consequently the question remains open.

Conclusions

Our study has four conclusions. The first is that often there are *particular theological* disagreements about how to explain the fact that some given doctrine has or has not been widely accepted as normative within the church. Frequently an influential element underlying the particular theological disagreements is a *general theological* disagreement about how normative doctrines emerge within the church (including how the Holy Spirit assists the church in believing and teaching). And frequently an influential element underlying a general theological disagreement, in turn, is a *philosophical* disagreement about how epistemically objective knowledge arises.

Second, precisely because the general theological and philosophical disagreements underlying a particular theological disagreement often are overlooked, they often are left unaddressed. On the other hand, any effort to address a particular theological disagreement that does not also address underlying general theological and philosophical disagreements is bound to be inadequate, for it is insufficiently radical.

Third, proponents of either of the first two general theological stances tend to collapse the other two stances together, always to the detriment of the third. That is to say, *classical cognitivists* tend to think that everyone who affirms that subjectivity is involved in knowing is a *noncognitivist*. Conversely, *noncognitivists* tend to think that everyone who affirms the possibility of epistemically objective knowing is a *classical cognitivist*. Such a blurring of stances deepens misunderstanding, because in both cases the *historical cognitivist* stance is given short shrift.

Fourth, the most promising concrete procedure for surfacing and addressing all three levels of disagreement would seem to be generous, candid, and self-critical dialogue involving all the disputants.

12

Watching from the Sideline: Recent Lutheran–Anglican Agreements[1]

Introduction

Roman Catholics are not participants in the agreements spelled out by *The Niagara Report*, *The Porvoo Common Statement*, and *Called to Common Mission*. But if we believe what we said at the Faith and Order Commission meeting at Santiago de Compostela about the unity of the one ecumenical movement,[2] then we know that agreements made by some churches will inevitably affect the remaining dialogue partner churches.

Anyone with a marriage partner knows this basic insight very well. The unmarried could quickly learn more about it by asking my husband to describe how his wife's ecumenical commitments have both enriched his life and altered his weekly schedule. Consequently, it is appropriate to wonder how Roman Catholics might evaluate the three recent agreements between the Lutheran and Anglican Churches, even if their effect on the Roman Catholic Church is only indirect.

---

[1] First presented on November 30, 2000, as "Toward a Roman Catholic Evaluation of the 'Niagara Report,' the 'Porvoo Common Statement,' and 'Called to Common Mission,'" at a meeting of the U.S. Lutheran–Roman Catholic Dialogue, Las Vegas, NV. Not previously published.

[2] World Conference on Faith and Order, "On the Way to Fuller Koinonia," *Mid-Stream* 33 (1994): 102–6; see n. 3.

At the same time, Roman Catholics should not undertake such an effort in a smug spirit. *Dominus Jesus* is critical of "ecclesial communities which have not preserved the valid Episcopate."[3] On the other hand, in his discussion on the validity of Lutheran orders Arthur Carl Piepkorn notes that the average Lutheran ordained minister "does not lose sleep through nocturnal doubts that he may really not be an ordained minister of Christ's one holy catholic and apostolic church after all."[4] And John Baycroft, Anglican bishop of Ottawa, has often pointed out the problems the Anglican communion finds with the arguments and practice against the ordination of women in the Roman Catholic Church. Making evaluations, in other words, is not limited to just one church. To utilize that fact for ecumenical benefit, offering evaluations of other churches' agreements should be part of every church's effort to heal divisive differences over ordained ministry—and, indeed, over everything else as well—throughout the entire church of Christ.

The *Joint Declaration on the Doctrine of Justification* asserts that developments affecting each of our churches not merely allow but "require the churches to examine the divisive questions and condemnations and see them in a new light."[5] The same theme is developed by Pope John Paul II in *Ut Unum Sint*, his encyclical on ecumenical dialogue. The pope stresses that the ecumenical journey requires purification of our bad memories about one another, memories that are sometimes mistaken but often enough are true; and the first step in such purification is repentance for our own pride, our own refusals to forgive, our own "unevangelical insistence on condemning 'the other side.'" Repentance is accompanied by the vision of new horizons, as we

---

[3] Congregation for the Doctrine of the Faith, *Dominus Jesus: On the Unicity and Salvific Universality of Jesus Christ and the Church* (Vatican City: Libreria Editrice Vaticana, 2000), n. 17. Also at http://www.vatican.va/roman_curia/congregations/cfaith/documents/rc_con_cfaith_doc_20000806_dominus-iesus_en.html.

[4] Arthur Carl Piepkorn, "A Lutheran View of the Validity of Lutheran Orders," in Paul C. Empie and T. Austin Murphy, eds., *Lutherans and Catholics in Dialogue*, vol. 4: *Eucharist and Ministry* (New York: U.S.A. National Committee of the Lutheran World Federation, and Washington, DC: Bishops' Committee for Ecumenical and Interreligious Affairs, 1970), 209.

[5] The Lutheran World Federation and the Roman Catholic Church, *Joint Declaration on the Doctrine of Justification* (Grand Rapids: Eerdmans, 2000), n. 7. Also at http://www.vatican.va/roman_curia/pontifical_councils/chrstuni/documents/rc_pc_chrstuni_doc_31101999_cath-luth-joint-declaration_en.html.

discover ways the Holy Spirit is at work in other churches.[6] Each of us needs to "change his or her way of looking at things."[7] "What is needed is a calm, clearsighted and truthful vision of things, a vision enlivened by divine mercy and capable of freeing people's minds and of inspiring in everyone a renewed willingness, precisely with a view to proclaiming the Gospel to the men and women of every people and nation."[8]

How can seeing in this new light and having the clearsighted and truthful vision that it enables contribute to the Roman Catholic evaluation of the Lutheran–Anglican agreements? I suggest three ways. For one thing, the new light can illuminate at least three recent developments that are relevant both to the overall ecumenical discussion about mutual recognition of ordained ministries and more specifically to a Roman Catholic appraisal of the agreements. The three developments are (i) the scholarly reassessment of historical data about ordained ministry during the medieval and Reformation periods, (ii) shifts in the Roman Catholic theology of ordained ministry and the liturgy of the sacrament of orders, and (iii) successive ecumenical agreements on ordained ministry.

For a second thing, the new light can illuminate both the *practices* of ordained ministry by Anglicans and Lutherans past and present and the *theological understandings* those practices express. But it also can illuminate something more fundamental: the *intentions* underlying the practices and understandings. For the meaning of ministerial practices encompasses not just their external features and how those features are understood by the ministers who perform them and those for whom they are performed. Most crucially, it also encompasses the principal aims, the main purposes, the key objectives that are intended by those involved in the performance. Consequently, a Roman Catholic evaluation of the meaning of Lutheran and Anglican ministerial practices—and, by extension, of the Lutheran–Anglican agreements about those practices—would at best proceed in the light that would illuminate the underlying intentions motivating those practices.

---

[6] John Paul II, encyclical *Ut Unum Sint*, *Origins* 25:4 (June 8, 1995) 49, 51–72; see n. 15. Also at http://www.vatican.va/holy_father/john_paul_ii/encyclicals/documents/hf_jp-ii_enc_25051995_ut-unum-sint_en.html.

[7] Ibid.

[8] Ibid., n. 2.

For a third thing, the new light does not just illuminate more widely and deeply than what might be called the "old" light: it also illuminates more clearly and reliably.[9] Hence it can enable a clearer and more trustworthy evaluation of Lutheran and Anglican practices and understandings of ordained ministry, the basic intentions underlying them, and the ecumenical agreements about them.

My paper, then, has three main parts. First, I will briefly review the three Lutheran–Anglican agreements. Second, I will sketch the recent developments I have just mentioned and explain why each of them supports an affirmative Roman Catholic evaluation of those agreements. Third, I will recount the significant additional support that is provided to an affirmative evaluation by enlightened discernment of underlying Lutheran and Anglican intentions.

1. Three Lutheran–Anglican Agreements

1.1. *"The Niagara Report"*

In 1988, after an international Anglican–Lutheran consultation on *episcope*, the Anglican-Lutheran International Continuation Committee published *The Niagara Report*.[10] The report observes that Anglican–Lutheran dialogue has repeatedly "identified differences in the *practice* of *episcope* (that is, pastoral leadership, coordination and oversight), especially the presence or absence of bishops in the historic episcopate, as the chief (if not the only remaining) obstacle to full communion" (NR 3). The differences in *episcope* include not only the presence or absence of "bishops in the historic episcopate" but also "difference in the significance" attributed to such bishops. These differences are the focal point of "mutual fears and suspicions,

---

[9] In its strengthening and corrective functions, the "new light" of the *Joint Declaration* would seem to have some affinity with what Bernard Lonergan calls "religious experience," experience that he interprets theologically as the presence of the Holy Spirit. See "The Holy Spirit's Assistance to the Magisterium in Teaching," chap. 11 of the present volume, nn. 18–19. (Ed.)

[10] Anglican–Lutheran International Continuation Committee, *The Niagara Report: Report of the Anglican–Lutheran Consultation on Episcope, Niagara Falls, September 1987* (London: Church House Publishing, 1988). Also at http://www.anglicancommunion .org/ministry/ecumenical/dialogues/lutheran/docs/niagara_report.cfm. Subsequent references to this document occur intratextually with the abbreviation "NR" followed by the section number.

prejudices and distorted perceptions" (NR 4). The report argues that the mission of the church "comes to special expression in the Church's apostolicity. For apostolicity means that the Church is sent by Jesus to be for the world, to participate his mission" and therefore in the mission intended by God—Father, Son, and Spirit (NR 21).

The document seeks "to identify the major requirements for carrying out the mission of the church in so far as they concern *episcope*" (NR 7). These requirements are found to be doxology, continuity, disciplined life together, nurture, direction and goal, and the development of structure. Regarding a key aspect of structure, the document asserts that "oversight or presiding ministry . . . constitutes the heart of the episcopal office, and that oversight is never to be viewed apart from the continuity of apostolic faith. The fact of bishops does not by itself guarantee the continuity of apostolic faith. A material rupture in the succession of presiding ministers does not by itself guarantee a loss of continuity of apostolic faith" (NR 54). How, then, should we evaluate "a situation in which there is a material rupture in the succession of presiding ministers in the name of preserving the continuity of apostolic faith?" (NR 54). The eventual answer to this question is that "neither tradition can, in good conscience, reject the apostolic nature of the other." Therefore "the continued isolation, one from another, of those who exercise this office of *episcope* in our two Churches is no longer tolerable and must be overcome" (NR 59).

The report goes on to propose many practical measures through which each church would recognize the ordained ministry of the other and would begin steps toward full communion. These steps would include the laying on of hands by both Lutherans and Anglicans exercising *episcope* at the installation of such a minister in either church (NR 87–96). The report concludes with suggestions for "reform and renewal in the area of *episcope*" for both churches (NR 99).

1.2. "The Porvoo Common Statement"

In 1993, conversations between the British and Irish Anglican Churches and the Nordic and Baltic Lutheran Churches resulted in the publication of *The Porvoo Common Statement*,[11] which was subse-

---

[11] Conversations between the British and Irish Anglican Churches and the Nordic and Baltic Lutheran Churches, *The Porvoo Common Statement* (1992) (London: Council for Christian Unity of the General Synod of the Church of England, 1993). Also at

quently accepted for implementation by the participating churches. The statement aims to harvest "the fruits of previous ecumenical dialogues" and so "to resolve the longstanding difficulties between" the partners "about episcopacy and succession" (PCS 6). An important note is struck in the first line of the section on the nature and unity of the church: "Our times demand something new of us as churches" (PCS 14). *The Porvoo Common Statement* reviews the partners' common vision of the church and their agreements in faith. It then draws on the work of earlier ecumenical dialogue step by step. The church as a whole is apostolic (PCS 37), and "the primary manifestation of apostolic succession is to be found in the apostolic tradition of the Church as a whole" (PCS 39). The succession is an expression of "permanence" and "continuity of Christ's own mission in which the Church participates" (PCS 39). Within the apostolicity of the whole church is "an apostolic succession of the ministry which serves and is a focus of the continuity of the Church in its life in Christ and its faithfulness to the words and acts of Jesus transmitted by the apostles" (PCS 40). Within the apostolic ministry is a ministry that coordinates the diverse gifts to the church, "ministry of oversight, *episcope,* a caring for the life of a whole community, a pastoring of the pastors and a true feeding of Christ's flock, in accordance with Christ's command across the ages and in unity with Christians in other places" (PCS 42). *Episcope* is required for the whole church (PCS 42) and is exercised personally, collegially, and communally (PCS 44).

The statement affirms that the ultimate ground of the church's fidelity, in continuity with the apostles, "is the promise of the Lord and the presence of the Holy Spirit at work in the whole Church" (PCS 46). But apostolic succession in the episcopal office is "a visible and personal way of focusing the apostolicity of the whole Church" (PCS 46). Continuity in apostolic succession "is signified in the ordination or consecration of a bishop" (PCS 47). But this continuity cannot be divorced from the continuity of life and witness of the diocese to which he is called. At the time of the Reformation "all our churches ordained bishops (sometimes the term superintendent was used as a synonym for bishop) to the existing sees of the Catholic Church, indicating their intention to continue the life and ministry

---

http://www.porvoochurches.org/whatis/resources-0201-english.php. Subsequent references to this document occur intratextually with the abbreviation "PCS" followed by the section number.

of the One, Holy, Catholic and Apostolic Church" (PCS 33). So the ordination of a bishop in historic succession is a sign that communicates the Church's "care for continuity in the whole of its life and mission" and that reinforces its "determination to manifest the permanent characteristics of the Church of the apostles" (PCS 50).

The use of the sign of historic episcopal succession is no guarantee of fidelity to all the aspects of apostolicity. "Nonetheless, the retention of the sign remains a permanent challenge to fidelity and to unity, a summons to witness to, and a commission to realise more fully, the permanent characteristics of the Church of the apostles" (PCS 51). All the partners "can affirm together the value and use of the sign of historic episcopal succession" (PCS 57) without implying "an adverse judgement on the ministries of those churches which did not previously make use of the sign" (PCS 53). In fact, "to the degree to which our ministries have been separated all our churches have lacked something of that fullness which God desires for his people" (PCS 54).

It is worth noting that the statement's recommendations for present and future shared life of worship, mission, and service, including mutual participation of the member churches in episcopal ordinations, have all been implemented.

1.3. "Called to Common Mission"

In 1999, the Evangelical Lutheran Church in America, acting through its churchwide assembly, ratified *Called to Common Mission: A Lutheran Proposal for a Revision of the Concordat of Agreement*.[12] The agreement was later ratified as well by the assembly of the U. S. Episcopal Church.

The purpose of the agreement is set forth as "the establishment of 'full communion'" between the Evangelical Lutheran Church in America and the U. S. Episcopal Church (CCM 1). The document understands full communion "to be a relation between distinct churches in which each recognizes the other as a catholic and apos-

---

[12] Evangelical Lutheran Church in American, Churchwide Assembly, *Called to Common Mission: A Lutheran Proposal for a Revision of the Concordat of Agreement* (Chicago: Evangelical Lutheran Church in America, 1999). Also at http://www.episcopalchurch .org/page/agreement-full-communion-called-common-mission. Subsequent references to this document occur intratextually with the abbreviation "CCM" followed by the section number.

tolic church holding the essentials of the Christian faith" (CCM 2). The churches will "become interdependent while remaining autonomous," with a diversity that "is not static" (CCM 2). Full communion is understood to include "the establishment locally and nationally of recognized organs of regular consultation and communication, including episcopal collegiality, to express and strengthen the fellowship and enable common witness, life, and service" (CCM 2).

After recognizing their agreement in faith (CCM 4–5), the partners go on to recognize an agreement in ministry. Affirming the ministry of all the baptized, they also acknowledge that "ordained ministers are called and set apart for the one ministry of Word and Sacrament" and that "personal, collegial, and communal oversight is embodied and exercised in both our churches in a diversity of forms, in fidelity to the teaching and mission of the apostles" (CCM 7). In order to share a "common pattern for the sake of common mission," the churches seek to share in the ministry of the bishop in "an evangelical, historic succession" (CCM 8). Mentioning the "deep desire" of the Lutheran confessional tradition to maintain the historic episcopate (CCM 11), the document commits the member churches "to include regularly one or more bishops of the other church to participate in the laying-on-of-hands at the ordinations/installations of their own bishops as a sign, though not a guarantee, of the unity and apostolic continuity of the whole church" (CCM 12). For both churches see ministry as one of the ways, "in the context of ordained ministries and of the whole people of God, in which the apostolic succession of the church is visibly expressed and personally symbolized in fidelity to the gospel through the ages" (CCM 12). But the Evangelical Lutheran Church is "free to maintain that this same episcopate, although pastorally desirable when exercised in personal, collegial, and communal ways, is nonetheless not necessary for a relationship of full communion" (CCM 13). Anglicans, however, can maintain that the episcopate is "necessary when Anglicans enter the relationship of full communion in order to link the local churches for mutual responsibility in the communion of the larger church" (CCM 13).

To implement this agreement, the two churches pledge to acknowledge immediately the full authenticity of each other's ordained ministries and to seek to incorporate all active bishops in the historic episcopal succession and to enter a continuing process of collegial consultation (CCM 14). Lutherans declare that their future bishops will be installed to serve the Gospel "with this church's intention to enter the ministry of the historic episcopate" (CCM 18), although in doing this the Evangelical Lutheran Church in America does not affirm that the historic episcopate "is necessary for the unity of the Church (*Augsburg Confession* 7.3)" (CCM 18). Bishops "already sharing in the sign of the episcopal succession" from the Lutheran churches and the Episcopal Church will participate in the installation of the next presiding bishop, and other installations of bishops will follow this same pattern of at least three bishops in historic succession (CCM 19). In addition, "a bishop shall regularly preside and participate in the laying-on-of-hands at the ordination of all clergy," while pastors shall continue to lay on hands as well. "Such offices are to be exercised as servant ministry, and not for domination or arbitrary control" (CCM 20). The document concludes with discussion of other forms of collaboration in ministry for common mission (CCM 22–26).

2. Three New Developments

2.1. *The Scholarly Reassessment of Historical Data about Ordained Ministry during the Medieval and Reformation Periods*

In my introduction I proposed three recent developments that affect the context in which Roman Catholic evaluation of the Lutheran–Anglican agreements takes place. The first of these developments is the scholarly reassessment of historical data about ordained ministry during the medieval and Reformation periods. A principal suggestion of the new findings is that the Reformers did not lightly depart from the apostolic tradition regarding ordained ministry for the sake of their own purposes, as the more familiar account would have it. On the contrary, they sought to remain faithful to that tradition despite the challenges they faced. Let me briefly indicate the three-element argument that supports this suggestion in relation to the Lutheran Reformers.[13]

The first element of the argument is the existence of a longstanding ecclesial view, known by the Reformers, that runs counter to the more

---

[13] For a similar argument in relation to the Anglican Reformers, see "Anglican Orders and Ecumenical Dialogue on Ordained Ministry," chap. 10 of the present volume, part 1. (Ed.)

common view in which the offices of presbyter and bishop are sharply distinguished.[14] Piepkorn sets out the patristic examples where the terms "presbyter" and "bishop" were used interchangeably. He cites at length from St. Jerome, who asserts, "Among the ancients bishops and priests [were] the same."[15]

But perhaps more important for reassessment of the historical material is the evidence throughout church history of ordinations done by presbyters. Here are some examples from Piepkorn's discussion of such ordinations.[16] The Council of Ancyra (314) was approved by St. Leo IV, bishop of Rome from 847 to 855. Its canon 13 "provided that neither chorepiscopi nor city presbyters may ordain presbyters or deacons outside their own *parochia*, unless the bishop has granted permission in the form of a letter for them to do so."[17] Again, even before their episcopal consecrations, Saints Willehad (730–789) and Liudger (742–809) were ordaining presbyters in their missionary districts. Further, following the opinion of Hugo of Pisa (who died in 1210), "many medieval canonists took the position that a simple presbyter was competent to ordain to the presbyterate if the pope empowered him to do so."[18] And in fact popes acted on this opinion. In 1400, Boniface IX gave an Essex abbot permission to ordain men not just to minor orders but also to the subdiaconate, diaconate, and presbyterate. When he withdrew this permission three years later he still understood that he had the power to give or withdraw such permissions. Martin V gave the same permission to a Cistercian abbot in Upper Saxony in 1427.

The second element of the argument is the tension, often severe, between the German bishops and the Lutheran Reformers. The bishops and archbishops in the Holy Roman Empire of the German Nation during Luther's day were also secular rulers, so that Dorothea Wendebourg concludes, "Die Kirche des Reiches war faktisch landesherrliche Kirche" ["The church of the Empire was in fact the

---

[14] In this paragraph and the next I rely mainly on Arthur Carl Piepkorn, "A Lutheran View of the Validity of Lutheran Orders," in Empie and Murphy, eds., *Lutherans and Catholics in Dialogue*, vol. 4: *Eucharist and Ministry*, 219–25.

[15] Ibid., 219.

[16] Ibid., 220–25.

[17] Ibid., 221.

[18] Ibid., 222–23.

church of the regional princes."][19] The Reformers strongly criticized this practice, because sometimes it led to a conflict of interest between a bishop's religious and secular roles. Moreover, at times the person who had been appointed bishop was unfit for his religious responsibilities and would designate others to represent him in that regard.

But the Reformers had more serious problems with the episcopate when the bishops adhering to the traditional faith prohibited evangelical preaching by presbyters attracted to the Reformation, persecuted such presbyters, and refused to ordain Reformation-minded theologians. The Reformers in Germany experienced this situation as an emergency in which they were required to choose between faithfulness to the apostolic tradition and continuation of the traditional forms of the ministry.

The third and concluding element of the argument is this: the Reformers resisted making that choice. Luther considered regional oversight as normal, instructing his pastors to choose one or more from among themselves who would visit each pastor and congregation to ensure the purity of Gospel proclamation. Melanchthon likewise insisted on pastors with a ministry of oversight. In line with such views, but needing pastors for the new reform-minded congregations that had emerged, the Reformers declared that as a matter of ecclesiastical order they would reserve the right of ordination to bishops if the bishops would accept and ordain reform-minded pastors.

It was only when that offer was deemed unacceptable that the Reformers began allowing ordinations by presbyters. But they did not do so lightly. Appealing to the longstanding albeit minority view that the offices of presbyter and bishop were not originally distinguished, they argued that such a practice remained in continuity with the tradition of apostolic oversight. Moreover, they took pains to implement the practice in a way that recognized the broad communal dimension of that tradition as they understood it. For example, the town pastor of Wittenberg was asked to ordain candidates for the ministry in his

---

[19] Dorothea Wendebourg, "Die Reformation in Deutschland und das bischöfliche Amt," 274–302, in *Visible Unity and the Ministry of Oversight: The Second Theological Conference Held under the Meissen Agreement between the Church of England and the Evangelical Church in Germany* (London: Church House Publishing, 1997), at 275. [English text at pp. 49–78, where the translation of the quoted passage is "The Church of the Empire was *de facto* a church run by the princes."—Ed.]

church—not in individual congregations—after the candidates had been examined for their doctrinal teaching. And Canon 4 of the Second Council of Nicea, according to which a bishop is to be consecrated by neighboring bishops, is cited frequently by the ordination certificates from this period.[20]

This sympathetic reassessment of the early history of the Reformation in Germany can help Roman Catholics appreciate more fully the positions taken by *The Niagara Report*, *The Porvoo Agreement*, and *Called to Common Mission* and to recognize what a significant achievement they constitute.

The Niagara Report, for example, emphasizes that "oversight or presiding ministry," the heart of the episcopal office, stands within the continuity of apostolic faith. But, as we have seen, it immediately goes on to state: "The fact of bishops does not by itself guarantee the continuity of apostolic faith" (NR 54). Roman Catholics can better identify with such a sentence when they recognize how deeply this lesson was learned by Lutherans during the emergency atmosphere of the Reformation.

In *The Porvoo Common Statement* Roman Catholics are pleased to find even more explicit emphasis on continuity in apostolic succession, though there too "the use of the sign of the historic episcopal succession does not by itself guarantee the fidelity of a church to every aspect of the apostolic faith, life and mission" (PCS 51). But the episcopal ordinations to the existing sees of the Catholic Church by the Reformation churches in the northern European lands is seen as a sign of "their intention to continue the life and ministry of the One, Holy, Catholic and Apostolic Church" (PCS 33). Roman Catholics welcome this emphasis on the historic continuity signified by apostolic succession of bishops, and welcome also the "[r]esumption of the use of the sign" as the ordinary means by which the ministry of *episcope* should be continued (PCS 53). The more sympathetic reassessment of the Reformation history should help them to understand why resumption of this sign "does not imply an adverse judgement on the ministries of those churches which did not previously make

---

[20] See the report of the Ecumenical Study Group of Protestant and Catholic Theologians in Germany, *The Condemnations of the Reformation Era: Do They Still Divide?*, ed. Karl Lehmann and Wolfhart Pannenberg, trans. Margaret Kohl (Minneapolis: Fortress Press, 1990), 153–55.

use of the sign" (PCS 53). This echoes a basic teaching of Roman Catholic sacramental theology, in which the reality of the thing signified can be present even when the sign is lacking, in this case because "[f]aithfulness to the apostolic calling of the whole Church is carried by more than one means of continuity" (PCS 52). Roman Catholics should not underestimate the massive step toward reconciliation with all episcopal traditions that is represented by *The Porvoo Common Statement*.

Similarly, Roman Catholics should welcome *Called to Common Mission* as a remarkable and positive achievement: the sharing by two church communions of an episcopal succession that is "both evangelical and historic" (CCM 12). This means that the Lutherans have agreed that "regularly" one or more Anglican bishops will participate in ordinations/installations of Lutheran bishops (CCM 12). Roman Catholics now can better grasp why Reformation history has made Lutherans insist on their freedom "to maintain that this same episcopate, though pastorally desirable when exercised in personal, collegial, and communal ways, is nonetheless not necessary for the relationship of full communion" (CCM 13)—though we might be inclined to point out that the loss of the "historic episcopate" at the time of the Reformation by some Lutheran churches did in fact contribute to a break in communion with our Roman Catholic forebears. Roman Catholics should also recognize that having a bishop "regularly" preside and participate in the laying-on-of-hands at all ordinations of clergy (CCM 20) represents a Lutheran acknowledgment of the emergency character of the Reformation practice. Lutherans here seek to return to the "regular" practice with a historic episcopate, but they do not intend to forget what they learned during the emergency period. The memories of this emergency period hence serve as a kind of "salutary warning." By the same token, the dissenting Lutheran "Word Alone" groups strike Roman Catholics as people who cannot recognize that the emergency has ended.

2.2. *Shifts in the Roman Catholic Theology of Ordained Ministry and the Liturgy of the Sacrament of Orders*

Recent Roman Catholic theological and liturgical shifts on ordained ministry constitute a second development that affects the context in which evaluation of the Lutheran–Anglican agreements takes place.

Let me review them briefly to show their relevance for my paper's topic.

In its teaching on the sacramentality of episcopal ordination, Vatican II asserts that "by episcopal consecration is conferred the fullness of the sacrament of orders . . . But episcopal consecration, together with the office of sanctifying, also confers the office of teaching and governing."[21] That is to say, unlike Aquinas and the sixteenth-century popes who followed his theology of orders when they judged Anglican bishops, the council teaches that the sacrament of orders itself gives the bishop jurisdiction. This also means that Vatican II makes the episcopacy, not the presbyterate, "the fundamental category for understanding ordained ministry," as Daniel Donovan explains.[22] Further, the council emphasizes the collegial character of the episcopacy: to be a bishop is to be received into the college of bishops and to share in the responsibility for *episcope* [oversight] of the whole church.[23] The bishop is the link between Christ and the local church that—gathered around the eucharist—is filled with the many charisms given to the ordained, the religious, and the laity.[24] Everyone shares the priesthood of the faithful, although the latter and the ministerial priesthood differ "in essence and not only in degree."[25]

What of the presbyter according to Vatican II? Besides taking the bishop as its starting point for understanding the sacrament of orders, the council shifts its theology of the presbyter—mainly by expanding it. It underlines the ministry of the word as a crucial complement to the presbyter's eucharistic ministry. For preaching holds an eminent place among the functions of bishops,[26] and this eminence extends as well to the preaching of presbyters.[27] Donovan notes that in

[21] Vatican II, *Lumen Gentium* (Dogmatic Constitution on the Church), n. 21. Also at http://www.vatican.va/archive/hist_councils/ii_vatican_council/documents/vat-ii_const_19641121_lumen-gentium_en.html.

[22] Daniel Donovan, *What Are They Saying about the Ministerial Priesthood?* (New York: Paulist Press, 1992), 10.

[23] Vatican II, *Lumen Gentium*, n. 22.

[24] Ibid., n. 26.

[25] Ibid., n. 10.

[26] Ibid., n. 25.

[27] Vatican II, *Presbyterorum Ordinis* (Decree on the Ministry and Life of Priests), in *The Documents of Vatican II*, n. 4. Also at http://www.vatican.va/archive/hist_councils/ii_vatican_council/documents/vat-ii_decree_19651207_presbyterorum-ordinis_en.html.

Presbyterorum Ordinis the council also argues that a proper understanding of Christian cult envisions it as including a ministry of the
word.[28] Indeed, the document relates the work of evangelization and
other pastoral work of the presbyter to the self-giving love of Christ's
sacrifice, expanding the meaning of sacerdotal language to include
all aspects of the presbyter's life.[29]

The council also endorses liturgical emphases and practices that
express various aspects of these theological shifts. For example, the
sacred liturgy should undergo a general restoration that makes its
primary aim the "full and active participation by all the people."[30]
Again: "The bishop is to be considered the high priest of his flock. . . .
[T]he Church reveals herself most clearly when a full complement of
God's holy people . . . exercise a thorough and active participation
at the very altar where the bishop presides."[31] Local parishes "under
a pastor who takes the place of the bishop . . . in a certain way represent the visible Church as it is established throughout the world."[32]
As with the other sacraments, to clarify the meaning of the sacrament
of orders "both the ceremonies and texts of the ordination rites are
to be revised."[33] And at an episcopal consecration "the imposition of
hands may be done by all the bishops present."[34]

These theological and liturgical shifts are relevant for a Roman
Catholic evaluation of the Lutheran–Anglican agreements in at least
four ways. First, rather than a narrow understanding of the sacerdotal
aspect of the ordained ministry, Vatican II elaborates an expanded
account of sacrifice and relates it to the preaching and pastoral work
of the ordained as well as to his liturgical role. Second, in its teaching
on the sacramentality of episcopal ordination the council gives the
episcopacy a more liturgical and communal grounding. Third, by
shifting its understanding of how episcopal jurisdiction is given, the
council moves away from the potential bifurcation of roles actually
experienced by the Reformers. Fourth, by emphasizing the collegiality of the bishops, the significance of the local church, and the priest-

---

[28] Donovan, *What Are They Saying about the Ministerial Priesthood?*, 14.

[29] Ibid.

[30] Vatican II, *Sacrosanctum Concilium* (Constitution on the Sacred Liturgy), in *The Documents of Vatican II*, n. 14.

[31] Ibid., n. 41.

[32] Ibid., n. 42.

[33] Ibid., n. 76.

[34] Ibid.

hood of the faithful shared by the whole people of God, Vatican II receives several teachings that had motivated Luther's call for reformation in the first place.

It follows that Roman Catholics today can applaud these emphases when they read them in the Lutheran–Anglican agreements. For example, they can agree with *The Niagara Report* when it describes the development of "an authoritative, but not authoritarian, ministry" (NR 19). And they can sympathize with *Called to Common Mission* when it insists that the historic catholic episcopate must be "exercised in personal, collegial, and communal ways" in order to be "pastorally desirable." Vatican II intended in part a reform of the episcopal office that would make it pastorally more effective.

I think Roman Catholics can especially welcome the elaborated theology of the episcopate present in *The Porvoo Common Statement*. According to that statement, apostolic succession in the episcopal office is "a visible and personal way of focusing the apostolicity of the whole Church" (PCS 46). But this continuity cannot be divorced from the continuity of life and witness of the diocese to which the bishop is called. Hence the continuity in the existing historic sees is seen as more than just personal, and the care for maintaining the church's pattern of life there "reflects an intention of the churches to continue to exercise the apostolic ministry of word and sacrament of the universal Church" (PCS 49). Hence the ordination of a bishop in historic succession is a sign that communicates the church's "care for continuity in the whole of its life and mission" and reinforces its "determination to manifest the permanent characteristics of the Church of the apostles" (PCS 50). The Roman Catholic Church can agree with *Porvoo* that the use of the sign of historic episcopal succession is in itself no guarantee of fidelity to all the aspects of apostolicity; but it should welcome *Porvoo*'s insistence that "the retention of the sign remains a permanent challenge to fidelity and to unity, a summons to witness to, and a commission to realise more fully, the permanent characteristics of the Church of the apostles" (PCS 51).

2.3. *Successive Ecumenical Agreements on Ordained Ministry*

Besides the scholarly reassessment of historical data about ordained ministry, and recent Roman Catholic theological and liturgical shifts on the same reality, successive ecumenical agreements on ordained ministry also constitute a development that is relevant to an evaluation of the three Lutheran–Anglican accords.

Roman Catholics can take confidence from the trajectory of increasing convergence in the successive ecumenical agreements, and they should take that convergence into account when evaluating full-communion accords between churches. To illustrate this point for Roman Catholics, let me examine two agreed statements: the "Ministry" statement of the World Council of Churches and *The Final Report* of the Anglican–Roman Catholic International Commission.

Both statements situate the ordained minister firmly in the midst of the church. The WCC affirms that the Holy Spirit bestows on the community diverse and complementary gifts,[35] but within that multiplicity of gifts, the ordained provide "a focus of its unity."[36] Indeed, "the ordained ministry has no existence apart from the community."[37] ARCIC also speaks of the many gifts of the Holy Spirit, among which is *episcope* by the ordained ministry, given for the edification of the church.[38]

At the same time, both statements emphasize the difference between the ordained ministry and other ministries in the church. The WCC argues that "in order to fulfill its mission, the Church needs persons who are publicly and continually responsible for pointing to its fundamental dependence on Jesus Christ."[39] Far from seeing the ordained simply as representatives of the community, "Ministry" explains that they are "representatives of Jesus Christ to the community," chosen and called by Christ, sent as "heralds and ambassadors" to "proclaim his message of reconciliation."[40] The presence of the ordained "reminds the community of the divine initiative, and of the dependence of the Church on Jesus Christ."[41] Such persons may be called "priests" because of their exercise of the royal and prophetic priesthood of the faithful "through word and sacraments,

---

[35] World Council of Churches, "Ministry," in *Baptism, Eucharist and Ministry* (Geneva: World Council of Churches, 1982), n. 5.

[36] Ibid., n. 8.

[37] Ibid., n. 12.

[38] Anglican–Roman Catholic International Commission, "Authority in the Church I," in *The Final Report*, n. 5.

[39] World Council of Churches, "Ministry," in *Baptism, Eucharist and Ministry*, n. 8.

[40] Ibid., n. 11.

[41] Ibid., n. 12.

through their prayers of intercession, and through their pastoral guidance of the community."[42]

The ARCIC discussion of ordained ministry also brings out its uniqueness. Although ordained ministers share through baptism in the priesthood of the people of God and represent the church in its priestly vocation of self-offering, the ministry of the ordained "is not an extension of the common Christian priesthood but belongs to another realm of the gifts of the Spirit."[43] Besides noting the basis for sacerdotal descriptions of the ordained ministry,[44] the ARCIC statement also gives a full job description: minister of the word, teacher, servant, shepherd, called to holiness and compassion.[45] The WCC statement also provides a long job description.[46]

When relating ordained ministry to its function of *episcope*, both statements provide an extensive and nuanced account. For the WCC every church needs a ministry of unity, of *episcope*, "in order to be the Church of God."[47] "Ministry" teaches that the Holy Spirit keeps the church in the apostolic tradition, and it lists a variety of characteristics through which continuity with the church of the apostles is maintained. Such characteristics include witness, proclamation and fresh interpretation of the Gospel, celebration of the sacraments, service to the sick and needy, and the transmission of ministerial responsibilities.[48] Succession of bishops became one way in which the church's apostolic tradition is expressed, the statement maintains.[49] It recommends that churches without episcopal succession recover it "as a sign, though not a guarantee, of the continuity and unity of the Church," yet as "part of a wider process by which the episcopal churches themselves also regain their lost unity."[50] In fact, the statement contends, the threefold pattern itself stands in need of "reform."[51]

---

[42] Ibid., n. 17.

[43] Anglican–Roman Catholic International Commission, "Ministry and Ordination," in *The Final Report*, n. 13.

[44] Ibid.

[45] Ibid., nn. 7–11.

[46] World Council of Churches, "Ministry," in *Baptism, Eucharist and Ministry*, n. 11.

[47] Ibid., n. 23.

[48] Ibid., n. 34.

[49] Ibid., n. 36.

[50] Ibid., n. 38.

[51] Ibid., n. 24.

For the ARCIC statement *episcope* is the work of the bishop, who symbolizes and maintains "[t]he communion of the churches in mission, faith, and holiness, through time and space."[52] ARCIC adds a lengthy discussion of the teaching authority exercised by bishops acting in conciliar or primatial ways.[53] It also affirms that the primacy of the bishop of Rome is part of "God's design for the universal *koinonia*,[54] and it declares that sometimes "[m]aintenance in the truth requires . . . a decisive judgment" on doctrine that becomes part of the church's "permanent witness,"[55] a judgment that can be made by council or "universal primate."[56] This recognition of the role of teaching authority as part of the doctrine of ordained ministry has brought the ecumenical discussion to a new level of depth.

We know, of course, that the discussion of *episcope* has not remained merely theoretical. In the Anglican and Lutheran churches of Northern Europe and of North America the members have decided to adopt a shared life of worship, mission, and service, including mutual participation of the partner churches in future episcopal and presbyteral ordinations. We should situate these decisions within the trajectory of successive ecumenical agreements. John Hotchkin envisages such decisions as standing within a third stage of the ecumenical movement. The first stage is the "pioneering and organizational stage" that began at the start of the twentieth century,[57] and the second stage is that of dialogue.[58] The third stage is "the stage of phased reconciliation."[59] During this stage, he explains, "the churches have coming before them proposals to redefine their relationships by decisive mutual action, leading in the end to increased direct participation in one another's ecclesial lives though without corporately merging."[60] With courage though not without struggle, Lutherans in Northern

---

[52] Anglican–Roman Catholic International Commission, "Ministry and Ordination," in *The Final Report*, n. 16.

[53] Anglican–Roman Catholic International Commission, "Authority in the Church I," in *The Final Report*, nn. 19–22.

[54] Anglican–Roman Catholic International Commission, "Authority in the Church II," in *The Final Report*, n. 15.

[55] Ibid., n. 24.

[56] Ibid., n. 26.

[57] John Hotchkin, "The Ecumenical Movement's Third Stage," *Origins* 25 (1995–96): 353–61, at 353.

[58] Ibid., 355.

[59] Ibid., 356.

[60] Ibid.

Europe and in North America have moved into this third stage and ratified not just one but two sets of agreements for increased communion with another church—with Anglicans and with the Reformed church tradition.

In 1984 the Lutheran–Roman Catholic International Commission for Dialogue published *Facing Unity*, which also foresaw a series of stages through which the two churches would move as they were healed of their divisions. In the first stage, as a "Community of Faith," they would renew their common and varied expressions of the apostolic faith and withdraw their condemnations and anathemas of each other.[61] In the second stage, as a "Community of Sacraments," the two churches would discover increasing agreement in the understanding and celebration of sacramental life.[62] In the third stage, *Facing Unity* foresaw a "Community of Service" gradually emerging as the churches moved toward a full communion in mutual recognition of ordained ministries.[63] This stage would include a series of healing steps in the exercise of *episcope*: first, joint exercise of *episcope*, then its collegial exercise, and finally a transition to a common ordained ministry through joint ordinations of bishops.[64] Such a process "could function at the universal level," noted the signers, "but could also be set in motion at local regional or national ecclesial levels"[65] and it could be joined by people "in other churches . . . who accompany us on this road."[66] Roman Catholics should recognize that this is precisely what has happened in the Lutheran–Anglican agreements.

It is important that Roman Catholics grasp that the Lutheran–Anglican agreements stand within the trajectory of the ongoing process of healing and reconciliation within the one church of Christ. This will allow them to recognize the agreements as the significant achievements they are, rather than criticizing them for their inadequacies. In those agreements Lutherans have chosen to recover the historic episcopate as a sign of continuity with the apostolic tradition,

---

[61] Joint Lutheran/Roman Catholic Study Commission on the Gospel and the Church, *Facing Unity: Models, Forms and Phases of Catholic–Lutheran Church Fellowship* (Geneva and New York: Lutheran World Federation, 1985), nn. 55–69. Also at http://www.prounione.urbe.it/dia-int/l-rc/doc/e_l-rc_facing.html.

[62] Ibid., nn. 70–85.

[63] Ibid., nn. 86–148.

[64] Ibid., n. 118.

[65] Ibid.

[66] Ibid., n. 149.

but to do so without minimizing the "salutary warning" that the emergency measures of the Reformation give to the entire church of Christ. For their part, Roman Catholics would want eventually to bring their concern for a ministry of unity and for the role of teaching authority into the discussion about *episcope*. But, as *Facing Unity* said, one step at a time. For the time being, Roman Catholics have a lot of work to do in reforming both their own ministry of unity and the way they have recently been exercising teaching authority.

The Enlightened Discernment of Underlying Intentions

In my introduction I pointed out that the meaning of ministerial practices crucially includes the principal aims, main purposes, and key objectives intended by both the ministers performing them and those for whom they are performed. I also noted that evaluating such underlying intentions is consequently a crucial part of evaluating Lutheran and Anglican ministerial practices and—by extension—evaluating the Lutheran–Anglican agreements about them. And I indicated my judgment that enlightened discernment of underlying Lutheran and Anglican intentions—seeing them in a new light—provides significant additional support to an affirmative Roman Catholic evaluation of those agreements. Let me conclude my paper by amplifying that judgment.

When Roman Catholics are able to reread the Reformation history in a spirit of repentance and purification of memories, they will be able to discern the underlying intention of the Reformers more clearly. That intention was the reform of the church, and the theology and liturgical changes of the Reformers—even if judged faulty by Roman Catholic standards—were guided by that intention. Given that fact, it is difficult to see how the Reformers did not "intend to do what the church does," as the resolution of the Donatist controversy put it.[67] Luther sought the reform of the ordained ministry of his day, and he did all that seemed faithfully possible to avoid breaking communion

---

[67] A somewhat parallel approach is suggested by George Tavard in his discussion of Anglican orders in *A Review of Anglican Orders: The Problem and the Solution* (Collegeville, MN: Liturgical Press, 1990). [See section 1 of "Anglican Orders and Ecumenical Dialogue on Ordained Ministry" in chapter 10 of the present volume. (Ed.)]

with the bishops. And it was the pope, after all, who excommunicated Luther, not vice versa.

But whatever Roman Catholics think of past Lutheran intentions, the ecumenical agreements help clarify the intentions of Lutherans today. The agreements I have cited, including the three Lutheran–Anglican accords, manifest an elaborate and nuanced theology of ordained ministry and apostolic succession that also touches on the teaching office. Furthermore, Vatican II incorporates changes into the Roman Catholic theology of ordained ministry itself, and these changes are reflected in today's Roman Catholic liturgical texts. Such theological developments manifest the convergence of understanding among Roman Catholics, Anglicans, and Lutherans. But they also demonstrate the point about underlying intention that emerged from the Donatist controversy: it is Christ who acts in the sacraments, regardless of the faith or theology of the minister. Even if Luther's understanding of ordained ministry was faulty, Roman Catholics today can see more clearly that he did his work so that the ordained might more faithfully do what the church does. Is it not time for Roman Catholics to conclude that today, at least, Lutherans certainly have the intention to do what the church does?

This is one reason the Anglican–Lutheran agreements have such an important role to play: they clarify current Lutheran intentions. For example, in *Called to Common Mission*, Lutherans express their "intention to enter the ministry of the historic episcopate" (CCM 18). Isn't that pretty clear? If we Roman Catholics cannot recognize in such steps the intention to do what the church does, then we face an awkward question about our own history: how can we confirm that the intention underlying our theologies and liturgies of ordination in the sixteenth century and today is the same?

Second, whose underlying intention should be evaluated? An earlier ecumenical approach first sought mutual recognition of ministries and then moved toward reconciliation of church communions, but today the reverse approach is preferred. This change of starting point reflects the shift from what Yves Congar called a "pyramidal" ecclesiology to an ecclesiology "of communion."[68] When we think about underlying intention, then, perhaps we can see a similar shift: from

---

[68] Yves Congar, "La 'réception' comme réalité ecclesiologique," *Revue des Sciences philosophiques et théologiques* 56 (1972): 369–403, at 392–93.

the intention of the ordaining presbyter or bishop to the intention of the whole community in which he ministers.

Jean-Marie Tillard underscores this idea in an article entitled "Recognition of Ministries: What Is the Real Question?"[69] The real question, he says, is not the intention of the ordained minister but that of the community he serves. Tillard argues that "the intention of causing a breach cannot be deduced simply on the basis of the ministers' doctrinal position."[70] And in discussing the churches emerging after the Reformation, he continues:

> it is not necessary for the threefold ministry—deacon, presbyter, bishop—to be attested in the classical form for apostolic *episkope* to exist. The *id quod requiritur et sufficit* [what is required and suffices] would consist in such cases in the fact that all the functions or services essentially required by the life of the Church in conformity with the apostolic institutions are present. . . . But it must be asked whether the essentially apostolic functions and services may not re-emerge in other forms.[71]

And in any case it is misleading to analyze the intention of the ordained ministers apart from the intention of the whole community they serve.[72]

Third, I think we should not underestimate the extent to which the signing of the *Joint Declaration on the Doctrine of Justification* is a sign of the underlying intention of both our churches to move toward visible unity. The resolution of misunderstandings during the year before the signing serves, if anything, to highlight the seriousness of both communions' intention to persevere despite difficulties. The document itself, the work on the "Annex" supplement,[73] the carefully planned event in Augsburg, the conferences and liturgical celebra-

---

[69] Jean-Marie R. Tillard, "Recognition of Ministries: What Is the Real Question?" *One in Christ* 21 (1985): 31–39.

[70] Ibid., 37.

[71] Ibid., 38–39.

[72] Ibid.

[73] The "Annex to the Official Common Statement" was issued by the Vatican at the time of the final signing of the *Joint Declaration*. It makes explicit the Roman Catholic endorsement of certain elucidations of Luther's assertion that a Christian is *simul justus et peccator* [justified and still a sinner]. The elucidations go beyond the text of the *Joint Declaration* itself, and they were worked out in response to tensions about

tions of this event worldwide—all these express in words and symbolic gestures the intention of the two communions to move closer together. I think the whole event of the *Joint Declaration* shows that the relationship of our two church communities today is shaped by a radical and persistent intention for the restoration of full communion. Indeed, we have become even more aware of our own limitations and seek at times to be corrected and converted by the other.

This attention to the underlying intention of the community as a whole, rather than that of just the ordained ministers, is also suggested by *The Porvoo Common Statement* with its emphasis on historic sees. It interprets the continuing use of such sees as a sign of the local churches' desire to remain in faithful continuity with the one, holy, catholic, and apostolic church.

Congar writes of this desire for unity: "Those involved in the ecumenical movement have by virtue of that a *votum unitatis, votum catholicitatis* [desire for unity, desire for catholicity], which gives to their present belief a dynamic dimension in which their intention of plenitude is fulfilled," he says.[74] Is not this growing *votum unitatis* with its accompanying openness to each other's history, theology, and practice a significant fact on which we should reflect more deeply? If our two communions were to be moving slowly into a new relationship with each other, would not their movement be characterized by this desire?

If they are able to see them in a new light, Roman Catholics can recognize this desire as patently present in the recent agreements Lutherans have made with Anglicans.

---

the assertion that surfaced during the year prior to the signing. (Ed.) See http://www.vatican.va/roman_curia/pontifical_councils/chrstuni/documents/rc_pc_chrstuni_doc_31101999_cath-luth-annex_en.html.

[74] Yves Congar, *Diversity and Communion*, trans. John Bowden (Mystic, CT: Twenty-Third Publications, 1984), 133.

13

Scripture and Tradition[1]

I often find myself at Saint John's Abbey, a Roman Catholic Benedictine monastery in Collegeville, Minnesota, when I take part in meetings at the nearby Collegeville Institute for Ecumenical and Cultural Research. Two years ago I attended a Vespers service in the Abbey Church that made a lasting impression on me. Saint John's Abbey had commissioned a group of calligraphers and artists to copy and illustrate the entire text of the Bible, and at this service the initial books prepared by the group (the four gospels and the Acts of the Apostles) were being used for the first time. Through the church filled with hundreds of people, mostly Roman Catholics, the beautifully copied and illustrated biblical books were carried reverently in procession, incensed, and solemnly proclaimed. The abbot preached on the importance of the written word of God. The books were enthroned on the altar in the center of the church, and they became the focus of visual attention as the entire congregation rose and sang a hymn of thanksgiving.

What struck me suddenly during the hymn was the shift of atmosphere this service revealed. Fifty years ago such an elaborate reverencing of biblical texts would not have been found in many Catholic

[1] First presented on April 12, 2002, as "Scripture and Tradition: A Roman Catholic Perspective," at a conference entitled "Catholics and Evangelicals in Conversation," Wheaton College, Wheaton, IL. Not previously published.

parishes. Processions, incensing, and enthronement on the altar would all have occurred—but to honor the reserved sacrament of the eucharist. Yet here these liturgical gestures of homage were directed instead to the inspired word of God.

After the service I asked my Evangelical colleague, with whom I have been in dialogue for many years, how he liked the service. He was quite positive. Although procession, incense, and enthronement on the altar were unfamiliar to him in the Church of the Nazarene he recognized in them the effort of Saint John's Abbey to honor the text of the Bible and to encourage its study. That seemed very good to him—though he might also have thought to himself, "Not bad, for Catholics."

Of course, Saint John's Abbey is hardly like a typical Roman Catholic parish. It has been a leader of liturgical and biblical renewal within the Roman Catholic Church for decades. But the image of the biblical books enthroned on the altar in the center of the Abbey Church has stayed in my mind, and it can help symbolize a shift that has taken place in the life of the Roman Catholic community, a shift to what Enzo Bianchi calls "the centrality of the Word of God." Commenting on the reception of the Second Vatican Council, Bianchi writes, "After centuries in exile the word of God once more occupies its central place in the life of the Catholic Church. . . . One might even speak of a *rediscovery* of the word of God by the Catholic faithful who for centuries did not experience or practice a direct contact with the word of God and did not even have occasion to appreciate the value of that word for the life of faith."[2]

When I was a little girl growing up in the 1950s, my deeply Catholic family kept the family Bible in a place of honor, heard biblical texts weekly at the eucharistic celebration, and read passages from the Bible at home together on such major feasts as Christmas and Easter. But the teachers at my Catholic grade school warned me not to read the Bible on my own because I might misinterpret it. Just ten years later, however, the biblical renewal within the Roman Catholic Church had affected my Catholic high school. I was studying the Bible in both religion class and my Young Christian Students leadership

---

[2] Enzo Bianchi, "The Centrality of the Word of God," in *The Reception of Vatican II*, ed. Giuseppe Alberigo, Jean-Pierre Jossua, and Joseph A. Komonchak (Washington, DC: Catholic University of America Press, 1987), 115–36, at 115.

group. The Second Vatican Council was meeting during that time, and it instructed me and all Roman Catholics that we are fed by God's word as well as by the eucharist,[3] and that we should read the Scriptures frequently.[4] It also taught that the Scriptures "impart the word of God Himself without change, and make the voice of the Holy Spirit resound,"[5] that all Catholic preaching "must be nourished and ruled by sacred Scripture,"[6] and that the study of the Scriptures "is, as it were, the soul of sacred theology."[7]

If we recognize the shift to the centrality of the word of God in the Roman Catholic Church, that should also help us to recognize the shift in thinking and practice on the more precise topic we are considering in this presentation: the Roman Catholic teaching on Scripture and tradition. This is an important issue of debate in Catholic–Evangelical discussion. The Theological Task Force on Ecumenical Issues of the World Evangelical Fellowship warns that "when a creed becomes the sole means through which the apostolic testimony is filtered, the creed tends to detract from the normative testimony of the apostles."[8] It notes that "the matter of biblical authority" will often determine the response of Evangelical churches to discussions of the value of, for example, the Nicene-Constantinopolitan creed.[9]

At first glance the texts of Vatican II about Scripture and tradition are not all that reassuring to Evangelicals. While the *Dogmatic Constitution on Divine Revelation* (*Dei Verbum*) does not articulate a two-source theory—as though some truths necessary for salvation are found in Scripture and some others in tradition—it nevertheless does emphasize the unity of Scripture and tradition, which are said to have "a close connection and communication."[10] The text continues, "For

---

[3] Vatican II, *Dei Verbum* (Dogmatic Constitution on Divine Revelation), n. 21. Also at http://www.vatican.va/archive/hist_councils/ii_vatican_council/documents/vat-ii_const_19651118_dei-verbum_en.html.

[4] Ibid., n. 25.

[5] Ibid., n. 21.

[6] Ibid.

[7] Ibid., n. 24.

[8] World Evangelical Fellowship Theological Task Force on Ecumenical Issues, "Confessing the One Faith: An Evangelical Response by the W.E.F. Theological Task Force on Ecumenical Issues," *Evangelical Review of Theology* 18 (1994): 35–46, at 38. In 2002 the World Evangelical Fellowship was renamed the World Evangelical Alliance.

[9] Ibid., 40.

[10] Vatican II, *Dei Verbum*, n. 9.

both of them, flowing from the same divine wellspring, in a certain way merge into a unity and tend toward the same end."[11] Evangelicals might be dismayed by this emphasis on the unity of Scripture and tradition. They could probably agree with a point the *Dogmatic Constitution on Divine Revelation* then makes: "it is not from sacred Scripture alone that the Church draws her certainty about everything which has been revealed."[12] But the next sentence will surely seem unwelcome to those who claim the heritage of the Reformation's *sola scriptura*: "Therefore both sacred tradition and sacred Scripture are to be accepted and venerated with the same sense of devotion and reverence."[13] While it affirms that the teaching office of the church "is not above the word of God but serves it," the document also affirms that tradition and Scripture together form "one sacred deposit of the word of God, which is committed to the Church."[14] How can Evangelicals and Roman Catholics get very far in their conversation together if Roman Catholics are so committed to emphasizing the unity of Scripture and tradition?

I think the key to understanding the Roman Catholic position here is to grasp what Roman Catholics mean by "tradition."

We know that the participants in the Second Vatican Council firmly rejected a two-source theory of revelation. First, they saw revelation as the basis for both Scripture and tradition,[15] and they did not want to equate revelation with the forms of its historical presentation. It is the Gospel, or more basically Christ, who is God's revelation to humankind and who is announced in the written Scriptures and in apostolic tradition. Second, the council participants did not wish to imply a kind of mechanical collection of propositions divided up between two separate sources.[16] Hence they emphasized the organic interdependence of Scripture and tradition.

---

[11] Ibid.
[12] Ibid.
[13] Ibid.
[14] Ibid., n. 10.
[15] Avery Dulles, "Revelation as the Basis for Scripture and Tradition," *Evangelical Review of Theology* 21 (1997): 104–20.
[16] Joseph Ratzinger, "Dogmatic Constitution on Divine Revelation: Chapter II, The Transmission of Divine Revelation," in *Commentary on the Documents of Vatican II*, vol. 3, ed. Herbert Vorgrimler, trans. William Glen-Doepel et al. (Freiburg: Herder; Montreal: Palm Publishers, 1968), 190–91.

In his commentary on the *Dogmatic Constitution on Divine Revelation*, Joseph Ratzinger notes[17] that the conciliar text defined Scripture by what it is: "Scripture is the word of God inasmuch as it is consigned to writing under the inspiration of the divine Spirit."[18] But when the *Constitution* turned to tradition, the discussion became more complex. It defined tradition by its function, by what it does. "[S]acred tradition hands on in its full purity God's word, which was entrusted to the apostles by Christ the Lord and the Holy Spirit," it said. Then it continued: "Thus, led by the light of the Spirit of truth," the successors of the apostles "can in their preaching preserve this word of God faithfully, explain it, and make it more widely known."[19] While Scripture is the word of God in writing, the task of tradition is its proclamation, preservation, and interpretation.

This means that tradition is not productive, explains Ratzinger, but "conservative"—it guards and expounds the Revelation written in Scripture. But precisely in order to give tradition a conserving function, the participants at Vatican II adopted a dynamic understanding of tradition's development. "Tradition . . . consisted not in particular truths but in a dynamic process of transmission under the guidance of the Holy Spirit," explains Avery Dulles.[20] Ratzinger agrees: tradition in Vatican II primarily "means simply the many-layered yet one presence of the mystery of Christ throughout all the ages."[21]

Because they saw tradition as a dynamic reality, the council participants taught that it "develops in the Church with the help of the Holy Spirit."[22] For "there is a growth in the understanding of the realities and the words which have been handed down," they continued. "[A]nd thus God, who spoke of old, uninterruptedly converses with the Bride of His beloved Son; and the Holy Spirit, through whom the living voice of the gospel resounds in the Church, and through her, in the world, leads unto all truth those who believe and makes the word of Christ dwell abundantly in them (cf. Col 3:16)."[23]

---

[17] Ibid., 194.

[18] Vatican II, *Dei Verbum*, n. 9.

[19] Ibid.

[20] Dulles, "Revelation as the Basis for Scripture and Tradition," 118.

[21] Ratzinger, "Dogmatic Constitution on Divine Revelation: Chapter II, The Transmission of Divine Revelation," in *Commentary on the Documents of Vatican II*, 184.

[22] Vatican II, *Dei Verbum*, n. 8.

[23] Ibid.

Some Evangelicals criticize this kind of language. During his presentation at the international dialogue between the World Evangelical Fellowship and the Roman Catholic Church, Henri Blocher accused this Vatican II text of manifesting a "vitalistic idea of development."[24] But I think that the Anglican–Roman Catholic International Commission [ARCIC], in a reflection on the nature of tradition, is more faithful to Vatican II's meaning. The "combination of permanence in the revealed truth and continuous exploration of its meaning," says ARCIC, "is what is meant by Christian tradition."[25] This sense of permanence of the Gospel but growth in our understanding of it is, I believe, what the council's portrayal of tradition as dynamic intended to express. The council wished to present tradition not as a source with content, but rather as a process by which the Gospel is preserved. This involves not a change in the Gospel, but rather a change in us: we grow in understanding.

To present in more detail the Roman Catholic view of Scripture and tradition, I want to highlight what Karl Rahner writes about the relationship of Scripture and tradition. Rahner was one of the leading Roman Catholic theologians of the twentieth century, and he was also deeply involved in ecumenical dialogue. In his reflections on Scripture and tradition he holds together two positions that have often been seen as contradictory: one a classically Catholic position, the other a classically Protestant position. On the one hand, he uses a Catholic insight: later dogmas that articulate the faith "need not simply be derived from Scripture in the sense that they are explicitly propounded there 'in other words'" or strictly deducible from the scriptural texts. "The faith which created Scripture did not eliminate itself by the formation of Scripture," writes Rahner. And in that sense, he continues, it is proper to say *"non sola scriptura."* But on the other hand, Rahner wants to draw on a Protestant insight as well: "no later dogmas," he writes, "are independent of Scripture and not subordinated to it." Further: "everything in the later utterances of faith must

---

[24] Henri Blocher, "Scripture and Tradition: An Evangelical Response," *Evangelical Review of Theology* 21 (1997): 121–27, at 124.

[25] Anglican–Roman Catholic International Commission, "Authority in the Church: Elucidations (1981)," in *The Final Report* (London: SPCK & Catholic Truth Society, 1982), n. 2. Also at http://www.vatican.va/roman_curia/pontifical_councils/chrstuni /angl-comm-docs/rc_pc_chrstuni_doc_1981_authority-elucidation-i_en.html.

be measured by Scripture." Hence it is correct to say *"sola scriptura,"* he explains, "since it is in the Scripture that the one whole apostolic faith has been objectivated and has given itself, and laid down for all future times, its *norma non normata* [unnormed norm]."[26]

Can both of these positions be maintained? In the past we thought they were contradictory, but Rahner teaches us they are complementary. We must hold them both. Later dogmas need not be simply a repetition of the words of Scripture (the Catholic insight); but later dogmas must be measured by Scripture, which remains the unnormed norm of all other norms (the Protestant insight). Both insights are true, I think. Sometimes they are held together with striking precision in ecumenical work, as for instance the sentence of ARCIC explaining the discernment of the canon of Scripture: "The Church's recognition of these Scriptures as canonical, after a long period of critical discernment, was at the same time an act of obedience and of authority."[27] An act of obedience and authority: in one sentence this statement affirms both Protestant and Catholic insights on Scripture and tradition.

I think that both points are increasingly maintained by both Evangelicals and Roman Catholics, but with different emphases. Each communion's emphasis is an important offering in the gift exchange that is central to ecumenical dialogue. Moreover, when we examine positions taken today by Roman Catholic theologians and members of ecumenical dialogues we find that both insights are part of Roman Catholic teaching on Scripture and tradition, but the first is easier to recognize than the second.

The first is the Catholic insight: tradition need not simply repeat the words of Scripture. This insight has several components. In its teaching, *Mysterium Ecclesiae* [*The Mystery of the Church*], the Congregation for the Doctrine of the Faith [CDF] says that sometimes new words must be found precisely in order to maintain the same mean-

---

[26] Karl Rahner, "Scripture and Tradition," in *Sacramentum Mundi: An Encyclopedia of Theology*, ed., Karl Rahner et al., vol. 6 (New York: Herder & Herder, 1970): 56.

[27] Anglican–Roman Catholic International Commission/Catholic Truth Society (Great Britain), *The Gift of Authority: Authority in the Church III, An Agreed Statement by the Anglican–Roman Catholic International Commission (ARCIC)* (London: SPCK & Catholic Truth Society, 1999), n. 22. Also at http://www.vatican.va/roman_curia/pontifical_councils/chrstuni/documents/rc_pc_chrstuni_doc_12051999_gift-of-autority_en.html.

ing. The CDF explains that it is the meaning of the Gospel that does not change, but sometimes the church, assisted by the Holy Spirit, finds new words to express that meaning.[28]

When it writes about dogmatic statements ARCIC seems to capture something of this insight as well. The purpose of dogmatic statements, ARCIC asserts, is to defend and translate the Gospel, sometimes to defend it precisely by translating it. "All generations and cultures must be helped to understand that the good news of salvation is also for them," says ARCIC. "It is not enough for the Church simply to repeat the original apostolic words. It has also prophetically to translate them in order that the hearers in their situation may understand and respond to them." But then it adds: "All such restatement must be consonant with the apostolic witness recorded in the Scriptures; for in this witness the preaching and teaching of ministers, and statements of local and universal councils, have to find their ground and consistency."[29] When it looks for an example of such restatement ARCIC uses the First Council of Nicea's *homoousion*, which was believed to express the content of faith about Christ contained in the Scriptures even though the word itself is not found there. "No endeavour of the Church to express the truth can add to the revelation already given," contends ARCIC, and all of the church's expression of revelation "must be tested by its consonance with Scripture," since "the Scriptures are the uniquely inspired witness to divine revelation." It goes on: "This does not mean simply repeating the words of Scripture, but also both delving into their deeper significance and unravelling their implications for Christian belief and practice." Hence often words different from the original text, but not alien to its meaning, will be found from current language and the thought of the day.[30] Walter Kasper notes that the *homoousion* of Nicea

[28] Congregation for the Doctrine of the Faith, *Mysterium Ecclesiae*, *The Tablet* 227 (14 July 1973): 667–70, at 668–69. Also at http://www.vatican.va/roman_curia /congregations/cfaith/documents/rc_con_cfaith_doc_19730705_mysterium -ecclesiae_en.html.

[29] Anglican–Roman Catholic International Commission, "Authority in the Church I," in *The Final Report*, n. 15. Also at http://www.vatican.va/roman_curia /pontifical_councils/chrstuni/angl-comm-docs/rc_pc_chrstuni_doc_197609 _authority-church-i_en.html.

[30] Anglican–Roman Catholic International Commission, "Authority in the Church I: Elucidations (1981)," in *The Final Report*, n. 2.

was in fact a countercultural position: while using the language and conceptual structures of its day, the Council of Nicea denounced the neoplatonism of Arius and proclaimed the divinity of Jesus taught by the Scriptures.[31]

Indeed, tradition can be understood in two ways, declares ARCIC.[32] On one approach, "under the guidance of the Spirit undiscovered riches and truths are sought in the Scriptures in order to illuminate the faith according to the needs of each generation." On the second approach to tradition, "[i]n the conviction that the Holy Spirit is seeking to guide the Church into the fullness of truth, it draws upon everything in human experience and thought which will give to the content of the revelation its fullest expression and widest application."[33] Both approaches capture the Catholic insight that teachings need not simply repeat the words of the Scripture.

I think that Evangelicals are joining Roman Catholics in appreciating this insight when they recognize the important role played by liturgical traditions of worship and by the great ecumenical councils and creeds from the first centuries of the church's life. At a time when the divinity of Christ, the Trinity, or the bodily resurrection of Jesus Christ are questioned or even dismissed by some exegetical studies, Evangelicals can share with Roman Catholics a deep appreciation for the liturgies, councils, and creeds as bearers of the Scriptural faith through the church's long history. The Evangelical–Roman Catholic Dialogue on Mission acknowledges the mutual appreciation of tradition. "Many of our teachers belong to the past," they write. "Both Evangelicals and Roman Catholics have inherited a rich legacy of tradition. We cherish creeds, confessions and conciliar statements. We peruse the writings of the Fathers of the Church. We read books and commentaries."[34]

Evangelicals and Roman Catholics share another aspect of this first Catholic insight, for both affirm that the Bible is the church's book

---

[31] Walter Kasper, *Jesus the Christ*, trans. V. Green (New York: Paulist Press, 1976), 178.

[32] Anglican–Roman Catholic International Commission, "Authority in the Church I: Elucidations (1981)," in *The Final Report*, n. 2.

[33] Ibid.

[34] Basil Meeking and John Stott, eds., *The Evangelical–Roman Catholic Dialogue on Mission 1977–1984: A Report* (Grand Rapids: Eerdmans, 1986), 22. Cited by George Vandervelde in "Justification between Scripture and Tradition," *Evangelical Review of Theology* 21 (1997): 128–48, at 132.

and that the Holy Spirit continues to guide the interpretation of the Bible within the church. The Evangelical–Roman Catholic Dialogue on Mission noted the danger of arbitrary individualistic exegesis,[35] a danger already recognized in 1963 by the Faith and Order statement on "Tradition and Traditions."[36] The dialogue maintains that "the Scriptures must be interpreted within the Christian community,"[37] which is the church. David Yeago, a Lutheran, makes the same point when he states that the correct interpretation of the Scriptures is done within the community of the church, under the guidance of the Holy Spirit.[38] Writing on this theme, ARCIC argues:

> The believer is incorporated into an "Amen" of faith, older, deeper, broader, richer than the individual's "Amen" to the Gospel. . . . Every baptised person shares the rich experience of the Church which, even when it struggles with contemporary questions, continues to proclaim what Christ is *for his Body*. Each believer, by the grace of the Spirit, together with all believers of all times and all places, inherits this faith of the Church in the communion of saints.[39]

The Roman Catholic theologian George Tavard writes: "the problem of tradition amounts to the question of discerning the Spirit. . . . Tradition emerges when the faithful interpret the memory of the past as normative for the faith of the future. But this can be done only through the discernment of the Spirit after a sustained and graceful *metanoia*."[40] I believe that Christians are moving toward an ecumenical consensus on the Bible's ecclesial character.

[35] Meeking and Stott, eds., *Evangelical–Roman Catholic Dialogue on Mission 1977–1984*, 22. Cited by Vandervelde in "Justification between Scripture and Tradition," 132.

[36] Faith and Order, "Scripture, Tradition and Traditions," *The Fourth World Conference on Faith and Order, Montreal 1963: The Report*, eds. Patrick C. Rodger and Lukas Vischer (London: SCM, 1964), 50–61.

[37] See above, n. 35.

[38] David S. Yeago, "The Spirit, the Church, and the Scriptures: Biblical Inspiration and Interpretation Revisited," in James J. Buckley and David S. Yeago, eds., *Knowing the Triune God: The Work of the Spirit in the Practices of the Church* (Grand Rapids: Eerdmans, 2001), 49–93.

[39] Anglican–Roman Catholic International Commission/Catholic Truth Society (Great Britain), *The Gift of Authority: Authority in the Church III*, n. 13.

[40] George Tavard, "Tradition in Theology: A Problematic Approach," 84–104, in *Perspectives on Scripture and Tradition: Essays*, ed. Joseph Kelly (Notre Dame, IN: Fides,

But what about Karl Rahner's second contention, the Protestant insight that later dogmas must be measured by the Scripture, which remains the unnormed norm of all other norms? How does this insight fare in the discussion between Evangelicals and Roman Catholics?

It is clear that Evangelicals make this insight the center of their position. "We as evangelicals confess the supreme authority of the Holy Scriptures for all matters of faith and conduct," wrote the World Evangelical Fellowship in their 1987 statement, "Roman Catholicism: A Contemporary Evangelical Perspective."[41] They add, "As evangelicals, we understand that our position is in conflict with the Roman Catholic acceptance of tradition and the so-called living voice of the church as sources of revelation and authority alongside of the Scriptures."[42] But what is the deep meaning of this *sola scriptura* position? In his discussion of justification at the international dialogue between Evangelicals and Roman Catholics, Evangelical George Vandervelde notes that the Reformation debate was not about abstract principles[43] but rather about the authority of Christ. Of course the heart of authority "resides not first of all in a book, but in a person," he observes.[44] "Biblical authority . . . was crucial to the Reformers for the sake of, in the service of, Christ's authority," he argues. "Justification by faith was not first of all a theological statement but an experience of forgiveness and peace that had been blocked by the practice of and promises surrounding penance"[45] in the life of the church of Martin Luther's time. In finding his way to the experience of forgiveness and peace won by Christ, Luther rediscovered the centrality of the Scriptures; but their centrality was in service of the authority of Christ, the crucified and risen one who remains present in his church as Lord.[46]

The implication of this understanding from the Reformation tradition, explains Vandervelde, is that "the Scripture must be accorded

---

1976), at 103–4; see also idem, "Tradition in Theology: A Methodological Approach," in the same volume at pp. 105–25.

[41] Paul G. Schrotenboer, ed., *Roman Catholicism: A Contemporary Evangelical Perspective* (Grand Rapids: Baker Book House, 1988), 42.

[42] Ibid., 43.

[43] Vandervelde, "Justification between Scripture and Tradition," 134.

[44] Ibid., 133.

[45] Ibid.

[46] Ibid.

its unique 'over-against' role."[47] Rahner agrees: the Scripture is the unnormed norm, the measure of all other norms.[48] But is this also the teaching of the Roman Catholic Church?

When we look again at the *Dogmatic Constitution on Divine Revelation*, this Protestant insight is surely less obvious than the Catholic one. Yes, I do believe the centrality of the Scriptures was a major reason that the council refused a two-source theory and instead adopted the dynamic view of tradition we have examined. And yes, I do believe we can see that centrality mirrored as well in the council's teachings on the importance of daily study of the Scriptures by all the faithful, their key place in the liturgy, and their role as foundation for theology and preaching. "[T]he Constitution as a whole marks a great step towards reconciliation" with Protestants, claims Ratzinger in his commentary on the text. But, he continues, "we shall have to acknowledge the truth of the criticism that there is, in fact, no explicit mention of the possibility of a distorting tradition and of the place of Scripture as an element within the Church that is *also* critical of tradition, which means that a most important side of the problem of tradition, as shown by the history of the Church—and perhaps the real crux of the question of the *ecclesia semper reformanda*—has been overlooked."[49] Since this council saw itself as a council of reform, continues Ratzinger, "and thus implicitly acknowledged the possibility and reality of distortion in tradition, it could have made here in its thinking a real achievement in theological examination. . . . That this opportunity has been missed can only be regarded as an unfortunate omission."[50] He judges that the council would have served ecumenical dialogue better by working out the possibility and necessity "of the criticism of tradition within the Church than to engage in what must be called an unreal controversy about the quantitative completeness of Scripture."[51]

Discerning which traditions are consonant with Scripture is not always easy. Most of our churches were slow to recognize the sinfulness of their traditions regarding slavery and racism. And think about

---

[47] Ibid., 144.

[48] Rahner, "Scripture and Tradition," in *Sacramentum Mundi*, vol. 6, 56.

[49] Ratzinger, "Dogmatic Constitution on Divine Revelation: Chapter II, The Transmission of Divine Revelation," in *Commentary on the Documents of Vatican II*, 192–93.

[50] Ibid., 193.

[51] Ibid., 186.

the following contrast in traditions of interpretation. Today many Evangelicals are members of churches whose reading of Scripture allows or even requires them to ordain women but does not consider certain teachings about Mary to be scriptural. On the other hand, I belong to a church that teaches that the Immaculate Conception and the Assumption of Mary do have a scriptural basis, but that women should not be ordained because Scripture teaches that it is against the practice and intention of Christ. Both positions claim a foundation in Scripture. Recognizing the irony in this situation is part of our ecumenical conversation.

But if Ratzinger is correct that Vatican II missed the opportunity to show clearly its commitment to Scripture as unnormed norm, I believe the Roman Catholic Church today has seized upon other opportunities. Let me briefly mention three. First, the council itself, as Ratzinger pointed out, was a council of reform. When it taught the church's need of continual reformation in the Decree on Ecumenism (*Unitatis Redintegratio*),[52] when it taught the priesthood of all the faithful in the Dogmatic Constitution on the Church (*Lumen Gentium*),[53] when it taught the dignity of all persons and their right to religious freedom in the Declaration on Religious Freedom (*Dignitatis Humanae*)[54]—all these teachings of reform were also teachings that show the dependence of the Roman Catholic Church upon the inspired word of God.

Second, in the apologies of Pope John Paul II, I think we see another acknowledgment of a norm that norms the church and its actions past and present. To mark the 2000th anniversary of the birth of Christ, Pope John Paul II asked forgiveness for the conduct of Catholics in the Crusades, forgiveness for the Holocaust and other acts of hatred against Jews, forgiveness for violence carried out in defending the truth, forgiveness for rending the unity of the church. He has

---

[52] Vatican II, *Unitatis Redintegratio* (Decree on Ecumenism), in *The Documents of Vatican II*, n. 6. Also at http://www.vatican.va/archive/hist_councils/ii_vatican _council/documents/vat-ii_decree_19641121_unitatis-redintegratio_en.html.

[53] Vatican II, *Lumen Gentium* (Dogmatic Constitution on the Church), in *The Documents of Vatican II*, n. 10. Also at http://www.vatican.va/archive/hist_councils/ii _vatican_council/documents/vat-ii_const_19641121_lumen-gentium_en.html.

[54] Vatican II, *Dignitatis Humanae* (Declaration on Religious Freedom) in *The Documents of Vatican II*, n. 2. Also at http://www.vatican.va/archive/hist_councils/ii _vatican_council/documents/vat-ii_decl_19651207_dignitatis-humanae_en.html.

acknowledged the contributions of thinkers once condemned by the church, such as Galileo and Matteo Ricci.[55] He has even asked forgiveness for the ways that Roman Catholic teaching about the papacy can be a difficulty for other churches, especially because of their painful memories of earlier popes.[56] He has asked as well for help with reshaping the form of his ministry. "This is an immense task," he writes, "which we cannot refuse and which I cannot carry out by myself."[57] He asks church leaders and theologians for "a patient and fraternal dialogue on this subject, a dialogue in which, leaving useless controversies behind, we could listen to one another, keeping before us only the will of Christ for his Church and allowing ourselves to be deeply moved by his plea 'that they may all be one . . . so that the world may believe that you have sent me' (Jn 17:21)."[58]

I find the third clue to the Roman Catholic Church's commitment to the normativity of Scripture in the ecumenical dialogue itself, the dialogue that Vatican II says calls for a "change of heart"[59] and that John Paul II says demands a "necessary purification of past memories"[60] and a recognition of the "sin of our separation."[61] George Vandervelde has explained that the real point of the *sola scriptura* of the Reformation era was the authority of Christ himself,[62] his overagainstness to the church.[63] By cosigning the *Joint Declaration on the*

---

[55] See John Paul II, apostolic letter *As the Third Millennium Draws Near* (*Tertio Millennio Adveniente*), *Origins* 24 (1994–95): 410–12. Also at http://www.vatican.va/holy _father/john_paul_ii/apost_letters/documents/hf_jp-ii_apl_10111994_tertio -millennio-adveniente_en.html; "Service Requesting Pardon," *Origins* 29 (1999–2000): 645, 647–48. Also at http://www.vatican.va/news_services/liturgy/documents/ns _lit_doc_20000312_prayer-day-pardon_en.html; John Paul II, "The Depths of the Holocaust's Horror," and "Report of Prayer at the Wailing Wall in Jerusalem," *Origins* 29 (1999–2000): 677, 679–80.

[56] John Paul II, encyclical *Ut Unum Sint*, *Origins* 25 (1995–96), 49, 51–72, see n. 88. Also at http://www.vatican.va/holy_father/john_paul_ii/encyclicals/documents /hf_jp-ii_enc_25051995_ut-unum-sint_en.html.

[57] Ibid., n. 96.

[58] Ibid.

[59] Vatican II, *Unitatis Redintegratio*, n. 7.

[60] John Paul II, *Ut Unum Sint*, n. 2.

[61] John Paul II, apostolic letter *Orientale Lumen*, *Origins* 25 (1995–96), 1, 3–13; see n. 17. Also at http://www.vatican.va/holy_father/john_paul_ii/apost_letters/1995 /documents/hf_jp-ii_apl_19950502_orientale-lumen_en.html.

[62] Vandervelde, "Justification between Scripture and Tradition," 133.

[63] Ibid., 144.

Doctrine of Justification with the Lutheran World Federation, the Roman Catholic Church in fact acknowledges this over-againstness. In that document the Catholics declare that the sixteenth-century condemnations, insofar as they relate to justification, "appear in a new light: the teaching of the Lutheran churches" presented in the *Joint Declaration* "does not fall under the condemnations of the Council of Trent."[64] In their turn the Lutherans acknowledge that "the condemnations in the Lutheran Confessions do not apply to the teaching of the Roman Catholic Church presented in this *Declaration*."[65]

When the Roman Catholic Church enters into ecumenical dialogue with other Christian communions, it does so precisely under the obligation it feels from the Lord to heal the division within the one church of Christ. Such division, said Vatican II, "openly contradicts the will of Christ, provides a stumbling block to the world, and inflicts damage on the most holy cause of proclaiming the good news to every creature."[66] In its commitment to the dialogue with other Christian communions, a commitment Pope John Paul II repeatedly called "irreversible," the Roman Catholic Church manifests to me a huge, vulnerable openness. When we enter into dialogue with others before God we show ourselves for what we are: our strengths and gifts from God, also our sins, our weaknesses, and our foolish idiosyncrasies. By this dialogue the Roman Catholic Church declares itself open to discovering the authority of Christ in the life and teachings of other Christian communions and to submitting to this authority. Here, I think, is where Evangelicals may recognize a submission to Scripture they may not have anticipated.

---

[64] The Lutheran World Federation and the Roman Catholic Church, *Joint Declaration on the Doctrine of Justification* (Grand Rapids: Eerdmans, 2000), n. 41. Also at http://www.vatican.va/roman_curia/pontifical_councils/chrstuni/documents/rc_pc_chrstuni_doc_31101999_cath-luth-joint-declaration_en.html.

[65] Ibid.

[66] Vatican II, *Unitatis Redintegratio*, n. 1.

Divine Law:
A Roman Catholic View[1]

The use of the category "divine law" (*ius divinum*) is not the focus of frequent discussion today in Roman Catholic theology. It receives little direct attention in *Lexikon für Theologie und Kirche, Sacramentum Mundi, New Dictionary of Theology,* the *New Catholic Encyclopedia,* or *The Catechism of the Catholic Church.* The *Catholic Guide to Periodical Literature* and the *Religion Index* for periodicals showed very few articles on the topic for the last twenty-five years.

But earlier and continuing claims about what is part of the church "by divine law" (*de iure divino*) continue to serve as a source of division between Christians. This paper will offer a brief Roman Catholic perspective on the meaning and viability of the category "divine law." I will not attempt to judge whether or not a particular sacrament or office of the church is divinely mandated. Instead, I will think about what it means to claim that anything is divinely mandated, and how the dialogue between Lutherans and Roman Catholics could address conflicting claims.

[1] Previously published as "A Roman Catholic Perspective on *Ius divinum*," in Randall Lee and Jeffrey Gros, eds., *The Church as Koinonia of Salvation: Its Structures and Ministries* (Washington, DC: U.S. Conference of Catholic Bishops, 2005), 226–46.

1. Lutheran–Roman Catholic Dialogue on Divine Law

Lutheran–Roman Catholic dialogue has regularly adverted to how claims about divine law have in the past been a source of division, and it has noted a new context for evaluating such claims. For example, the Malta Report of the Lutheran–Roman Catholic International Study Commission (1971) stated that "[g]reater awareness of the historicity of the church in conjunction with a new understanding of its eschatological nature, requires that in our day the concepts of *ius divinum* and *ius humanum* [human law] be thought through anew." In addition, the Malta Report said that the two "can never be adequately distinguished" from each other.[2]

In the discussion of papal primacy by the U.S. Lutheran–Roman Catholic Dialogue the idea of divine law came up again. In "Differing Attitudes toward Papal Primacy," the Common Statement notes that Roman Catholics have affirmed that "the papacy is a matter of divine law (*ius divinum*)" and "consequently have viewed it as an essential part of the permanent structure of the church," while "Lutherans have held, in opposition to this, that the papacy was established by human law, the will of men, and that its claims to divine right are nothing short of blasphemous."[3] At the end of the Common Statement the signers note that they "do not wish to understate" their remaining disagreements. "While we have concluded that traditional sharp distinctions between divine and human institution are no longer useful, Catholics continue to emphasize that papal primacy is an institution in accordance with God's will," but Lutherans find this "a secondary question." The one thing necessary, Lutherans insist, "is that papal primacy serve the gospel and that its exercise of power not subvert Christian freedom."[4]

---

[2] Lutheran–Roman Catholic [International] Study Commission, "The Gospel and the Church [The Malta Report]," in Harding Meyer and Lukas Vischer, eds., *Growth in Agreement: Reports and Agreed Statements of Ecumenical Conversations on a World Level* (Geneva: World Council of Churches, 1984), 175 n. 31. Also at http://www.prounione .urbe.it/dia-int/l-rc/doc/e_l-rc_malta.html.

[3] U.S. Lutheran–Roman Catholic Dialogue, "Differing Attitudes toward Papal Primacy: Common Statement," in *Papal Primacy and the Universal Church*, ed. Paul C. Empie and T. Austin Murphy (Minneapolis: Augsburg Publishing House, 1974), n. 7. Also at http://www.usccb.org/beliefs-and-teachings/ecumenical-and-interreligious /ecumenical/lutheran/attitudes-papal-primacy.cfm.

[4] Ibid., n. 30.

In their reflections the Lutheran participants give their opinion that "the traditional distinction between *de iure humano* and *de iure divino* fails to provide usable categories for contemporary discussion of the papacy." Instead, the Lutheran participants suggest a different set of questions: "In what way or ways has our Lord in fact led his church to use particular forms for the exercise of the Petrine function? What structural elements in the church does the gospel require for the ministry which serves the unity of the empirical church?"[5] Roman Catholics, for their part, affirm that the papacy is divinely instituted, "imperative" because "it is willed by God for his church." But since the term "*ius divinum*" used to mean institution by a formal act of Jesus and a clear apostolic record of such an act, today "the term itself does not adequately communicate what we believe concerning the divine institution of the papacy." Instead, Roman Catholics continue, "we are convinced that the papal and episcopal form of Ministry, as it concretely evolved, is a divinely-willed sequel to the functions exercised respectively by Peter and the other apostles according to various New Testament traditions."[6]

In his discussion of the idea of *ius divinum*, Avery Dulles includes in its meaning the notions "divine right," "divine law," "divine institution," and "divine ordination," which he notes are not synonymous but "may be used almost interchangeably for the purposes of this essay."[7] Unless otherwise indicated, I will intend this broad sense of *ius divinum* (and its correlatives) and "divine law" in my paper as well.[8]

---

[5] U.S. Lutheran–Roman Catholic Dialogue, "Differing Attitudes toward Papal Primacy: Reflections of the Lutheran Participants," in *Papal Primacy and the Universal Church*, n. 35. Also at http://www.usccb.org/beliefs-and-teachings/ecumenical-and -interreligious/ecumenical/lutheran/attitudes-papal-primacy.cfm.

[6] See U.S. Lutheran–Roman Catholic Dialogue, "Differing Attitudes toward Papal Primacy: Reflections of the Roman Catholic Participants," in *Papal Primacy and the Universal Church*, nn. 34–35. Also at http://www.usccb.org/beliefs-and-teachings /ecumenical-and-interreligious/ecumenical/lutheran/attitudes-papal-primacy.cfm.

[7] Avery Dulles, "*Ius Divinum* as an Ecumenical Problem," *Theological Studies* 38 (1977): 681–708, at 681.

[8] Discussions of moral theology and its relationship to the divine command tradition focus on a different set of issues from those of this paper; e.g., Oliver O'Donovan, "How Can Theology Be Moral?" *Journal of Religious Ethics* 17 (1989): 81–94; Jean Porter, "Christianity, Divine Law and Consequentialism," *Scottish Journal of Theology* 48 (1995): 415–42.

But what is the basic value intended by "divine law" talk? Why is it worth understanding or reconceptualizing? Though noting the difficulties with this older terminology and its accompanying world-views, Dulles suggests that we not eliminate it until we find substitutes. "After all," he observes, "it is important to find ways of expressing that the Church is not its own Lord."[9] I believe this is an important purpose that the idea "divine law" has served: to show that the church is not its own Lord. Dulles explains that "there has to be some terminology that allows us to distinguish what the officers of the Church decide as a matter of free discretion and what they hold because fidelity to God's revelation so requires. The traditional *ius divinum* terminology, for both Protestants and Catholics, provided ways of making this distinction."[10]

The Anglican–Roman Catholic International Commission provides another suggestion for understanding "divine law" talk. Discussing the primacy of the bishop of Rome, members propose reconceptualizing "divine right" to mean that the primacy of the bishop of Rome is "part of God's design for the universal *koinonia*,"[11] or that for Roman Catholics it expresses "God's purpose for his Church."[12] But they continue by observing that Anglicans might be able to affirm the development of the Roman primacy as a gift of providence, "in other words, as an effect of the guidance of the Holy Spirit in the Church." Moreover, ARCIC members state, "it is reasonable to ask whether a gap really exists between the assertion of a primacy by divine right (*jure divino*) and the acknowledgement of its emergence by divine providence (*divina providentia*)."[13]

---

[9] Dulles, "*Ius Divinum* as an Ecumenical Problem," 698.

[10] Ibid.

[11] Anglican–Roman Catholic International Commission, "Authority in the Church I [1976]," in *The Final Report* (London: SPCK & Catholic Truth Society, 1982), n. 24b. Also at http://www.vatican.va/roman_curia/pontifical_councils/chrstuni/angl-comm -docs/rc_pc_chrstuni_doc_197609_authority-church-i_en.html.

[12] Anglican–Roman Catholic International Commission, "Authority in the Church II [1981]," in *The Final Report*, n. 11. Also at http://www.vatican.va/roman_curia /pontifical_councils/chrstuni/angl-comm-docs/rc_pc_chrstuni_doc_1981_authority -church-ii_en.html.

[13] Ibid., n. 13.

2. Roman Catholic Conciliar Texts and Present-Day Roman Catholic Theology on Divine Law

2.1. *Roman Catholic Conciliar Texts*

Roman Catholics inherit the use of "divine law" claims made in conciliar texts. Dulles draws our attention to three councils. The Council of Trent was "remarkably nuanced" in its discussion of the sacrament of penance, he thinks, since Trent "saw the substance of the sacrament as having been instituted by Christ, but conceded that the form of its celebration was a matter of human legislation."[14] Carl Peter also emphasizes the council's nuanced approach to the sacrament of penance. Trent distinguished between the necessity of confessing serious sin to a priest, which it taught was a matter of divine law, and the rules regarding frequency of confession, which it taught were required by the church.[15]

In *Pastor Aeternus*, Vatican I taught that by the institution of Christ himself (*de iure divino*) Peter has a perpetual line of successors in his primacy within the church. Dulles finds this approach "a static and objectivistic notion of divine institution," which seems "to refer to the actions of the historical Jesus in his earthly and risen life."[16]

Finally, Vatican II left open whether the distinction between bishop and presbyter is of divine institution,[17] but it asserted that the variety of ministries in the church is indeed by divine institution, and that bishops are successors of the apostles by divine institution as well. It also taught that the church has by divine mandate the duty to preach the Gospel to every creature. Dulles thinks that Vatican II had a "dynamic" understanding of divine law as "something given only

---

[14] Dulles, "*Ius Divinum* as an Ecumenical Problem," 687.

[15] Carl J. Peter, "Dimensions of *Jus Divinum* in Roman Catholic Theology," *Theological Studies* 34 (1973): 227–50, at 238–39; cf. André Duval, "Le 'droit divin' de l'intégrité de la confession selon le canon 7 'De Poenitentia' du Concile de Trente: examen de l'interprétation du P. A. Amato," *Revue des Sciences philosophiques et théologiques* 63 (1979): 549–60; Pierre-Marie Gy, "Le précepte de la confession annuelle et la nécessité de la confession," *Revue des Sciences philosophiques et théologiques* 63 (1979): 529–47.

[16] Dulles, "*Ius Divinum* as an Ecumenical Problem," 689.

[17] Ibid.

inchoatively at the beginning—that is to say, as something that unfolds in the history of the Church."[18]

2.2. *Present-Day Roman Catholic Theology*

How do Roman Catholics understand divine law today? Three articles by earlier members of the U.S. Lutheran–Roman Catholic Dialogue (Avery Dulles, Carl Peter, and George Lindbeck) discuss a wide variety of views on this issue. Let me summarize some of their findings.

Dulles finds four schools of thought among twentieth-century Roman Catholic and Lutheran theologians. He calls the first the *neo-Lutheran* view. Exemplified by Edmund Schlink, this view sees four essential elements in the New Covenant: (1) the mission of proclamation, (2) baptism, (3) the Lord's Supper, and (4) the power of binding and loosing. All these elements rest on the word of the Lord and are unexpendable, but the church can regulate how they are to be conducted. Dulles thinks Hans Küng held a position close to Schlink's, which puts a strong emphasis on the apostolic period's understanding of divine law but does not read the New Testament in a literal way.[19]

Dulles labels a second view *nonhistorical orthodoxy*, previously exemplified by Francisco Suarez and in the nineteenth and twentieth centuries respectively by Johann Baptist Franzelin and Emmanuel Doronzo. "According to this view, everything essential to the Church in any period of its existence must have been actually contained in the apostolic deposit; for the Lord alone could give the Church what it needed for its supernatural mission, and he would not have failed to supply it with anything truly requisite."[20] Proponents of this approach held that Jesus personally established the Mass as a sacrifice, instituted each of the seven sacraments directly, and conferred primacy upon Peter. While New Testament texts could be used to support such views, their proponents also drew on oral traditions considered to be apostolic.

Dulles identifies a third group, represented by Karl Rahner, as the *developmental* school. This group holds that "by divine law" does not

---

[18] Ibid., 690.
[19] Ibid., 690–91.
[20] Ibid., 692.

necessarily mean that the structure being considered was given directly by Christ himself during his earthly ministry. Instead, Rahner thinks the notion can be extended to include decisions made by the church in apostolic times that were consonant with the church's nature and now may be irreversible.[21] Rahner argues that such a sacrament or office "may draw its *iure divino* character from its being an indispensable way of insuring the necessary continuation of that which Jesus did found."[22] Rahner finds revelation within this process of free decision-making by the apostolic church, and he thinks that "the irreversibility of an action and decision is not something particularly strange and surprising, but rather is exactly what one should expect in the light of the nature of freedom."[23]

Peter also comments on Rahner's approach to divine law, noting that Rahner's writings on this topic before Vatican II had a major impact on Roman Catholic theology.[24] Dulles places Peter himself within the "developmental" school represented by Rahner. But while Rahner leaves open the question of whether any institutional developments of the post-apostolic church were irreversible, Peter holds that some are definitely irreversible. Peter also lays strong emphasis on the process of discernment used by the church to discover whether something is a matter of divine law; such discernment is not "reducible to the laws of inductive or deductive reasoning"[25] or to the explicit language of the New Testament.[26] Details of application are worked out by the church in history.

Dulles observes that both Rahner and Peter, though holding the possibility of irreversible developments in the post-apostolic church that are also matters of divine law, still "are reluctant to specify exactly what in the later development was in fact irreversible."[27] Dulles continues: "If the episcopate is such a development, does this mean that the monarchical episcopate is forever necessary—or could you,

---

[21] Ibid., 693.

[22] Ibid., 694.

[23] Karl Rahner, "Reflections on the Concept of '*Ius Divinum*' in Catholic Thought," in *Theological Investigations*, vol. 5: *Later Writings*, trans. Karl-H. Kruger (Baltimore: Helicon, 1966), 219–43, at 237.

[24] Peter, "Dimensions of *Ius Divinum* in Roman Catholic Theology," 227.

[25] Ibid., 246.

[26] Ibid., 248.

[27] Dulles, "*Ius divinum* as an Ecumenical Problem," 695.

for example, have a college of presbyters collectively filling the office of bishop? If papal primacy is an essential and irreversible feature of the Church after a certain date, what exactly does that mean? Must the primacy always be that of the bishop of Rome? Could it be exercised by a group of bishops rather than by a single individual? Could the papacy rotate from see to see according to a cycle of a certain number of years? Could the pope be required always to consult the synod of bishops when he exercises his primacy of jurisdiction or infallible teaching functions? These questions are not easily answered."[28]

In his writing after Vatican II, Rahner makes clear the flexibility with which he approached even institutions such as the papacy and the episcopate, which he regarded as part of the church by divine intention. He says that the forms of these institutions could vary greatly from one time to another. He maintains that "the concrete forms in which . . . papal authority" is exercised could "undergo such far-reaching transformations that so far as the average everyday impression of an individual Christian is concerned the directive power of the pope may be encountered in some new form in which it seems to retain only a slight connection with that authority which was once and for all defined in the First Vatican Council as permanently enduring."[29] The episcopal structure of the church as well could perhaps be altered so that it was ascribed to a "small collegiate body" and was complemented by "many structures and institutions . . . built into the Church which give the people of the Church a more active role than that which they have previously had in the life of the Church itself."[30]

In his commentary on the Dogmatic Constitution on the Church (*Lumen Gentium*) Rahner sees as unresolved the extent to which the later church is bound by the early church's decision to have "two limited degrees" of the office of bishop (priesthood and diaconate)."[31]

---

[28] Ibid.

[29] Karl Rahner, "Basic Observations on the Subject of the Changeable and Unchangeable Factors in the Church," in *Theological Investigations*, vol. 14: *Ecclesiology, Questions in the Church, The Church in the World*, trans. David Bourke (New York: Seabury, 1976), 3–23, at 17.

[30] Ibid., 19.

[31] See Karl Rahner's commentary on Article 20 of the Dogmatic Constitution on the Church (*Lumen Gentium*), in Herbert Vorgrimler, ed., *Commentary on the Documents of Vatican II*, vol. 1, trans. Kevin Smyth (New York: Herder and Herder, 1967), 192.

He comments: "And here we may leave it an open question, whether this decision also binds the Church which came after, that is, is part of the process of revelation of divine law in the apostolic Church, or represents Church law of human institution in the apostolic age."[32] He continues: "The full office in its essence, its collegiate form and its union with the Pope is in any case of divine institution."[33]

Dulles identifies a fourth school of thought, represented by Johannes Neumann and Edward Schillebeeckx, which he calls the *functionalist* group. Neumann, for example, held that a post-apostolic development could be by divine law for a certain period in the life of the church but then later be modified. Schillebeeckx likewise "rejects Rahner's suggestion that the development of the monarchical episcopate since New Testament times could be irreversible."[34] However, the mere fact that post-apostolic developments do not come from Jesus in his earthly ministry but are influenced by sociological factors does not make them simply human, for "the Holy Spirit is continually operative in the Church."[35]

Dulles himself proposes a fifth approach to "what is unchangeable about the Church." He calls this approach *relational*. The church is constituted by its relationship to Jesus Christ, a stable reference point, and its relationship to those to whom it mediates Christ's presence, the people of each time and place. Though always recalling and reliving the mysteries of Christ's life, death, and resurrection, the church must relate and adapt to various ages and cultures. Dulles asserts: "The abiding structures of the Church, therefore, must undergo ceaseless modification, not in order to weaken or dissolve its bonds in Christ, but precisely in order to keep them intact."[36] With this in mind Dulles proposes four spheres of functions and structures, with the spheres having progressively less binding relations to divine law: (1) the inner core of the church's mission, which requires a ministry of proclamation, baptism, eucharist, and binding and loosing, (2) institutional features that appeared after the apostolic age but are irreversible—such as the anointing of the sick or the episcopate—and "may

---

[32] Ibid.
[33] Ibid.
[34] Dulles, "*Ius Divinum* as an Ecumenical Problem," 696.
[35] Ibid.
[36] Ibid., 700.

be called *iure divino* in a somewhat more extended sense than structures that pertain to our first category,"[37] (3) temporary, reversible developments "truly willed by Christ and inspired by the Holy Spirit"[38] could also be envisioned, such as collegiality of the bishops and greater cultural pluralism, and, finally (4) discretionary matters that are provisional and subject to the church's decision. Eric Doyle makes a somewhat similar suggestion, saying that "it is evident on historical grounds that there must be a hierarchy of elements of divine institution in the church of Christ on an analogy with the hierarchy of truths."[39]

Dulles notes the difficulty of distinguishing between the second and third spheres—between the irreversible and the reversible post-apostolic developments. He sees the papacy as an irreversible development, while (writing in 1977)[40] he sees the exclusion of women from ordination as perhaps a reversible development. Regarding the latter, he states: "As with the papacy, so here, it would not be enough to argue simply from apostolic precedent or from unbroken continuity in the past. If the exclusion of women from ordination is to be sustained, a justification must be given in terms of the biblical and liturgical symbolism and the need of the Church as a sign of Christ in the world today."[41]

Finally, Dulles suggests an alternative terminology, in which the most essential sphere would be envisioned as *ad esse ecclesiae* (pertaining to the church's very being), the second, irreversible sphere as *ad plene esse ecclesiae* (pertaining to the church's perfection), the third, reversible sphere as *ad bene esse ecclesiae* (pertaining to the church's flourishing), and the fourth sphere as not pertaining at all to the

---

[37] Ibid., 701.

[38] Ibid., 703.

[39] Eric Doyle, "The Essential Unity of the Church: Some Consequences for Ecumenism," *Journal for Ecumenical Studies* 20 (1983): 245–56, at 253.

[40] In 1976 the Congregation for the Doctrine of the Faith issued "Declaration on the Question of the Admission of Women to the Ministerial Priesthood (*Inter Insigniores*)," *Origins* 6 (1976–77): 517, 519–24. Also at http://www.vatican.va/roman_curia /congregations/cfaith/documents/rc_con_cfaith_doc_19761015_inter-insigniores _en.html; in 1994 John Paul II issued "*Ordinatio Sacerdotalis*," *Origins* 24 (1994–95): 49, 51–52. Also at http://www.vatican.va/holy_father/john_paul_ii/apost_letters /documents/hf_jp-ii_apl_22051994_ordinatio-sacerdotalis_en.html.

[41] Dulles, "*Ius Divinum* as an Ecumenical Problem," 705.

church's essence. Whether these or other terms are found, Dulles points out, "it will be necessary to differentiate . . . between the biblical and the nonbiblical, the apostolic and the nonapostolic, the reversible and the irreversible." Dulles ends his discussion by calling for "a more modest and nuanced view of *ius divinum*," noting that his suggestion takes account of both continuity and mutability. "The Church's abiding essence actually requires adaptive change; and such change, if it is healthy, serves to actuate and express more vividly the true and permanent nature of the Church itself."[42]

Lindbeck in his article suggests that discussions of *ius divinum* in relation to papal primacy show a good deal of agreement between Lutherans and Roman Catholics. He makes five observations about present-day Lutherans: (1) they recognize the importance of the Petrine function; (2) they are open to the possibility that it should be more effectively institutionalized in Lutheranism; (3) they do not exclude the possibility that the papacy could rightly exercise this function; (4) they maintain that such right exercise would require that the papacy be reformed theologically and practically to make clear its subordination to the primacy of the Gospel; and (5) even if this were to happen, "Lutherans do not agree that the papacy is the necessary institutionalization of the Petrine function."[43] But in fact many Roman Catholics take the same stands as Lutherans on the first four points, Lindbeck contends. For instance, Roman Catholics insist on the Reformation thesis "that the authority and rights of the ecclesiastical office (and of the church as a whole) are not to be viewed in static juridical or ontological terms as attributes which it continues to possess independently of what it does, but must rather be seen as functions of 'service to the word.' "[44] Thus "the one remaining point of dispute on the level of theological principle is whether it [the papacy] is a necessary instrument (Thesis 5)" for carrying out the Petrine function.[45]

But even this fifth thesis is uninformative, Lindbeck continues, since the word "necessary" could have two different meanings: (1) the

---

[42] Ibid., 708.

[43] George A. Lindbeck, "Papacy and *Ius divinum*: A Lutheran View," in *Papal Primacy and the Universal Church*, 193–208, at 196.

[44] Ibid., 198.

[45] Ibid., 198–99.

papacy could be the "contingently (and perhaps only temporarily) necessary means for carrying out the Petrine function simply because it happens at present (and we don't know about the future) to be the only historically available instrumentality which could effectively do this job for the church as a whole," or (2) the "unconditional necessity" of the papacy.[46] But, he notes, there is nothing un-Lutheran in attributing the first, contingent kind of necessity to papal primacy. And he wonders: Are Roman Catholics actually obligated to affirm an unconditional necessity for papal primacy, the kind that Lutherans must deny?[47]

Surveying contemporary views on divine law, Lindbeck sees only two truly distinct schools of thought: (1) functionalists, who might call something a matter of divine law if it is a historically and functionally conditioned necessity, as he earlier suggested might be thought about papal primacy; and (2) irreversibilists, who hold that a divinely mandated structure must be irreversible or permanent. "Lutherans see no biblical grounds for asserting this irreversibility, at least not as a matter of faith, and consequently deny that the papacy is *de iure divino* in this second sense. In contrast, they have no difficulty with the functionalist interpretation of the *ius divinum* character of certain postbiblical developments, for this simply affirms that what is historically and functionally necessary for the welfare of the church is also what God wills that the church be and do."[48]

In fact, Lindbeck continues, "divine law" in present discussion differs so much from earlier understandings that its meaning has become fluid. "Perhaps some things which were prohibited by divine law in biblical and post-biblical times are now in our day commanded (e.g., the ordination of women)."[49] Because the difference between Lutherans and Roman Catholics on divine law has narrowed so much and the terms of the discussion have changed, Lindbeck thinks that "the traditional controversy over the *de iure divino* character of the papacy is now of only historical interest."[50] He contends that "the only meaningful contemporary manner of posing the question of

---

[46] Ibid., 199.
[47] Ibid.
[48] Ibid., 203.
[49] Ibid., 204.
[50] Ibid., 207.

papal primacy is to ask whether it is a possible—or perhaps even the best or only—way of effectively institutionalizing the Petrine function now or in the foreseeable future. On this point," he continues, "Lutherans are open to persuasion."[51]

A final perspective was provided by an interesting discussion of "divine law" in canon law. Although canon law is outside the scope of my paper, there is one article I wish to mention. In "*Ius divinum* as a Canonical Problem: On the Interaction of Divine and Ecclesiastical Laws," Joseph Koury compares the canons of the 1917 Code with the revised 1983 Code on their claims and comments about what is "divine law" or "by divine institution."[52]

Koury finds instances in which something attributed to divine law by the 1917 Code lacks such attribution in the 1983 Code—some liturgical matters, for example.[53] Moreover, sometimes the 1917 Code speaks of divine law in one way but the 1983 Code speaks of it in a different way. For example, the more recent Code shifts its claim of divine institution from the distinction between clergy and laity in the church to the existence of both clergy and laity in the church.[54] In another example, a rule regarding sanations of marriage is actually reversed, although the same reference to impediments from divine law is maintained.[55] In a discussion of *communicatio in sacris* (participation in non-Catholic religious services), the boundaries of what divine or ecclesiastical law forbid "have been dramatically redrawn."[56] The 1983 Code also adds some new uses of "divine law." For example, it states that all the Christian faithful are bound to do penance "in virtue of divine law."[57] Another section of the Code on marriage impediments and dispensations shows a movement in the "boundaries" of "divine law." As one example of this boundary shift Koury

[51] Ibid., 208.

[52] Joseph J. Koury, "*Ius Divinum* as a Canonical Problem: On the Interaction of Divine and Ecclesiastical Laws," *The Jurist* 53 (1993): 104–31; cf. Ad Van der Helm, "Le droit divin dans une perspective oecuménique," *Praxis Juridique et Religion* 3 (1986): 225–31; Marie Zimmermann, "Le chrétien catholique romain face au droit de son Église," *Praxis Juridique et Religion* 5 (1988): 72–81.

[53] Koury, "*Ius divinum* as a Canonical Problem," 106.

[54] Ibid., 108.

[55] Ibid., 114.

[56] Ibid., 116.

[57] Ibid., 120.

notes that the 1917 Code refers to the divine prohibition of a mixed marriage where there is a danger of perversion of the Catholic spouse and the children. But in the 1983 Code's treatment of mixed marriage the phrase "forbidden by divine law" has been deleted. Finally, sometimes an invocation of divine law is maintained but its object is changed. For example, the 1917 Code affirms a divinely mandated right and duty to acquire knowledge of doctrine and embrace the true church of God. The 1983 Code says that all persons "are bound to seek the truth in matters concerning God and God's Church" (n. 748.1), and that they also have a divinely mandated duty and right to embrace and observe the truth they have recognized.[58]

At the end of his article Koury observes that "rigid and exaggerated claims for *ius divinum* have in the past created and contributed to divisions among the churches."[59] Knowing and communicating the boundaries between divine and ecclesiastical laws and "the different ways in which they are recognized, enacted, or changed" remains "an unfilled yet important task of church officials and ministers." He also deems that claims about divine law "should not be easily made," lest in later changes of them "the claim . . . lose some of its weightiness, the rule being urged lose some of its effectiveness, and the Church lose some of its credibility."[60]

3. My Reflections

By now it must be clear that, as ARCIC stated, in Roman Catholic conviction "there is no universally accepted interpretation" of "divine law" language.[61] In discussing the primacy of the bishop of Rome, ARCIC notes that "it means at least that this primacy expresses God's purpose for his Church."[62] Beyond that basic meaning, a number of different interpretations of "divine law" coexist today in Roman Catholic theology. At the same time claims about divine law in past conciliar documents and present understandings continue to cause

[58] Ibid., 114–15.
[59] Ibid., 130.
[60] Ibid, 131.
[61] Anglican–Roman Catholic International Commission, "Authority in the Church II," in *The Final Report*, n. 11.
[62] Ibid.

division between Roman Catholics and Lutherans. In this situation I offer reflections on three points: (1) an emerging consensus in the Roman Catholic Church regarding historicity, (2) a range of views regarding divine law within this consensus, and (3) a way forward in thinking about divine law.

3.1. *An Emerging Consensus in the Roman Catholic Church regarding Historicity*

The Roman Catholic Church is well on its way to making the shift in understanding from what Bernard Lonergan calls a "classicist" worldview to "historical-mindedness." Both in the work of Catholic theologians and in official expressions of church teaching, a genuine consensus in this regard is clearly emerging.

Writing a decade before the benefits of inclusivist language became commonly recognized, Bernard Lonergan contended that insofar as one takes the classicist approach, one will tend to "apprehend man abstractly through a definition that applies *omni et soli* and through properties verifiable in every man. In this fashion one knows man as such; and man as such, precisely because he is an abstraction, also is unchanging."[63] On the other hand, insofar as one takes the historical-minded approach one will tend to

> apprehend mankind as a concrete aggregate developing over time, where the locus of development and, so to speak, the synthetic bond is the emergence, expansion, differentiation, dialectic of meaning and of meaningful performance. On this view intentionality, meaning, is a constitutive component of human living; moreover, this component is not fixed, static, immutable, but shifting, developing, going astray, capable of redemption; on this view there is in the historicity, which results from human nature, an exigence for changing forms, structures, methods; and it is on this level and through this medium of changing meaning that divine revelation has entered the world and that the Church's witness is given to it.[64]

[63] Bernard Lonergan, "The Transition from a Classicist World-View to Historical-Mindedness," in *A Second Collection: Papers by Bernard J. F. Lonergan, SJ,* ed. William Ryan and Bernard Tyrrell (Philadelphia: Westminster, 1974), 1–9, at 5.
[64] Ibid., 5–6.

By historical-mindedness Lonergan does not mean relativism, as he is at pains to indicate. He means rather the recognition of the historicity of human understanding, a recognition that characterizes contemporary thought and profoundly enriches how we envision our knowledge of the truth.[65] Ladislas Örsy puts the point more simply when he describes our time as "the age when the Church was coming to grips with the law of evolution, especially in doctrinal matters."[66] Or again, we could describe it with Rahner as the recognition that there dwell in the church together "changeable and unchangeable factors," some part of the permanent witness to the faith and some not.[67] Once the shift to historical-mindedness is made, Frederick Crowe asserts, we can grasp that the church is not only a teacher but also a learner. He argues that for the church, even for the writers of Scripture, even for the magisterium, learning comes before teaching.[68] Indeed, "we have laid so much stress on the teaching Church—and this not as a function related to and integrated with a learning function, but as an office belonging to certain people—that we have not attended to the learning function, though it is primary."[69]

In its official teaching as well the Roman Catholic Church is in the process of making the shift from a classicist worldview to historical-mindedness. We can see this shift symbolized in the emphases of the two Vatican councils. Vatican I taught that "the meaning of the sacred dogmas is perpetually to be retained which our Holy Mother Church has once declared"[70] and spoke of definitions that are "irreformable."[71] But Vatican II affirmed—without denying the earlier points—that "there is a growth in the understanding" by the church "of the

---

[65] Ibid., 6. More generally, "Philosophy and Theology," in *A Second Collection*, 193–208.

[66] Ladislas Örsy, "Magisterium: Assent and Dissent," *Theological Studies* 48 (1987): 473–97, at 473.

[67] Rahner, "Basic Observations on the Subject of Changeable and Unchangeable Factors," 3.

[68] Frederick E. Crowe, "The Church as Learner: Two Crises, One *Kairos*," in *Appropriating the Lonergan Idea*, ed. Michael Vertin (Washington, DC: Catholic University of America Press, 1989), 370–84, at 371.

[69] Ibid., 373.

[70] First Vatican Council, *Dei Filius*, in DS 3020; The *Teaching of the Catholic Church as Contained in her Documents*, ed. Karl Rahner (Staten Island, NY: Alba House, 1967), 38.

[71] DS 3074; *The Teaching of the Catholic Church*, 229.

realities and the words which have been handed down." It continues, "For as the centuries succeed one another, the Church constantly moves forward toward the fullness of divine truth until the words of God reach their complete fulfillment in her."[72] And some practical implications of this affirmation of the historicity of understanding are embraced in the endorsement of historical critical tools for the study of Scripture.[73]

The shift to historical-mindedness is confirmed more thoroughly by the Congregation for the Doctrine of the Faith in the 1973 teaching *Mysterium Ecclesiae*. The CDF affirms that "the meaning of the pronouncements of faith depends partly upon the expressive power of the language used at a certain point in time and in particular circumstances," that "some dogmatic truth is first expressed incompletely (but not falsely), and at a later date . . . it receives a fuller and more perfect expression," and finally, that truths taught through dogmatic formulas sometimes "bear traces" of "the changeable conceptions of a given epoch."[74]

To reiterate, I am suggesting that the worldview of the Roman Catholic Church, in both its theological reflection and its official documents, is shifting from classicism to historical-mindedness. The growing consensus in this regard seems difficult to deny.

3.2. *A Range of Views regarding Divine Law within the Roman Catholic Consensus*

It remains true that sometimes Roman Catholics differ about how to take account of the shift to historical-mindedness when dealing with issues of divine law. Although they affirm historical-mindedness in general, they may continue to treat particular questions within a classicist worldview. Alternatively, they may affirm historical-mindedness more concretely but then struggle in particular cases with the range of historicity-affirming stances sketched by Dulles

---

[72] Vatican II, Dogmatic Constitution on Divine Revelation (*Dei Verbum*), n. 8. Also at http://www.vatican.va/archive/hist_councils/ii_vatican_council/documents /vat-ii_const_19651118_dei-verbum_en.html.

[73] Ibid., n. 12.

[74] Congregation for the Doctrine of the Faith, *Mysterium Ecclesiae*, *The Tablet* 227 (14 July 1973): 668–69. Also at http://www.vatican.va/roman_curia/congregations /cfaith/documents/rc_con_cfaith_doc_19730705_mysterium-ecclesiae_en.html.

that I recounted above, stances that can include both developmentally irreversible and developmentally reversible perspectives on church structures. Three examples can help us appreciate this variety.

A first example appears when comparing arguments about the papacy and the ordination of women. In the U.S. Lutheran–Roman Catholic Dialogue on papal primacy, the Roman Catholic participants explain that an earlier notion of divine law emphasized the divine institution of an ecclesial structure or function by a formal act of Jesus and the clear witness of this act in the New Testament or in some apostolic tradition.[75] But such a notion is inadequate, the Roman Catholics believe. In the New Testament they have not found a clear and direct affirmation about the papacy itself, but this does not "surprise or disconcert" them, they say.

> We believe that the New Testament is given to us not as a finished body of doctrine but as an expression of the developing faith and institutionalization of the church in the first century. . . . As Roman Catholics we are convinced that the papal and episcopal form of Ministry, as it concretely evolved, is a divinely-willed sequel to the functions exercised respectively by Peter and the other apostles according to various New Testament traditions.[76]

Here we see a clear argument for the papacy, well grounded in historical-mindedness, probably drawing on the developmental school of thought represented by Rahner's position. ARCIC members state this more explicitly: "Yet it is possible to think that a primacy of the bishop of Rome is not contrary to the New Testament and is part of God's purpose regarding the Church's unity and catholicity, while admitting that the New Testament texts offer no sufficient basis for this."[77]

But if we compare this argument's rationale to the argument that women cannot be ordained, we see an interesting contrast of grounds.

---

[75] U.S. Lutheran–Roman Catholic Dialogue, "Differing Attitudes toward Papal Primacy: Reflections of the Roman Catholic Participants," in *Papal Primacy and the Universal Church*, 34.

[76] Ibid., 34–35.

[77] Anglican–Roman Catholic International Commission, "Authority in the Church II [1981]," in *The Final Report*, n. 7.

In *Ordinatio Sacerdotalis*, Pope John Paul II bases his argument against women's ordination on the conscious will and practice of Christ in choosing "the twelve men whom he made the foundation of his Church."[78] The gospels and the Acts of the Apostles show that "this call was made in accordance with God's eternal plan; Christ chose those whom he willed. . . . after having spent the night in prayer," explains the Pope. And he continues: "The Church has always acknowledged as a perennial norm her Lord's way of acting."[79] Avoiding the argument from Christ's maleness and using instead this biblical argument from Christ's conscious will and practice, John Paul declares "that the Church has no authority whatsoever to confer priestly ordination on women and that this judgment is to be definitively held by all the Church's faithful."[80]

I am not focusing here on the contents asserted in the three documents; rather, I am focusing simply on the striking contrast in the foundations on which the assertions rest. In their assertion of papal primacy the first two documents employ a developmental notion of divine law that grounds the primacy not in acts of the historical Jesus but in a divinely willed sequel to New Testament *Gestalt*, seeing the Spirit active in the post-apostolic church. By contrast, in its assertion of the exclusion of women from ordination the third document is grounded in a biblical interpretation of the historical Jesus, and it emphasizes the limits of the church's authority for any post-apostolic deviation from the conscious will and practice of Jesus in this matter.

A third example showing the range of Roman Catholic applications of historical-mindedness comes from the commentary by Joseph Ratzinger and Tarcisio Bertone on *Ad Tuendam Fidem*. In this commentary the authors set out to explain the meaning of the category "taught definitively" that had been officially inserted into the Code of Canon Law by *Ad Tuendam Fidem*. A definitive teaching, Ratzinger and Bertone maintain, is not a part of revelation, but it is connected with revelation and proposing it is an exercise of infallibility. Why should believers accept such definitive teaching? The authors argue

[78] John Paul II, *Ordinatio Sacerdotalis: Apostolic Letter on Reserving Priestly Ordination to Men Alone*, n. 2. See http://www.vatican.va/holy_father/john_paul_ii/apost_letters/1994/documents/hf_jp-ii_apl_19940522_ordinatio-sacerdotalis_en.html.

[79] Ibid.

[80] Ibid., n. 4.

that assent to a definitive teaching is based "on faith in the Holy Spirit's assistance to the magisterium and on the Catholic doctrine of the infallibility of the magisterium."[81] Though such a teaching is not a part of revelation, it is necessary for the support of revelation.

Furthermore, Ratzinger and Bertone indicate, definitive teaching is, as it were, inside a kind of "waiting room" (my term) for revelation: although the church may not yet have recognized that a given definitive teaching can be known infallibly to be part of divinely revealed truth, in time such recognition may emerge. The authors give an example from the past: the teaching on papal infallibility, which was once definitive teaching, they say, because it seemed at least connected to revelation. But then at Vatican I it moved beyond the "waiting room" and was recognized and infallibly taught as divinely revealed truth. Another example, they suggest, may be the exclusion of women from ordination. This teaching is now taught merely definitively, in *Ad Tuendam Fidem*, but perhaps someday it will be taught infallibly as divinely revealed truth.

Within this unusual presentation can be found a clear statement of historical-mindedness (though applied wrongly here to the question of women's ordination, I believe): "Moreover, it cannot be excluded that at a certain point in dogmatic development the understanding of the realities and the words of the deposit of faith can progress in the life of the church, and the magisterium may proclaim some of these doctrines as also dogmas of divine and catholic faith."[82] Some truths have been defined, the authors explain; "other truths, however, have to be understood still more deeply before full possession can be attained of what God, in his mystery of love, wished to reveal to men for their salvation."[83] These statements use different arguments and manifest a different worldview than that of *Ordinatio Sacerdotalis*, even though they wish to defend both the conclusion and the reasoning of that document.

---

[81] Joseph Ratzinger and Tarcisio Bertone, "Commentary on Profession of Faith's Concluding Paragraphs," *Origins* 28 (1998–99): 116–19, n. 8. Also at http://www.vatican.va/roman_curia/congregations/cfaith/documents/rc_con_cfaith_doc_1998_professio-fidei_en.html.

[82] Ibid., n. 7.

[83] Ibid., n. 3.

These three examples illustrate a range of positions taken by Roman Catholic theologians on the interpretation and application of divine law within the worldview of historical-mindedness. Although the term "divine law" is not always used, the examples clearly manifest the diversity.

3.3. *A Way Forward in Thinking about Divine Law*

When reading Lindbeck's article I was struck by some of its similarities with the successful method of the *Joint Declaration on the Doctrine of Justification*.[84] Like the *Joint Declaration*, Lindbeck emphasized that many points affirmed by Roman Catholics are not denied by Lutherans. Lutherans, he said, "have no difficulty with the functionalist interpretation of the *ius divinum* character of certain postbiblical developments, for this simply affirms that what is historically and functionally necessary for the welfare of the church is also what God wills that the church be and do."[85] Many Roman Catholic theologians as well as Lutherans "now emphasize the primacy of the gospel and employ chiefly functional categories when dealing" with questions about papacy or ministerial orders in general.[86] For instance, both see papal primacy as necessary "only as a means, only as an instrument, for the proclamation of the gospel."[87] Even Lutherans who criticize the views of their irreversibilist Roman Catholic colleagues may not really be denying their viewpoints, since the irreversibilists "insist on the difficulty of specifying exactly what is divinely mandated and therefore irreversible in any given development."[88]

Lindbeck's position suggests a way forward for the dialogue between Lutherans and Catholics. Rather than trying to decide between the many historically minded approaches to divine law now being used in both of our communions—some of them internally inconsistent—perhaps we should take the more modest route of clarifying

---

[84] The Lutheran World Federation and the Roman Catholic Church, *Joint Declaration on the Doctrine of Justification* (Grand Rapids: Eerdmans, 2000). Also at http://www.vatican.va/roman_curia/pontifical_councils/chrstuni/documents/rc_pc_chrstuni_doc_31101999_cath-luth-joint-declaration_en.html.

[85] Lindbeck, "Papacy and *Ius Divinum*: A Lutheran View," 203.

[86] Ibid., 194.

[87] Ibid., 199.

[88] Ibid., 205.

that the denials of one church do not contradict the affirmations of the other church regarding divine law. So, for example, we might argue:

(1) When Roman Catholics affirm that the primacy of the bishop of Rome is divinely mandated, they do not deny that this primacy and all offices in the church must be under the word of God and must serve it.

(2) When Lutherans deny that the primacy of the bishop of Rome is divinely mandated, they do not deny that papal primacy could be conditionally necessary today for the effective proclamation of the Gospel in the contemporary world.

(3) When Roman Catholics affirm that the episcopate is a divinely mandated part of the ordained ministry, they do not deny that the exercise of the episcopate must be reformed.

The Anglican–Roman Catholic Commission's discussion of divine law gives additional suggestions for such an approach. "*Ius divinum* in this context need not be taken to imply that the universal primacy as a permanent institution was directly founded by Jesus during his life on earth," ARCIC comments.

> Neither does the term mean that the universal primate is a "source of the Church" as if Christ's salvation had to be channelled through him. Rather, he is to be the sign of the visible *koinonia* God wills for the Church and an instrument through which unity in diversity is realized. It is to a universal primate thus envisaged within the collegiality of the bishops and the *koinonia* of the whole Church that the qualification *jure divino* can be applied.[89]

Commission members go on to note that "[t]he doctrine that a universal primacy expresses the will of God does not entail the consequence that a Christian community out of communion with the see of Rome does not belong to the Church of God."[90] In addition, they note, Anglican theologians have sometimes affirmed "that, in changed

---

[89] Anglican–Roman Catholic International Commission, "Authority in the Church II [1981]," in *The Final Report*, n. 11.
[90] Ibid., n. 12.

circumstances, it might be possible for the churches of the Anglican Communion to recognize the development of the Roman primacy as a gift of divine providence—in other words, as an effect of the guidance of the Holy Spirit in the Church."[91] And they ask "whether a gap really exists between the assertion of a primacy by divine right (*jure divino*) and the acknowledgement of its emergence by divine providence (*divina providentia*)."[92]

These points suggest two further possible theses:

(4) When Roman Catholics affirm that the papacy is a divinely mandated part of the church, they do not deny that a Christian communion out of communion with the see of Rome may belong to the one church of Christ.

(5) When Lutherans affirm that God will always provide instruments for the proclamation of the Gospel in every age, they do not deny that the episcopate could be an instrument chosen by God for this age.

This approach would allow us to draw on divine law traditions in a positive way, while also responding to the fears and misunderstandings that such traditions carry. In addition, it would absolve us from choosing between the different, sometimes conflicting approaches to divine law employed today in the Roman Catholic communion and, I suspect, in the Lutheran communion as well. And it would help clarify which issues related to divine law, if any, still divide us.

Conclusion

Dulles is correct when he underlines the importance of what is intended by the idea of divine law. It is a way of highlighting the permanence of the Gospel and the church's dependence on the Lord. At the same time, Roman Catholic theology now attributes a variety of meanings to the term "divine law." This is why I suggest that a way forward involves clarifying what is affirmed and what is denied by each of our communions in this regard, with the suspicion that on this matter we are not finally at odds.

[91] Ibid., n. 13.
[92] Ibid.

15

Teaching Authority:
Catholics, Disciples of Christ,
and Lutherans[1]

This study focuses on the findings of two international dialogues on which I have served: the Disciples of Christ–Roman Catholic International Commission for Dialogue and the Lutheran–Roman Catholic International Commission on Unity. Each of these dialogues did a great deal of its work on the topic of ordained ministry. Each contributes in important ways to the development in our understanding of ordination and apostolic succession, a widespread development within the ecumenical movement during the three decades since the publication of *Baptism, Eucharist and Ministry* in 1982. It would be possible to highlight this work and show its vital link to the wider discussion. However, I have chosen to highlight another theme that also threads its way through the work of these dialogues, a theme that has not yet been addressed as fully. That theme is the teaching authority that serves the Gospel and allows the church to remain in the truth.

[1] Original version completed in August 2010 and entitled "Remaining in the Truth: Catholics in Dialogue with Disciples of Christ and Lutherans about Teaching Authority," for Donald Bolen and Nicholas Jesson, eds., *Toward the Restoration of Unity: Ecumenical Achievements and Hopes on the Eve of 2017. Festschrift in honor of Monsignor John A. Radano* (Grand Rapids: Eerdmans, forthcoming).

The latter theme is a fundamental one, and each of the two dialogues makes a distinctive contribution to our current understanding of it. Moreover, studying the two contributions together reveals a shared pattern of thought that future investigations of teaching authority might fruitfully pursue. That is to say, in a small way this study both validates and participates in the much broader project of "harvesting the fruits" that Cardinal Walter Kasper has initiated and exhorted other ecumenists to extend—a thematic investigation of agreed statements made by all the ecumenical dialogues since the Second Vatican Council.[2]

1. Two Agreed Statements of the Disciples of Christ–Roman Catholic International Commission for Dialogue

1.1. *From the Second Phase of the Dialogue (1983–1992)*

The second phase of the Disciples of Christ–Roman Catholic International Commission for Dialogue began in 1983 and was completed in 1992 with the publication of "The Church as Communion in Christ."[3] While the statement considered the eucharist as well as teaching authority, here I focus mainly on the latter.

As the statement notes, the dialogue between Disciples and Catholics has a specific character among dialogue commissions. Because Disciples of Christ participate in what the statement calls a "protestant ethos," they share such Protestant emphases as the proclamation of the Word, the binding of conscience by individual judgment, and personal appropriation of the word of God (CCC 6). Yet because the Disciples movement actually emerged as a break from Protestant churches in the nineteenth century, "it had nothing to do with a deliberate break from the Roman Catholic Church and lacked the memories of sixteenth and seventeenth-century controversies" (CCC 8).

---

[2] Walter Kasper, *Harvesting the Fruits: Aspects of Christian Faith in Ecumenical Dialogue* (London and New York: Continuum, 2009).

[3] Disciples of Christ–Roman Catholic International Commission for Dialogue, "The Church as Communion in Christ: Report of the Disciples of Christ/Roman Catholic International Commission for Dialogue," *Mid-Stream* 33 (April 1994): 219–39; reprinted as "The Church as Communion in Christ (1983–1992)," *Mid-Stream* 41 (October 2002): 96–114. Also at http://www.prounione.urbe.it/dia-int/dc-rc/doc/e_dc-rc_1992_printable.html. Subsequent references to this document occur intratextually with the abbreviation "CCC" followed by the section number.

And Disciples broke from the Presbyterian tradition precisely over their commitment to the centrality of the eucharist in the church's life and to the unity among Christians that it symbolized and effected. Hence their distinctive history has much in common with that of the Roman Catholic Church, which also "proclaims that it has a specific mission for the unity of the world, and affirms that this unity is signified and given by the eucharistic communion," and "teaches that the restoration of unity among all Christians is linked with the salvation of the world" (CCC 8). So Disciples and Roman Catholics in our dialogue set out to explore "whether all of these affirmations and convictions are not in fact the expression of a very profound communion in some of the most fundamental gifts of the grace of God" (CCC 8).

On the question of teaching authority it seemed at first that differences between the two church traditions were irreconcilable. While Roman Catholics see the church "throughout its history as continuous with the teaching of the apostles," Disciples have the conviction that "some discontinuities in the life of the Church have been necessary for the sake of the Gospel" (CCC 11). In fact, the Disciples emerged from the Presbyterian Church as a reform movement that underlined the need for such discontinuity precisely for the sake of the centrality of the eucharist and the unity of the church. This also made Disciples "distrustful of many of the creeds, confessions and doctrinal teachings" of the Christian tradition, "finding in the way they have been used a threat to unity," whereas Roman Catholics regard creeds and doctrinal definitions as a "sign of the assistance of the Holy Spirit to bind the Church into one and to lead it into all truth" (CCC 11). Both desire to be faithful to the apostolic church of the New Testament, but this has led Disciples to be distrustful of the structure of episcopal authority, while Roman Catholics have found it "a necessary means for maintaining continuity with the apostles and with their teaching" (CCC 11). In addition, Disciples found that they are "readily critical of some developments in the history of the Church," finding sin and error among these developments, while Roman Catholics approach such teachings with more appreciative eyes, slow to find sin and error there and "quick to see continuity with the apostolic teaching" (CCC 15).

We summarized our findings on differences with a contrast: "Roman Catholics are convinced that, although they must decide for themselves, they cannot decide by themselves. Disciples, on the other hand, are convinced that, although they cannot decide by themselves, they must decide for themselves" (CCC 16). At first, the notion that such differences between Disciples and Catholics could be overcome seemed "nearly incredible" (CCC 17).

Despite these differences, we found real convergence about teaching authority in the church. With our strong conviction that the eucharist brings us into communion with God and with other members of the body of Christ and gives us a foretaste "of what will come in fullness through the Spirit at the end of time" (CCC 24), we realize as well, members report, that the church must "live in the memory of its origin, remembering with thanksgiving what God has done in Christ Jesus" (CCC 25). Living in this memory means, for both church traditions, being in continuity with the witness of the apostolic generation. "The New Testament speaks of those called apostles in the earliest period in a variety of ways; and they played a unique and essential role in formulating and communicating the Gospel. The Church is founded on their proclamation" (CCC 26). We could affirm that we each "share an intention to live and teach in such a way that, when the Lord comes again, the Church may be found witnessing to the faith of the apostles" (CCC 27). Both Disciples and Roman Catholics believe that they maintain continuity with the apostolic witness by preserving the memory of the apostolic teaching and by proclaiming and living it anew (CCC 27). Such remembering, proclaiming, and witnessing is made possible by the Holy Spirit, who acts especially in the eucharist to make Christ present. So the commitment of the two traditions to live in the memory of the apostolic teaching is highlighted by their central emphasis on the frequent celebration of the eucharist, where "the essential elements of Christian faith and life are expressed" (CCC 30).

Disciples and Roman Catholics both intend to remain in continuity with the apostles, and they "understand what this demands in different ways" (CCC 33). We explored together the ways such continuity has been maintained by each and also the possibility of receiving new enriching gifts from the other tradition. A striking agreement was noted on the Scriptures and the tradition of the church.

> Both receive the Scriptures as a normative witness to the apostolic faith. Both agree as well that the history of the Church after the writing and formation of the New Testament canon belongs to the Church's continuity in Apostolic Tradition, even though

they have different emphases in understanding the significance of that history. Both find within this history many developments which, because they are the work of the Holy Spirit, are normative for the Church. Both affirm that the Gospel is embodied in the Tradition of the Church. (CCC 34)

Members noted that the two traditions are committed "in different ways" to continuity with the church's history when evaluating earlier formulations of doctrine. But they also agreed that such statements "never exhaust the meaning of the Word of God and that they may need interpretation or completion by further formulations" (CCC 35) for clarity, and that fresh doctrinal statements may actually sometimes be needed to preserve the Gospel or proclaim it in new contexts.

Although agreeing that the pilgrim church is affected by both finitude and sin in its remembering of the Gospel, the members also were able to reach significant breakthroughs about God's assistance to the church in its teaching. They write: "But both Roman Catholics and Disciples are agreed that the Holy Spirit sustains the Church in communion with the apostolic community because Christ promised that the Spirit 'will teach you everything and remind you of all that I have said to you' (Jn 14:26 NRSV)." They agree that "[t]he Spirit guides the Church to understand its past, to recall what may have been forgotten, and to discern what renewal is needed for the Gospel to be proclaimed effectively in every age and culture" (CCC 36). The Holy Spirit helps the church adopt fresh understandings or practices precisely in order to maintain continuity with the apostolic tradition and to preach the Gospel in different contexts and circumstances (CCC 37), and even to be given "a foretaste of [the] transformation" it will know fully in the future (CCC 38). Through all of this "the Holy Spirit guarantees that the Church shall not in the end fail to witness faithfully to the divine plan," members agree (CCC 37). This is a striking convergence.

As Disciples and Roman Catholics consider the means by which the church is enabled to maintain continuity with apostolic tradition, they agree that individual members receive the gift of faith within and for the communion of the church (CCC 40), and that the Spirit gives a variety of charisms to the church that enable it to maintain continuity. In addition to the charisms enabling the everyday living of the Gospel, there are the charisms of teaching by parents and others in Christian formation, of care for the poor and needy, as well as the charisms of especially vivid witness to the Gospel. Within the many complementary charisms given to the church, members agree that there is also "a particular charism given to the ordained ministry to maintain the community in the memory of the Apostolic Tradition." Such ordained ministry "exists to actualize, transmit, and interpret with fidelity the Apostolic Tradition" originating in the first generation and continuing to spread through space and time (CCC 44).

Turning to the issue of the episcopacy, the members acknowledge that Disciples come from those traditions "which at the Reformation rejected episcopacy as the Reformers knew it in the Roman Catholic Church" (CCC 45). They then give the following explanation:

> Disciples have always recognized that the work of the ministry, shared in the local congregation by ordained ministers and ordained elders, is essential to the being of the Church and is a sign of continuity with the Apostolic Tradition. Roman Catholics believe that the bishop, acting in collaboration with presbyters, deacons and the whole community in the local church, and in communion with the whole college of bishops throughout the world united with the Bishop of Rome as its head, keeps alive the apostolic faith in the local church so that it may remain faithful to the Gospel. (CCC 45)

While showing the differences between the two church communions, this explanation also shows their similarities and underlines their common purpose: continuity with the apostolic tradition. This point is made again when the statement notes that the whole church shares in the priesthood and ministry of Christ, that the ordained ministers "have the specific charism of re-presenting Christ to the Church," and that "their ministries are expressions of the ministry of Christ to the whole Church" (CCC 45). The whole church, shaped by the Gospel, enables it to hold fast to the "faith which was once for all delivered to the saints (Jude 3, NRSV)," and the ordained ministry "is specifically given the charism for discerning, declaring and fostering what lies in the authentic memory of the Church" (CCC 45). In this process, members note, "this charism of the service of memory is in communion with the instinct for faith of the whole body," and they conclude: "Through this communion the Spirit guides the Church" (CCC 45).

By focusing only on one aspect of the statement's content—its discussion of teaching authority—I have in a certain sense distorted it. In fact, the perspectives on teaching authority that I have high-lighted are embedded within the larger discussion that also shows the centrality of the eucharist in both traditions, where the faithful hear the Gospel proclaimed with authority by those ordained for this ministry, receive the body and blood of Christ, enter into communion with the saints, and are sustained for continuing the mission of the church. For each tradition the communion in Christ that is the church "is realized especially in the celebration of the Eucharist" (CCC 48). Nevertheless, focusing just on the remarkable amount of agreement about teaching authority makes it easy to see why we agreed "that our diversities are real but not all of them are necessarily signs of division" (CCC 46).

1.2. *From the Third Phase of the Dialogue (1993–2002)*

The third phase of the Disciples of Christ–Roman Catholic International Commission for Dialogue began in 1993 and was completed in 2002 with the publication of the agreed statement, "Receiving and Handing on the Faith: the Mission and Responsibility of the Church."[4] This statement built strongly on the agreement from the second phase, but it addressed a different question: how can the two church traditions succeed in handing on the Gospel? Disciples wondered whether the "more elaborate hierarchical structure" of the Roman Catholic Church with "an apparent emphasis on uniformity" could give "sufficient freedom of conscience" to people, while Roman Catholics wondered "how Disciples, with an apparent lack of structure and creedal formulations, have handed on the Gospel" (RHF 1.4). From the outset, then, this statement addressed the question of teaching authority, but, unlike the previous statement with its emphasis on the eucharist, it emphasized the relationship of teaching authority and individual conscience.

The statement begins with the agreement that "the Church is essentially a missionary community" (RHF 2.1) and that the proclama-

---

[4] Disciples of Christ–Roman Catholic International Commission for Dialogue, "Receiving and Handing on the Faith: the Mission and Responsibility of the Church (1993–2002)," *Mid-Stream* 41/4 (October 2002): 51–79. Also at http://www.vatican.va /roman_curia/pontifical_councils/chrstuni/information_service/pdf/information _service_111_en.pdf. Subsequent references to this document occur intratextually with the abbreviation "RHF" followed by the section number.

tion of God's word takes place as a "living tradition of scriptural interpretation and prayer" through which each Christian is linked to other Christians and to other generations of Christians who have preceded them (RHF 2.4). The members repeat their conviction that "the Holy Spirit guides the Church, which because of this guidance will not finally fail in its task of proclaiming the Gospel" (RHF 2.4).

Turning again to the recognition of "the need to hold on to the memory of the apostolic community about what God has done in Christ," the members explore their recognition that the canon of the Scriptures, councils of the church, and creeds were "developed as instruments to do this, under the guidance of the Holy Spirit (Jn 14:26)" (RHF 3.1). They also consider the process that first led the church to discern "these instruments of faithfulness" and that continues "whenever the Church seeks to confess the Gospel with courage in the face of new situations and challenges" (RHF 3.1).

Considering the canon of the Scriptures, the agreed statement focuses on the procedure by which this canon was set. "The intention of the canon is to indicate where the heart of Christian faith is authentically to be found" (RHF 3.5); in the books of the Scripture "the Church recognized the authentic Word of God in its written form inspired by the Holy Spirit" (RHF 3.2). Disciples and Roman Catholics understand that the setting of the canon "was at the same time an act of obedience and of authority" (RHF 3.6), and they recognize the close relation between the canon and the unity of the church. "Because it is held in common by Christians, the Bible holds Christians together with one another as they read and proclaim the same Word of God received from the Church of the apostles" (RHF 3.10).

Perhaps the agreements in the next section, on councils and declarations of the faith, are a more surprising section of the statement. While Roman Catholics turn more readily to the patristic period of the church's history than do Disciples, we discovered that "Disciples for their part have received the major teachings of the patristic period without necessarily always using its texts explicitly" (RHF 3.11). When considering the authority of the first seven ecumenical councils, members found "more agreement" than previously recognized, since both Disciples and Roman Catholics "recognize the first seven councils as authentic gatherings of the Church able to speak in the name of the whole Church" (RHF 3.13). In probing the reasons for this recognition the statement notes that councils remained conscious that they were under the Gospel and that Christ was in their midst as they articulated and defined the mystery of the triune God revealed in Christ. Furthermore, the councils of bishops, seen as succeeding the apostolic community, wished to serve the Scriptures; their definitions "clarified and made explicit the main affirmations of the Scriptures" (RHF 3.13). After the councils ended, all local churches were drawn into their decisions through reception (RHF 3.13).

Roman Catholics "believe that their life continues to be shaped by the work of the seven ecumenical councils" and that later councils can define doctrine as divinely revealed (RHF 14). While the situation is not the same for Disciples, still "the Disciples tradition has never held the theological positions condemned by the early ecumenical councils," which Disciples regard as part of God's providential ordering of the church on the path of the Gospel (RHF 3.15). Members write: "To the extent that they have accepted the decisions of those councils, Disciples have acknowledged their authority" (RHF 3.15). Certainly early Disciples were critical of confessions of faith used as tests of fellowship at the communion table during previous centuries. The main targets of their criticism were not the Apostles' or Nicene Creeds, but Reformation and post-Reformation confessions such as the *Westminster Confession* and the *Secession Testimony* (RHF 3.16). So Disciples have preferred New Testament confessions of faith, and "they emphasize the dependence of conciliar creeds on the New Testament" (RHF 3.16). But today both Disciples and Roman Catholics "draw on the central teachings of the first seven councils when judging new ideas or practices" without necessarily affirming the "world view or conceptual structure" of their formulations (RHF 3.17). For clarity may require that some formulations be redone at a later time. In fact, members agree that councils "demonstrate that sometimes the Church finds such restatement necessary precisely in order to remain in continuity with the faith it has received" (RHF 3:17).

This consideration brings members to reflect on the process of the discernment of the Gospel in history, a process that takes place over time (RHF 3.22) and as the fruit of the presence of the *sensus fidei* (the sense of the faith) in all of the faithful (RHF 3.24). A process of mutual reception takes place that is the result of all of the charisms given to the members of the church. "To be authentic, ecclesial agreement in matters of faith will include ordained ministers with responsibility for teaching in the Church, scholars working within the community of faith, and the body of the faithful who receive and celebrate this consensus in their worship and witness," the statement observes

(RHF 3.24). Disciples and Roman Catholics recognize that an immediate discernment of some questions is impossible because of the time needed for reception by the whole community; they "are not unanimous on the ways in which reception is achieved, but they agree on its necessity" (RHF 3.26).

With this set of agreements about the process of the formation of the Scriptures, about councils and declarations of faith, and about the process of discerning the Gospel in every age, the statement now turns to the difficult question of the individual within the community of the church. With different emphases, Disciples and Roman Catholics both agree that "obedience to the Word of God has priority" (RHF 4.1). Furthermore, they agree that persons must obey their conscience, understood at the first level as the voice of God present within each human being (RHF 4.4), and that they must also shape their conscience, understood at the second level as a reasoned response to God's revelation (RHF 4.5). "It is their responsibility to form a conscience which is open to what God is saying," members agreed. "Nothing can oblige them to act against their perception of the will of God" (RHF 4.5).

While the church has a duty to teach the Gospel, sometimes Christians disagree with church teaching of their day because of obedience to the word of God as they discern it. Given that Disciples' memory has been shaped by their origins, when "their leaders were unwilling to accept the restrictions which Presbyterians placed on access to the Lord's Table," their "attitude toward the issue of disagreement with prevailing views" has also been affected. Roman Catholics have "no similar dominant memory" and place their "strong emphasis on unity" (RHF 4.6). Despite these differences of memory and emphasis, members recognize "two important agreements." They explain: "Disciples and Roman Catholics both recognize that commitment to the Gospel should be freely made. They also recognize that living the Christian life is a continuous process of receiving and living by the teaching handed on in the Church and making personal decisions which are themselves shaped by life in communion with other believers" (RHF 4.8).

In the next section the members explore the question of teaching with authority. Both agree that "discernment of the authentic meaning of the revealed Word belongs to the whole community," and both agree that ordained ministers "are called and empowered by the Spirit to teach the Word of God. These are the pastors" (RHF 4.9). But

Disciples and Roman Catholics "locate and describe the exercise of ministerial authority in different ways." In the Roman Catholic Church the bishops in communion with the bishop of Rome are responsible for the ordinary teaching of the church, serving to inform the faithful and "also to form their consciences so that they may take responsible decisions" (RHF 4.12). The Roman Catholic Church, through its teaching office, today articulates "an increasingly large number of positions on new challenges or questions" (RHF 4.12), and the bishops "can at times make decisions binding on the conscience of Roman Catholics" (RHF 4.16). For Disciples, teaching is "the function of theologically educated, ordained ministers" who teach in consultation with their colleagues nationally and internationally (RHF 4.11). "Disciples are more reluctant than Roman Catholics to provide official teaching on a wide range of matters. They often do not seek to articulate an official position when a question is under debate" (RHF 4.13), and the decisions of their General Assembly or regional Conference "do not bind the conscience of individual members" (RHF 4.16).

The section on teaching with authority ends with a trenchant observation:

> For both Roman Catholics and Disciples the authority of the Church's teaching derives from a combination of elements: the truths of revelation, the theological arguments based upon them to guide human thought and behavior, the position and experience of those responsible for teaching, and reception by the whole Church. However, the relative weight attached to the elements differs between Roman Catholics and Disciples. Thus the claims made for the authority of the Church in matters of conscience differ in our two communities. (RHF 4.16)

While highlighting differences, the statement has also revealed the deep similarities behind these differences. In order to serve the same goal each communion has developed somewhat different approaches on teaching authority and individual conscience.

The last sections of the statement discuss the ways that both Disciples and Roman Catholics equip the faithful for evangelization. While "all Christians are called to the work of evangelization" (RHF 5.11), some have special roles of formation: parents, catechists, scholars, members of religious orders, ordained ministers, missionaries. Here the purpose of the statement's argument about the individual and the church's teaching authority is shown: "[e]vangelization and the unity of the Church go together" (RHF 5.12). The church's mission of receiving and handing on the faith is undermined by the disunity of the church, a concern that marks both Disciples and Roman Catholics (RHF 5.12). The members conclude: "In this dialogue, we have increasingly come to recognize that the structures and instruments for the visible unity of the Church of God are part of the necessary obedience to the command of Christ who said, 'Go . . . and make disciples of all nations' (Mt 28:19)" (RHF 5.13).

In its views of ordained ministry and the nature of discerning the Gospel the agreed statement culminating the dialogue's third phase builds with great consistency on the earlier statement. To that foundation it adds a detailed discussion of how teaching authority has been exercised during the church's history and of the significance of such authority for personal reception of the faith within community. Taken together, these two statements express a notable convergence regarding teaching authority.

2. A Study Document of the Lutheran–Roman Catholic International Commission on Unity

The fourth phase of the Lutheran–Roman Catholic International Commission on Unity began in 1995 and was completed with the publication of a study document in 2006, *The Apostolicity of the Church*.[5] When compared with the two agreed statements of the Disciples of Christ–Roman Catholic International Commission for Dialogue that we have just examined, it is roughly four times as long and significantly different in form. While the Disciples of Christ–Roman Catholic statements are concise in style and largely systematic in structure,

---

[5] Lutheran–Roman Catholic Commission on Unity, and Pontifical Council for Promoting Christian Unity, *The Apostolicity of the Church: Study Document of the Lutheran–Roman Catholic Commission on Unity [of] The Lutheran World Federation [and] Pontifical Council for Promoting Christian Unity* (Minneapolis: Lutheran University Press, 2006). Also at http://www.vatican.va/roman_curia/pontifical_councils /chrstuni/information_service/pdf/information_service_128_en.pdf. Except for three instances, where the document itself cites other documents, subsequent references to sections of this document are made intratextually with the abbreviation "AC" followed by the section number.

the Lutheran–Roman Catholic study document is more discursive and contains lengthy exegetical and historical sections. But, like the earlier statements examined, this document also contains significant agreements about teaching authority in the church. Hence it allows us to compare its conclusions with those of the earlier statements and to appreciate the common pattern of agreement emergent in the work of the two international commissions.

The document focuses on the apostolicity of the church and is organized into four parts: (I) the apostolicity of the church: New Testament foundations, (II) the apostolic Gospel and the apostolicity of the church, (III) apostolic succession and ordained ministry, and (IV) church teaching that remains in the truth. One of the significant achievements of this document is its ambitious perspective that refuses to consider apostolic succession and ordained ministry in isolation from apostolic teaching that remains in the truth. Hence its structure in itself is already an important statement about the topic. For my present purpose, however, I will leave aside its first and third parts and examine only its general discussion of the apostolic Gospel and the apostolicity of the church in Part II and its consideration of teaching that remains in the truth in Part IV. These parts address teaching authority directly and also may be less well known than the more familiar discussion of biblical foundations of apostolicity and the issues of apostolic succession and ordained ministry.

After noting the witness of the Scriptures to the importance of the teaching that comes from the apostles, Part II treats the early affirmations of apostolicity. In the fourth and fifth centuries "great preaching bishops brought the Scriptures to bear on both doctrinal questions and Christian life, so as to make the churches apostolic in an intense manner, without however linking this with the notion of apostolicity" (AC 84). The Creed of the Council of Constantinople (381) confessed the church to be "apostolic" (AC 85), religious orders sought a lifestyle in conformity with the church's apostolic beginnings (AC 89), and the artwork of late antiquity and the medieval period regularly presented the foundational role of the apostles. Different claims about the special apostolicity of the seat of the bishop of Rome began in the second century, but these claims were contested at the time of the Reformation.

Luther himself rarely spoke about the apostolic church, but he emphasized continuity in proclaiming the message of the apostles and in apostolic practices: baptism, the Lord's Supper, the office of the keys, the call to ministry, public worship of praise and confession, and the bearing of the cross as Christ's disciples. For Luther these are the marks of the church, and among these marks "the gospel message . . . is the decisive criterion of continuity in practice with the apostolic church" (AC 95). Thus the Reformation wished to "refocus" church life on the Gospel, the document argues, by centering church life on Scripture and its exposition through these other apostolic practices. In its apologetic reaction to Luther the Council of Trent narrowed the understanding of apostolicity. Trent did teach that Christ as preached by the apostles is the source and norm of all saving truth and practice. But it also focused on the authority of the institution where the truth of Christ is normatively taught, his efficacious sacraments administered, and pastoral governance legitimately exercised, "especially by reason of apostolic succession of Pope and bishops in a church assuredly still sustained by Christ's promised assistance" (AC 105).

Turning to contemporary discussions of the church's apostolicity, the document examines Vatican II's restatement of Trent's declaration "on the gospel as source of all saving truth" (AC 107). Locating the ministry of the bishop of Rome firmly within the college of bishops, the council also makes clear that "the heritage of teaching, liturgy and witness . . . is thus bound to a corporate body of living teachers, whose apostolic succession makes them normative witnesses to what comes from Christ through the apostles" (AC 109). Vatican II also links the episcopal office with preaching the Gospel, a major Reformation concern, and it emphasizes the complex reality of the apostles' message: "the spoken word of their preaching, by the example they gave, by the institutions they established, [as] they themselves had received" (AC 114). By presenting apostolic tradition as dynamic and interwoven strands of teaching that foster faith and a life consonant with faith (AC 116), and by recognizing many of these "elements of sanctification and truth" in church communions beyond the visible boundaries of the Catholic Church (AC 119), Vatican II took important steps in responding to the concerns of the Reformation.

Meanwhile, contemporary Lutheran emphases also see apostolicity "as a complex reality embracing multiple elements" (AC 127). Lutherans look at the apostolicity of the church not simply as the presence of these elements within a community, but look "much more to the pattern of their configuration and to the understanding and use of them" (AC 127). The Reformers saw that all the elements of apostolicity were present in the late medieval church, but they wanted them reconfigured around their proper center, the Gospel of forgiveness and salvation. However, Lutherans today also recognize that the Gospel is embedded in community and is handed down in historically contingent expressions. "Around the central expression of the gospel in word and sacrament, the life of the community takes shape in offices and institutions, doctrines, liturgies and church orders, and an ethos and spirituality animated by the message of God's grace," members explain (AC 130). When Lutherans hear the Roman Catholic Church emphasizing the centrality of the apostolic gospel at Vatican II or hear the doctrine of justification rightly taught in the *Joint Declaration on the Doctrine of Justification*, they are able to reevaluate their earlier judgment that the Roman Catholic Church's teaching and practice was discontinuous with the apostolic legacy (AC 139).

The new emphases allow the dialogue members to close this part with a set of shared foundational convictions about the apostolicity of the church, and also to record new "shared understandings discovered" (AC 149–59). Among these shared understandings is the centrality of the Gospel now taught by Roman Catholics as well as Lutherans. In addition, Vatican II's definition of tradition sees it as

> an ensemble of gospel preaching, sacraments, different types of ministry, forms of worship, and the apostles' example of selfless service of the churches founded by the gospel . . . The apostolic heritage, expressed in a special manner in Scripture, "comprises everything that serves to make the People of God live their lives in holiness and increase their faith."[6]

But the document notes the "remarkable correspondence" of this definition by Vatican II with Luther's view connecting the Gospel

> with a set of practices through which the saving message comes to individuals and gives shape to community life . . . Christ rules and works through the gospel proclaimed, but this comes to expression in baptism, the sacrament of the altar, and the ministry of the keys for the forgiveness of sins. The church is

---

[6] Ibid., n. 156, citing Second Vatican Council, *Dei Verbum*, n. 8.

apostolic by holding to the truth of the gospel that is embodied continually in practices coming from the apostles in which the Holy Spirit continues the communication of Christ's grace. (AC 158)

With this convergence in their understandings of tradition the two church communions can also converge in their reevaluations of one another's apostolic character (AC 157, 159): "we therefore mutually recognize, at a fundamental level, the presence of apostolicity in our traditions" (AC 160). While important differences on apostolicity remain, the extent of convergence on the nature of apostolic tradition is striking.

In Part IV the document considers "church teaching that remains in the truth," beginning again with biblical perspectives and then considering "doctrine and apostolic truth" in the early and medieval periods of the church. In a distinctive approach, the document sets three developments alongside each other in time: attention to the rule of faith, the emergence of creeds for professing the apostolic faith, and the formation of the canon of Scripture. The document relates these to one another. It observes, for example:

> Earlier creeds and Church Fathers were decisive in councils because in doctrinal controversy both sides appealed to Scripture, as in the Arian appeal to texts subordinating the Son to the Father. Later Councils deliberated in the presence of the open gospels, but the doctrines that they taught served to renew for their time what they received from their predecessors in the conciliar tradition. (AC 341)

This discussion of the three interlocking topics is followed by an extended reflection on scriptural interpretation in the early and medieval church, with its consideration of allegory, the plain sense of the text, the problem of diverse interpretations, and the relation between scriptural interpretation and creeds and conciliar definitions.

Next there is a lengthy presentation of the centrality the Lutheran Reformation gave to "being maintained in the truth of the gospel" (AC 355). In the Reformation dispute "both Luther and his opponents agreed that Holy Scripture is normative for church teaching," the members observe. "The dispute however was about the precise relationship between the church and Scripture" (AC 361). Another section follows that probes Catholic doctrine on the canon of Scripture, scriptural interpretation, and the teaching office. Members maintain that "Catholic doctrine . . . does not hold what Reformation theology fears and wants at all costs to avoid, namely, a derivation of scriptural authority as canonical and binding from the authority of the church's hierarchy which makes known the canon" (AC 400). The document makes the obvious point that "the teaching office of the Catholic Church has taken on a structure and mode of operation notably different from Lutheran teaching ministries" (AC 413), but it argues that even obligatory magisterial teachings necessary in a given situation "are not the church's last word" since they must still be "received by the faith of the church, in order to be recognized in their lasting significance for keeping the church in the truth of the gospel" (AC 427).

In the conclusion to Part IV members indicate areas of shared foundational convictions where "full consensus" (AC 431) is shared, and areas of reconciled diversity where the two traditions can "mutually recognize in each other the shared truth of the apostolic gospel of Jesus Christ" (AC 435) and so the diversity is "not . . . church-dividing" (AC 431). With full consensus the members affirm that God in Christ has issued a saving message to humankind (AC 432) that "continues to be announced in the gospel of Christ that the apostles first preached and taught" (AC 433). Again with full consensus the document affirms that "for Lutherans and Catholics the source, rule, guideline, and criterion of correctness and purity of the church's proclamation, of its elaboration of doctrine, and of its sacramental and pastoral practice" are the Scriptures, which "emerged, under the Holy Spirit's inspiration, through the preaching and teaching of the apostolic gospel" (AC 434). By the biblical canon, the document explains, "the church does not constitute, but instead recognizes, the inherent authority of the prophetic and apostolic Scriptures." It concludes: "Consequently, the church's preaching and whole life must be nourished and ruled by the Scriptures constantly heard and studied. True interpretation and application of Scripture maintains church teaching in the truth" (AC 434).

Turning to topics of reconciled diversity that are therefore not church dividing, the document examines the history of discussions about the canon of Scripture and its relation to the church, and it concludes that remaining differences on the extent of the canon are not of sufficient weight to justify continued division (AC 441). Furthermore, Catholics and Lutherans agree as well that "Scripture is oriented toward a process of being interpreted in the context of ecclesial tradition" (AC 442).

In discussing tradition, Catholics affirm that tradition is indispensable in the interpretation of the word of God in order to connect the Gospel and Scripture with faith as it is transmitted in history and maintained by the Holy Spirit (AC 443). But they have reappropriated the patristic and high-medieval conviction that Scripture contains all revealed truth, and so today they see tradition as the living process by which the entirety of the Word is transmitted (AC 444). Lutherans, on the other hand, while rejecting human traditions that lack grounding in Scriptures (AC 445), have used creeds and confessions to orient the church properly in its witness to the Gospel and its reading of Scripture (AC 446). This section concludes with a striking convergence:

> Lutherans further insist that while Scripture and tradition are connected, Scripture should not be absorbed into the tradition-process, but should remain permanently superior as a critical norm, coming from the apostolic origins, which is superior to the traditions of the church. Catholics agree with this, because Scripture is "the highest authority in matters of faith" and Scripture continues to direct the church in the "continual reformation" of its life and teaching of which it has need.[7]

Hence different emphases on Scripture and tradition do not justify maintaining the present division of the churches, members agree (AC 448).

In its last section of reporting areas of reconciled diversity the document focuses on the teaching office, its necessity, and its context. Lutherans locate the ministry of teaching primarily in ordained ministers in the local congregation, but "the Lutheran confessional tradition also holds that a supra-local teaching responsibility is essential in the church, for oversight of discipline and doctrine."[8] In addition,

---

[7] Ibid., n. 447, citing Pope John Paul II, *Ut Unum Sint*, n. 79, and Second Vatican Council, *Unitatis Redintegratio*, n. 6.

[8] Ibid., n. 450, citing *Augsburg Confession*, Art. 28.

Lutherans take account of the processes of interaction among those in office, those practicing the common priesthood of the baptized, and theologians. "Lutheran churches earnestly hope that through these processes the Holy Spirit is maintaining them in the truth of the gospel" (AC 451). The Roman Catholic magisterium includes the college of bishops with the pope as its head, exercising their office within an extensive network of other ministers, including ordained pastors of parishes and theologians, but "the magisterium functions in virtue of a capacity for discerning the truth of God's word, based on a charism conferred by episcopal ordination" (AC 452). In spite of the different configurations of teaching ministries today among Lutherans and Roman Catholics, they agree "that the church must designate members to serve the transmission of the gospel, which is necessary for saving faith." Furthermore, without a teaching office functioning both locally and regionally "the church would be defective" (AC 453).

The two communions also agree that those exercising the teaching office carry out their responsibilities within a network of other historical and contemporary witnesses to the word of God (AC 457). Certainly "the teaching office or ministry is a necessary means by which the church is maintained in the truth of the gospel of Christ" (AC 458). The teaching office or ministry must proclaim the Gospel, interpret biblical witness, and reject doctrine contrary to the Gospel. Lutherans and Roman Catholics agree that the teaching ministry especially should give public voice to the saving acts of God in Christ. But because the church exists in history, its witness to the truth has "aspects of both finality and provisionality" (AC 460). This requires "an ongoing search for appropriate doctrinal expressions adequate to God's truth in this time before the ultimate eschatological manifestation of Christ as Lord and Savior of all" (AC 460). On this, too, the members are agreed.

Conclusion

When we compare the agreements about teaching authority that have been reached in these three documents we can discern a remarkable degree of convergence. First, perhaps most notable is the virtual end of debate about the authority of the canon of the Scriptures and the authority of creeds, councils, and dogmatic formulations in church history. With careful nuances, each of the documents reports genuine convergence on these topics and hence on the relationship of Scripture and tradition.

Second, each document reports real convergence on the necessity of an ordained ministry with responsibility for oversight in teaching. But none envisions that such responsibility is exercised apart from the witness of other ordained ministers, of theologians, or indeed of all the baptized in their various roles and states—witness given in such diverse ways as through holiness of life, critical discernment of Scripture, and striving for justice.

Third, each of the documents focuses explicitly on the historical character of the church's search for doctrinal expressions that are, as the Lutheran–Roman Catholic document puts it, "adequate to God's truth in this time" (AC 460), emphasizing that the search takes time and involves the whole church. It is in this process of ecclesial searching that the documents situate the Holy Spirit's guidance of the church, assisting it to remain in the truth of the Gospel.

More broadly, reading these documents side by side clearly illustrates the significant contribution bilateral dialogues make to ecumenism. When two partner churches probe deeply into a single divisive topic for a period of years, genuine theological breakthroughs occur that would not be possible in shorter and less focused investigations. And when the fruit of many such dialogues is made available to the entire ecumenical movement there emerges the possibility of a rich harvest.

Ecumenical Dialogue:
The Next Generation[1]

Introduction

In my title, *Star Trek* fans among us will recognize the name of the second series that followed the first famous group of space travelers in *Star Trek* who set out on a spaceship to explore new worlds. The next generation that followed them faced both old and new challenges: "to explore new worlds . . . to boldly go where no one has gone before." In some ways ecumenical dialogue does boldly explore new worlds, and it presents Catholic theologians today with a number of important challenges.

This convention on the theme "Generations" has given us many exciting opportunities to explore theological shifts from one generation to another. For our closing reflection I decided to talk about what a new generation of ecumenists will face as they explore this new world.

To begin, I want to note my personal obligations to the generation in my own family who helped prepare the Roman Catholic Church

[1] First presented on June 8, 2008, as the presidential address at the sixty-third annual convention of the Catholic Theological Society of America, Miami, FL. Previously published in *Origins* 38 (2008–09): 154–63; and *Catholic Theological Society of America Proceedings* 63 (2008): 84–103.

for entrance into the ecumenical movement. Long before the Second Vatican Council passed its Decree on Ecumenism, I had learned about ecumenism from my parents, James and Joan O'Gara, fervent Chicago Catholics who met in a discussion group at the Chicago Catholic Worker and became committed to the renewal of the Catholic Church. During the 1930s and 1940s my mother helped direct the Chicago Inter-Student Catholic Action movement and my father ran the Chicago Catholic Worker House. For both of them dialogue with other Christians was part of what the renewal of Catholicism meant. When I was four years old my father became managing editor of *Commonweal* magazine; when I was twelve years old I decided to become a theologian. By the time my father headed to Rome during my high school years to report on the Second Vatican Council for *Commonweal* I had already written my first essay about ecumenism, drawing on what I had learned not from my school but from my parents. The potent mix of ideas from Catholic Worker and from *Commonweal* became my intellectual heritage, and in gratitude to my parents for this precious gift I dedicate my remarks this morning to their memory.

We all know that a good meeting handles both business arising from the minutes and new business. This is not a bad image for the challenge facing a new generation of ecumenists as they enter into the joys and challenges of dialogue with other Christians. I will structure my remarks into two sections, then: old business and new business.

1. Old Business

In this section I want to talk about three areas of old business that the next generation of ecumenists must still address: historic sources of division, reforming the exercise of authority, and rereading our past.

1.1. *Historic Sources of Division*

Catholic scholars entering dialogue with Protestant, Anglican, and Orthodox churches encounter a large corpus of scholarly agreement on the topics that led to earlier divisions between the churches. Since the start of the modern ecumenical movement, and then more extensively since the Roman Catholic Church officially entered these discussions, theologians have reached consensus on a large number of divisive topics. We all know the list of these topics: baptism, eucharist, ordained ministry, Mary the Mother of God, the nature of the ministry of *episcope* (oversight), the person of Jesus Christ, justification, the nature and mission of the church, the papacy, teaching authority. When I consider agreements reached just during the thirty-two years of my own involvement in ecumenical work I am amazed at how broad a consensus has been achieved through ecumenical discussion. Today it is commonplace among ecumenists to speak easily of the mutual recognition of our baptism, of the real and unique presence of Christ in the eucharist, of justification by faith through grace, of the church as a communion, of a universal ministry by the bishop of Rome as something desirable for all the churches to recover, and of diverse forms of devotion to Mary as an authentic inculturation of the Gospel. This is an impressive growth in mutual understanding, developed patiently through hour after hour of discussion and study by ecumenical partners.

How should we understand this growth in consensus? I have compared ecumenical dialogue on these divisive questions to a gift exchange.[2] I married into a large family, and at Christmas each member of my husband Michael's family brings one gift to the family exchange and receives one in return. Ecumenism is partly like a gift exchange, where each Christian communion brings one or many gifts to the dialogue table and receives riches from their dialogue partners as well. But in the ecumenical gift exchange the gift-giving enriches all, since we do not lose our gifts by sharing them with others. The gift exchange of ecumenical dialogue means a mutual reception of gifts received in fact from God and given for the good of the whole church, now offered for sharing by all.

In *Lumen Gentium*, the Second Vatican Council taught that the catholicity of the church results in a gift exchange: "In virtue of this catholicity each individual part of the Church contributes through its special gifts to the good of the other parts and of the whole Church."[3]

---

[2] Margaret O'Gara, *The Ecumenical Gift Exchange* (Collegeville, MN: Liturgical Press, 1998).

[3] Vatican II, *Lumen Gentium* (Dogmatic Constitution on the Church), n. 13. Also at http://www.vatican.va/archive/hist_councils/ii_vatican_council/documents/vat-ii _const_19641121_lumen-gentium_en.html.

Pope John Paul II referred to this insight in his encyclical on commitment to ecumenism, *Ut Unum Sint:* "Dialogue is not simply an exchange of ideas," he said. "In some way it is always an 'exchange of gifts.'"[4]

But ecumenical partners exchange gifts in different ways.

A first kind of gift exchange is exemplified by the *Joint Declaration on the Doctrine of Justification* of 1999, in which Lutherans and Catholics at the world level saw each other, they said, "in a new light."[5] In this new light they could see that the contrasting emphases of present-day Lutheran and Catholic teachings on justification are not contradictory but complementary, and they concluded as well that one another's teachings today on this topic do not fall under the doctrinal condemnations of the sixteenth century.[6] In this gift exchange the distinctive emphases and language of each tradition are maintained and recognized as valid alternative formulations of the commonly held faith. This first way of exchanging gifts, recognizing different formulations of the same faith, is reflected as well in the even more historic agreements about Christ between the Roman Catholic Church and the Oriental Orthodox churches. The agreement between Pope John Paul II and Patriarch Moran Mar Ignatius Zakka I Iwas (patriarch of Antioch and All the East and head of the Syrian Orthodox Church), for example, recognizes that the two churches profess a common faith about Christ with different formulas that were "adopted by different theological schools to express the same matter."[7] Here again, agreement on a common faith permits varying emphases and articulations.

[4] John Paul II, encyclical *Ut Unum Sint, Origins* 25 (1995–96), 49, 51–72, n. 28. Also at http://www.vatican.va/holy_father/john_paul_ii/encyclicals/documents/hf _jp-ii_enc_25051995_ut-unum-sint_en.html.

[5] The Lutheran World Federation and the Roman Catholic Church, *Joint Declaration on the Doctrine of Justification* (Grand Rapids and Cambridge: Eerdmans, 2000), n. 7. Also at http://www.vatican.va/roman_curia/pontifical_councils/chrstuni/documents /rc_pc_chrstuni_doc_31101999_cath-luth-joint-declaration_en.html.

[6] Ibid., n. 41.

[7] John Paul II and Mar Ignatius Zakka I Iwas, "Common Declaration [23 June 1984]," in *Growth in Agreement II: Report and Agreed Statements of Ecumenical Conversations on a World Level, 1982–1998*, ed. Jeffrey Gros et al. (Geneva: WCC Publications; Grand Rapids: Eerdmans, 2000), 691–93, at 691, n. 3. Also at http://www.vatican.va/roman _curia/pontifical_councils/chrstuni/anc-orient-ch-docs/rc_pc_christuni_doc _19840623_jp-ii-zakka-i_en.html.

Discussions about the eucharist often show a second kind of gift exchange when ecumenical partners combine several insights, each representing a point made by one partner that needs to be balanced with another point. So in the 1971 agreement of the Anglican–Roman Catholic International Commission (ARCIC) on "Eucharistic Doctrine," the members recognized that the eucharist does not repeat the once-for-all character of Christ's death on the cross, which is sufficient for removing the sins of the world. But this classically Anglican point is immediately balanced by a Catholic understanding of the eucharist as "no mere calling to mind of a past event or of its significance, but the Church's effectual proclamation of God's mighty acts," such that the church even "enter[s] into the movement" of Christ's self-offering.[8] By holding these two points together the statement corrects distortions in the approach to the sacrificial aspect of the eucharist that have resulted when either partner's position is considered in isolation.

A third kind of gift exchange can be found in the popular movement for dialogue between Mennonites and Catholics called "Bridgefolk."[9] In this gathering each tradition desires to receive a distinct kind of gift from the other. Mennonites ask to recover a richer liturgical and sacramental heritage, one they feel they lost at the time of the Reformation. Roman Catholics seek a deeper set of practices to sustain long-term peacemaking. While Mennonites explore more frequent and liturgically richer eucharistic celebrations at Saint John's Abbey during our meetings, Catholics inch closer to a pacifist position in their strict reinterpretation of the just war theory. With such recent Catholic rethinking of peace and war, Mennonites feel right at home.

The ecumenical exchange of gifts can take many forms, then, and I have used examples to illustrate three kinds of exchange. But what is the meaning of such a gift exchange? Is it really possible to say the same things in other words or to discover parts of the Gospel that have been neglected or overlooked?

To such a question, Catholic theology of course can easily answer "yes." Catholic theologians are very clear that, as Vatican II taught,

---

[8] Anglican–Roman Catholic International Commission, "Eucharistic Doctrine (1971)," in *The Final Report* (London: SPCK & Catholic Truth Society, 1982), n. 5. Also at http://www.vatican.va/roman_curia/pontifical_councils/chrstuni/angl-comm -docs/rc_pc_chrstuni_doc_1971_eucharistic-doctrine_en.html.

[9] See http://www.bridgefolk.net.

there is a "growth in the understanding" of the apostolic faith that occurs within the church over the centuries through conversation with the Lord under the guidance of the Holy Spirit.[10] Describing such growth that comes about through ecumenical and interreligious dialogue, Walter Kasper observes: "No concrete historic form or formula of Christianity will ever be able adequately to exhaust its richness. . . . Dialogue helps us to know all the depth and dimensions of Jesus Christ."[11]

My colleagues in ecumenism can take heart from the perspective of Pope John Paul II, who thought that ecumenical dialogue makes "surprising discoveries possible." Sometimes, he said, "[i]ntolerant polemics and controversies have made incompatible assertions out of what was really the result of two different ways of looking at the same reality." So, he explained, "[o]ne of the advantages of ecumenism is that it helps Christian Communities to discover the unfathomable riches of the truth."[12] This is very different from the relativism against which John Paul II warned. Because East and West became progressively estranged, the pope maintained, "the other's diversity was no longer perceived as a common treasure, but as incompatibility."[13] I think this is a very interesting idea: that "the other's diversity was no longer perceived as a common treasure, but as incompatibility." Instead, John Paul II wanted us to recognize that some kinds of diversity are a richness, a common treasure, rather than a sign of incompatibility. They present us with an opportunity not for relativism but for an exchange of gifts.

For the last fifty years ecumenical dialogue groups have explored such a gift exchange, and their intellectual breakthroughs are an important part of the heritage our future colleagues must appropriate. But the implications of this heritage wait as unfinished business on the ecumenical agenda. Despite widespread consensus on many

---

[10] Vatican II, *Dei Verbum* (Dogmatic Constitution on Divine Revelation), n. 8. Also at http://www.vatican.va/archive/hist_councils/ii_vatican_council/documents/vat-ii_const_19651118_dei-verbum_en.html.

[11] Walter Kasper, "The Nature and Purpose of Ecumenical Dialogue," in idem, *That They May All Be One: The Call to Unity Today* (London and New York: Burns & Oates, 2004), 40.

[12] John Paul II, *Ut Unum Sint*, n. 38.

[13] John Paul II, apostolic letter *Orientale Lumen*, *Origins* 25 (1995–96): 3–13, n. 18. Also at http://www.vatican.va/holy_father/john_paul_ii/apost_letters/1995/documents/hf_jp-ii_apl_19950502_orientale-lumen_en.html.

issues that once divided the churches, only two areas of consensus have received official reception: the agreements on justification and on the incarnation. All the others, a large group of fresh innovative theological conclusions that were even vetted by the Congregation for the Doctrine of the Faith under Joseph Ratzinger—these remain stacked up on the sidelines, gathering dust as our churches procrastinate about ratifying and implementing them. Harvesting these theological advances will be a significant step in completing our unfinished ecumenical business.

1.2. *Reforming the Exercise of Authority*

Another distinctive and emotionally sensitive piece of unfinished business on the ecumenical agenda is the reform of the papacy. This is at the same time one of the most complicated, because it involves changes not just in understanding but also in practice.

Recognition that the papacy needs reform is widespread. On the one hand, such reform was a theme at the Second Vatican Council, with its emphasis on the local church, the collegiality of the bishops, and the infallibility of the whole people of God. Hermann Pottmeyer echoes many Catholic theologians when he discusses the changes required if the papacy is to turn away from what Yves Congar called a "pyramidal ecclesiology"[14] and to appropriate instead the ecclesiology of communion recovered from the biblical and patristic texts by Vatican II.[15] Exercise of the primacy of the bishop of Rome within an ecclesiology of communion would be less centralized, more collegial, and more respectful of local churches' diversity. Pope John Paul II echoed this theme in Roman Catholic theology when, in his encyclical on ecumenism, he himself recognized that the papacy needs renewal—being "open to a new situation" is how he puts it[16]—and asked for the help of pastors and theologians from other churches in reenvisioning and reforming this ancient ministry.

From ecumenical partners the invitation to rethink the papacy has received many positive responses. Many other Christian communions

---

[14] Yves Congar, "La 'réception' comme réalité ecclésiologique," *Revue des Sciences philosophiques et théologiques* 56 (1972): 369–403, at 392–93.

[15] Hermann J. Pottmeyer, *Towards a Papacy in Communion: Perspectives from Vatican Councils I & II*, trans. Matthew J. O'Connell (New York: Crossroad, 1998).

[16] John Paul II, *Ut Unum Sint*, n. 95.

have looked with some longing, even jealousy, at the ministry of unity for the whole church. Today the pope provides leadership as a global spokesperson for the Gospel, facing new moral questions at a time of cultural change and serving as a uniquely credible witness of the church's tradition. Papal teaching on social justice and peace since *Rerum Novarum* has shaped an integral vision of the social implications of sin and grace. Many Christian churches desire this ministry of unity as well, and they seek to regain full communion with the bishop of Rome. Ecumenical dialogues have gone even further in their agreements on the need for a universal ministry. The Anglican–Roman Catholic International Commission calls such a ministry "part of God's design" for the church,[17] and the U.S. Lutheran–Roman Catholic dialogue seeks again a "petrine ministry" to witness to the Gospel at the world level[18]—a ministry Lutherans acknowledge they lost at the time of the Reformation.[19] At the same time, these other churches refuse to be reconciled with the present form of papal authority, which they find often too centralized and authoritarian.

If we Catholics look at the last pontificate through the eyes of our ecumenical partners we can see the mixed message the modern papacy sends to them. On the one hand, Pope John Paul II presented an engaging figure for Protestants, Anglicans, and Orthodox. Many welcomed his strong criticism of both capitalism and communism, his commitment to mission and to a new evangelization, his outreach to non-Christians, and his opposition to abortion, war, capital punishment, and euthanasia. Under his pontificate the global possibilities available to a world-level spokesperson were demonstrated in new ways. John Paul II revived a modern form of pilgrimage that celebrated

[17] Anglican–Roman Catholic International Commission, "Authority in the Church II (1981)," in *The Final Report*, n. 15. Also at http://www.vatican.va/roman_curia/pontifical_councils/chrstuni/angl-comm-docs/rc_pc_chrstuni_doc_1981_authority-church-ii_en.html.

[18] U.S. Lutheran–Roman Catholic Dialogue, "Differing Attitudes toward Papal Primacy: Common Statement," in *Papal Primacy and the Universal Church*, ed. Paul C. Empie and T. Austin Murphy (Minneapolis: Augsburg Publishing House, 1974), n. 28. Also at http://www.usccb.org/beliefs-and-teachings/ecumenical-and-interreligious/ecumenical/lutheran/attitudes-papal-primacy.cfm.

[19] U.S. Lutheran–Roman Catholic Dialogue, "Teaching Authority and Infallibility in the Church: Common Statement," in *Teaching Authority and Infallibility in the Church*, ed. Paul C. Empie, T. Austin Murphy, and Joseph A. Burgess (Minneapolis: Augsburg Publishing House, 1980), n. 39. Also at http://www.ts.mu.edu/readers/content/pdf/40/40.1/40.1.5.pdf.

the variety of local churches by becoming a pilgrim himself, an itinerant preacher of the Gospel to the nations, and then inviting the young at World Youth Days to become pilgrims as well. During his pontificate ecumenical dialogue at the world and local levels was systematically supported. Perhaps even more intriguing to Protestants, Anglicans, and Orthodox was John Paul II's call to repent for the sins of former Christians, including "the use of violence in the service of truth"[20] and the sins "which have rent the unity of the Body of Christ and wounded fraternal charity."[21] Hearing a pope apologize was a new experience for most Christians, and it changed the tone of many ecumenical discussions.

It would be inattentive, however, for Roman Catholics not to recognize the large problems posed to our ecumenical partners by the last pontificate. Protestants, Anglicans, and Orthodox Christians had welcomed Vatican II's emphasis on collegiality and the local church, and so they are disappointed when they see signs that Rome is unable or unwilling to extend this emphasis into its practice. John Garvey complained that "[c]ollegiality was a principle, but not really a practice" in the Roman Catholic Church.[22] During the last pontificate Protestants, Anglicans, and Orthodox watched uneasily as the synod of bishops remained merely advisory to the pope and the authority of episcopal conferences was restricted. In "Some Aspects of the Church Understood as Communion," our ecumenical partners read that the petrine ministry is "interior to each particular Church,"[23] and in *Dominus Iesus* that Protestant and Anglican communities are not "churches in the proper sense" at all.[24] Our ecumenical partners

---

[20] John Paul II, apostolic letter "As the Third Millennium Draws Near" (*Tertio Millennio Adveniente*), *Origins* 24 (1994–95): 401, 403–16, n. 35. Also at http://www .vatican.va/holy_father/john_paul_ii/apost_letters/documents/hf_jp-ii_apl _10111994_tertio-millennio-adveniente_en.html.

[21] John Paul II, "Service Requesting Pardon [12 March 2000]," *Origins* 29 (1999–2000): 647. Also at http://www.vatican.va/news_services/liturgy/documents/ns_lit_doc _20000312_prayer-day-pardon_en.html.

[22] John Garvey, "The New Pope: An Orthodox View," *Commonweal* 132 (May 20, 2005): 7.

[23] Congregation for the Doctrine of the Faith, *Letter to the Bishops of the Catholic Church on Some Aspects of the Church Understood as Communion*, *Origins* 22 (1992–93): 108–12, at 110. Also at http://www.vatican.va/roman_curia/congregations/cfaith /documents/rc_con_cfaith_doc_28051992_communionis-notio_en.html.

[24] Congregation for the Doctrine of the Faith, *Dominus Iesus: On the Unicity and Salvific Universality of Jesus Christ and the Church*, *Origins* 30 (2000–01): 209, 211–19, n. 17.

looked hopefully for a more collegial exercise of the papacy with attention to local diversity, but instead they heard the complex debate between Joseph Ratzinger and Walter Kasper about whether the local or the universal church had priority. Our ecumenical partners heard that *subsistit* as used at Vatican II meant that the church of Christ "continues to exist fully only in the Catholic Church"[25] and that the teaching against the ordination of women was now one "to be definitively held by all the Church's faithful."[26]

Moreover, the volume of papal teaching from the last pontificate was enormous, much larger than in previous pontificates. While Roman Catholics themselves puzzled together over the authority of these many encyclicals, apostolic letters, apostolic exhortations and declarations, our ecumenical partners looked on with concern. What role would such teachings play in the life of sister churches in the future if our divisions could be overcome? Often Roman Catholics themselves could not answer this question.

The pontificate of John Paul II thus leaves a mixed heritage on ecumenism. And many of the same issues persist in the present pontificate. They indicate the unfinished business regarding the renewal of the papacy for the sake of Christian unity.

Let me be clear. I believe the papacy is one of the gifts we Catholics bring to the dialogue table. The Anglican–Roman Catholic International Commission calls the papacy a gift "to be shared," a gift Anglicans should prepare themselves to receive, a gift that "could be offered and received even before our churches are in full communion."[27] But the statement also says something further, something I think is very interesting. It says that Roman Catholics should desire

---

Also at http://www.vatican.va/roman_curia/congregations/cfaith/documents/rc _con_cfaith_doc_20000806_dominus-iesus_en.html.

[25] Ibid., n. 16.

[26] John Paul II, *Ordinatio Sacerdotalis: Apostolic Letter on Reserving Priestly Ordination to Men Alone* [May 22,1994], *Origins* 24 (1994–95): 49, 51–52, n. 4. Also at http://www .vatican.va/holy_father/john_paul_ii/apost_letters/1994/documents/hf_jp-ii_apl _19940522_ordinatio-sacerdotalis_en.html.

[27] Anglican–Roman Catholic International Commission/Catholic Truth Society (Great Britain), *The Gift of Authority: Authority in the Church III, An Agreed Statement by the Anglican–Roman Catholic International Commission (ARCIC)* (London: SPCK & Catholic Truth Society; New York: Church Publishing, 1999), n. 60. Also at http://www .vatican.va/roman_curia/pontifical_councils/chrstuni/documents/rc_pc_chrstuni _doc_12051999_gift-of-autority_en.html and at http://www.prounione.urbe.it/dia-int /arcic/doc/e_arcicII_05.html.

not just that such a gift be received but also that they should want to offer it to the whole church of God.[28] This text suggests that receiving gifts is not the only difficult part of the ecumenical gift exchange; even offering them suitably can be a challenge.

This reminds me of something that used to happen in my husband's large family. For many years at Christmas my mother-in-law Kathleen used to offer my father-in-law Joe a gift. It was the same gift, offered over and over again: a sundial. Kathleen had painted it and wrapped it up nicely, and the first time Joe opened this gift he said he liked it. But he didn't really want it; he never set it up and used it, and then he forgot about it. So the next year she wrapped up the sundial again and offered it to him again, and of course everybody laughed. After that, every year for a few years, Kathleen would re-wrap the sundial, and Joe would take off the wrappings, and everyone would clap.

By that time it had become a joke. But I think it is an interesting story because it shows that sometimes a gift needs to be repaired or changed before it is offered. This is what Roman Catholics know about the papacy: it is a gift for the whole of Christ's church, but it needs repair. Could the bishop of Rome once more in the future exercise a ministry of unity for the entire church of Christ throughout the world? Could he serve again as shepherd and teacher for the whole church? Yes, I believe that he could; but to do so his ministry needs repair. The papacy needs to exercise the ministry of ecclesial unity in a more pastoral way, in a less centralized way, in a way that respects the diversity of the local churches. This was what Pope John II acknowledged in his request to other churches for help in repairing this ancient and precious gift. "This is an immense task," he wrote, "which we cannot refuse and which I cannot carry out by myself."[29]

Of course, some Roman Catholics don't want to reform the papacy so it can be shared with others: they want it all for themselves, as a sign of their "identity." So we Roman Catholics must learn to want to share the papacy with others as a gift to them. Other churches have to want to receive it, but we must be willing to offer it suitably. We must be willing not just to keep wrapping it up and offering it, but

---

[28] Ibid., n. 62.
[29] John Paul II, *Ut Unum Sint*, n. 96.

first to do the hard work of reforming it. However, reforming—repairing—a gift is hard work. It takes imagination, faithfulness, and perseverance. These are virtues that will be needed by the next generation of ecumenists.

1.3. *Rereading Our Past*

When churches enter into dialogue with each other about past controversies they invite a new look at our history. It is a new look because it is done with new partners, people who offer us new eyes to see and new perspectives from which to understand many points about our history that we have distorted or neglected. Karl Rahner comments that the history of theology is a history of forgetting as well as remembering,[30] and in this sense ecumenical dialogue makes a direct contribution to theology's work. It becomes a work of reception or even re-reception of the past. Mennonites and Catholics in their international commission for dialogue reported that rereading certain periods of church history together in an atmosphere of openness was "invaluable."[31] It can lead to "a shared new memory and understanding," and "in turn, a shared new memory can free us from the prison of the past."[32] Such a newly shared interpretation of both early Christian history and the Reformation period allowed the commission to reach important breakthroughs in appreciation of both Catholic and Mennonite developments on the topic of war and peace.[33]

Of course, we know that Pope John Paul II was also strongly aware of the power of memory. He believed that part of the ecumenical journey includes what he called "the necessary purification of past

---

[30] Karl Rahner, "Current Problems in Christology," 149–200, in *Theological Investigations*, vol. 1: *God, Christ, Mary and Grace*, trans. Cornelius Ernst (Baltimore: Helicon Press, 1961), 151.

[31] Willard Roth and Gerald W. Schlabach, eds., *Called Together to Be Peacemakers: Report of the International Dialogue between the Catholic Church and Mennonite World Conference, 1998–2003*, abridged ed. (Kitchener, ON: Pandora Press, 2005), n. 26. For the unabridged text see http://www.vatican.va/roman_curia/pontifical_councils /chrstuni/mennonite-conference-docs/rc_pc_chrstuni_doc_20110324_mennonite _en.html.

[32] Ibid., n. 27.

[33] Ibid., nn. 145–89.

memories."[34] He thought that Christians in different churches do not know each other well, and they have misunderstandings and prejudices about each other inherited from the past. Some of these past memories are true; some are distorted—a kind of false-memory syndrome. But none of them, John Paul II taught, should be ignored. They should be faced and purified.

For him a first step toward this purification is repentance and conversion. "The sin of our separation is very serious," he writes.[35] We need to change our "way of looking at things."[36]

In a sense the entire ecumenical movement rests on recognizing the need for repentance, a willingness to ask whether we have a beam in our own eye before concerning ourselves with the mote in the other's eye. The Second Vatican Council had taught that there is no true ecumenism without a change of heart,[37] and John Paul II returned repeatedly to this theme of repentance and conversion, linking it to a new perspective on the past. Catholics, he explains, are called by the Holy Spirit to make a "serious examination of conscience" that will lead the churches into a "dialogue of conversion."[38] Of course he put theory into practice on the Day of Pardon at the time of the millennium, when he asked forgiveness from God for earlier offenses committed by Christians who went before us.

After Christians have repented of their sins toward each other they are ready for a new look at the past, acknowledging with "sincere and total objectivity the mistakes made and the contingent factors at work at the origins of their deplorable divisions. What is needed," he affirms, "is a calm, clearsighted and truthful vision of things, a vision enlivened by divine mercy and capable of freeing people's minds and of inspiring in everyone a renewed willingness, precisely with a view to proclaiming the Gospel to the men and women of every people and nation."[39]

---

[34] John Paul II, *Ut Unum Sint*, n. 2.

[35] John Paul II, *Orientale Lumen*, n. 17.

[36] John Paul II, *Ut Unum Sint*, n. 15.

[37] Vatican II, *Unitatis Redintegratio* (Decree on Ecumenism), in *The Documents of Vatican II*, n. 7. Also at http://www.vatican.va/archive/hist_councils/ii_vatican _council/documents/vat-ii_decree_19641121_unitatis-redintegratio_en.html.

[38] John Paul II, *Ut Unum Sint*, n. 82.

[39] Ibid., n. 2.

"A calm, clearsighted and truthful vision of things": this is what re-reception of history means. Note that re-reception is not just a new spin. Bernard Lonergan makes clear the difference between a relativist notion that envisions truth as fabricated, constructed, and a historical-minded notion that envisions it as discovered, recognized.[40] This distinction between construction and recognition is carefully noted in ecumenical work on reception. The Anglican–Roman Catholic International Commission explains that reception does not create truth,[41] and the same is true of our re-reception of history together.

Nor is re-reception the elimination of history. Sometimes our students wonder why a new generation must bother with debates from the past, when the church of the present and the future beckons us forward. But I think that if we ignore the past we are like persons who suffer abuse in childhood and later try to ignore or stifle the problems of that history rather than facing them with the loving help of others. The *Joint Declaration on the Doctrine of Justification*, for example, notes that the condemnations of the sixteenth century "were not simply pointless." They "remain for us 'salutary warnings' to which we must attend in our teaching and practice."[42] But like our *anamnesis* at the eucharist, our remembering of history is not locked in the past, Rather, as the Mennonite–Catholic international dialogue argued, remembering together can "free us from the prison of the past"[43] to enable peacemaking for the future. In that sense we will never be completely finished with old business in ecumenical work, even though we treat it no longer as our own business arising but rather as new business because we see it in a "new light."[44]

---

[40] Bernard Lonergan, "The Transition from a Classicist World-View to Historical-Mindedness," in *A Second Collection: Papers by Bernard J. F. Lonergan, SJ*, ed. William Ryan and Bernard Tyrrell (Philadelphia: Westminster, 1974), 1–9; idem, "Philosophy and Theology," in ibid., 193–208.

[41] Anglican–Roman Catholic International Commission, "Authority in the Church: Elucidations (1981)," in *The Final Report*, n. 3. Also at http://www.vatican.va/roman_curia/pontifical_councils/chrstuni/angl-comm-docs/rc_pc_chrstuni_doc_1981_authority-elucidation-i_en.html.

[42] *Joint Declaration on the Doctrine of Justification*, n. 42.

[43] Roth and Schlabach, eds., *Called Together to Be Peacemakers*, n. 27.

[44] *Joint Declaration on the Doctrine of Justification*, n. 7.

2. New Business

In this section I will again discuss three areas: new sources of division, rethinking the understanding of authority, and anticipating the future.

2.1. *New Sources of Division*

While the generation of theologians entering ecumenical dialogue today cannot neglect old sources of division, today they are faced with a bewildering new cluster of arguments that cause new divisions between and within the churches.

Of course, it is possible to exaggerate the importance of these new arguments. Karl Rahner spoke of the neurotic fear shown by those who, when faced with an ecumenical agreement, suspect that it is not "really" an agreement "in depth." He observes: "Such fears then give rise to those strange efforts . . . to find new sets of ever more subtle formulae and nuances so as to prove the existence of mutual dissent."[45] When I hear of yet another new reason for slowing down our ecumenical work I do sometimes suspect the presence of this neurotic fear that we may be in disagreement, or worse, the neurotic fear that we may be in agreement. But today it does seem that a new set of arguments has arisen that frequently function to divide.

Some of these arguments are about moral matters. Positions taken on homosexual behavior, same-sex marriage, abortion, and the justification of war are often cited by Christians from many churches as a cause for hesitation about ecumenical work. But these issues are also sources of new, unexpected alliances: Evangelicals and Catholics band together to oppose abortion while mainline Protestants join Mennonites and Catholic religious orders in sending Christian peacemaker teams to Iraq. Churches of many kinds find new alliances in developing sanctuary movements for immigrants.

Another set of issues hovers at the edge of these moral matters. The issue of women's ordination, though many see it as a moral matter, also involves questions about doctrine and the exercise of authority. And interreligious dialogue raises questions as well. The

---

[45] Karl Rahner, "Questions of Controversial Theology on Justification," 189–218, in *Theological Investigations*, vol. 4: *More Recent Writings*, trans. Kevin Smyth (Baltimore: Helicon Press; London: Darton, Longman & Todd, 1966), at 196.

work of Christ and the Holy Spirit, the salvation of non-Christians, and the relationship of the church to non-Christian religions have become new issues facing ecumenical dialogue today. Finally, the voices of the young churches in countries where the Gospel was recently planted by missionary outreach pose new queries to the ecumenical dialogue.

How should we think about these many questions? One way to understand them is as fruits of our separation. Because the churches have been separated from one another for centuries, they have emphasized different parts of the Gospel, valued different cultural insights, developed different areas of moral outrage. Different parts of the Gospel: Mennonites have maintained a pacifist identity, while Anglicans love the liturgy. Different cultural insights: Lutherans have modeled their decision-making structures more on modern democracies than have Catholics. Different areas of moral outrage: Evangelicals are outraged by abortion while Disciples of Christ are outraged when women cannot be ordained. In our separation from each other we have learned to value and to oppose different things. The fruit of these centuries of separation is now bitter in our mouth.

A second way to understand these conflicts is as encounters between Gospel and culture. In discussing the issue of the ordination of women, the Anglican–Roman Catholic Dialogue of Canada pointed out that each church must answer this question: is the ordination of women a sign of the times—a positive inculturation of the Gospel in our day—or is it a capitulation to secular culture that waters down our witness?[46] The present painful debate within the Anglican communion itself about same-sex marriage must answer the same kind of question. This is surely an issue of generations as well, since many young Catholics are attracted to the faith precisely because they yearn for a countercultural witness: they reject what Charles Péguy named "bourgeois Catholicism."[47] These Catholics share my admiration for John Paul II's fully pro-life teaching, a teaching that opposes abortion, euthanasia, capital punishment, and war, and they enter ecumenical work ready to defend such a countercultural vision.

---

[46] Anglican–Roman Catholic Dialogue of Canada, "Agreed Statement of the Anglican–Roman Catholic Dialogue of Canada on the Experience of the Ministries of Women in Canada," *Origins* 21 (1991–92): 605, 607–18.

[47] Cited by Gilles Routhier during the Peter and Paul Seminar, Québec City, March 2, 2008.

But of course we must also ask: counter to which culture? My African students are totally opposed to abortion, but they also are scandalized by nursing homes for the elderly. "Why do you isolate your old people from their children and grandchildren and leave them so lonely?" they keep asking me. Within the Anglican communion right now, this kind of intercultural discussion is a painful one. The African Anglicans say to North American Anglicans: "Our cultures and the Bible you brought us teach that homosexuality is wrong." These African Anglicans preach the need of re-evangelizing the mother church. And some North American Anglicans reply: "But you are misinterpreting those precious biblical texts we entrusted to you."

Again: which culture? My students from South America and from Hispanic or Latin cultures in the United States had hesitations about ecumenism that had nothing to do with the Decree on Ecumenism. For them the experience of Protestants was of fundamentalist Protestants, often committed not to dialogue but to proselytism. And I still remember clearly the first Protestant student from mainland China in my course on ecumenical dialogue twenty years ago. After puzzling at length over my contrast between the teachings of late medieval Catholicism and of Luther on the eucharist, she finally said hesitantly: "But in our church in China we hold both of those positions." How necessary today in Asia is it to teach the history of the European Reformation?

All of these new questions raise the issue of discernment of gifts: how do we distinguish between offering bread and offering a stone? Churches engaged in dialogue are familiar not just with the joy of having a gift accepted but also with the pain of having a gift refused out of fear that it is actually poison.

Commenting on this dynamic, the "Princeton Proposal for Christian Unity" criticizes the ecumenical movement for sometimes giving in to a kind of "liberal indifference," a sort of relativism. It observes that some churches, trying to avoid such relativism, focus instead on older formulations to define their identity over against other churches in a "divisive sectarianism."[48] They fear the gifts of others. But in fact, the Princeton Proposal argues, both liberal relativism and divisive

[48] Carl E. Braaten and Robert W. Jenson, eds., *In One Body through the Cross: The Princeton Proposal for Christian Unity* (Grand Rapids: Eerdmans, 2003), n. 24.

sectarianism often are marked by their shift away from the question of truth and toward the question of identity. Rather than asking "Is it true?" some Christians ask instead " 'Is it authentically Catholic?' . . . 'Is it Evangelical?' . . . 'Is it congruent with the dynamics of the Reformation?' "[49] The Princeton Proposal calls this shift from truth to identity a kind of "tribalization" (in the bad sense) of Christian communities, tempting them to secular nationalism, ethnic conflict, or consumerism.[50]

Such reflections spotlight the need for repentance before any exchange of gifts is possible. The Princeton Proposal speaks of the "wound" of disunity affecting all Christians,[51] a language also used by Walter Kasper,[52] and it calls for disciplines of unity that are "penitential" and "ascetical."[53] Christians require an attitude of repentance to help them learn whether it is relativism or love for Gospel truth that leads them to reject a position offered as a gift by a partner church. Such discernment is not easy, and it presents ecumenical dialogue with a new agenda.

Refusing gifts is a complicated issue. What seems to one communion like a gift of God for the church's upbuilding may strike another communion as a deeply unfaithful betrayal of the Gospel. Two examples reveal the complexity here.

Many Evangelicals are deeply troubled by the teaching of the Second Vatican Council that non-Christians and even atheists may be saved.[54] While mainline Protestants and some Catholics cringed at the line from *Dominus Iesus* that said non-Christians were objectively in a "gravely deficient situation," these Evangelicals were pleased.[55] I repeatedly explain to my Evangelical colleagues that the teaching of Vatican II shows an increasing testimony to the wideness of God's mercy, but some Evangelicals find this teaching a capitulation to secular culture and a diminishment of Christ's saving work. For them, official Catholic teaching on this point is not a gift offered but a stone. The discussion with Evangelicals about this topic is not finished.

[49] Ibid., n. 41.
[50] Ibid., n. 42.
[51] Ibid., n. 10.
[52] Kasper, "Nature and Purpose of Ecumenical Dialogue," 42.
[53] Braaten and Jenson, eds., *In One Body through the Cross*, n. 71.
[54] Vatican II, *Lumen Gentium*, n. 16.
[55] Congregation for the Doctrine of the Faith, *Dominus Iesus*, n. 22.

In the discussion about the ordination of women we again have a topic where the churches disagree about which teaching and practice is truly the gift. In 1976 the Congregation for the Doctrine of the Faith argued that "the Church . . . does not consider herself authorized to admit women to priestly ordination" because the practice of Jesus and the apostolic community did not include women among the twelve apostles or invest them with "the apostolic charge."[56] In 1994, Pope John Paul II argued from the will and practice of Christ "that the Church has no authority whatsoever to confer priestly ordination on women" and that this judgment is to be held "definitively."[57] But in explaining the decision of some Anglicans to ordain women, Robert Runcie, then archbishop of Canterbury, also appealed to a christological basis. In a letter to Cardinal Jan Willebrands he noted that since in Jesus Christ the eternal word of God assumed a human nature inclusive of both men and women, some Anglicans believe that ordaining women as well as men would "more perfectly . . . represent Christ's inclusive high priesthood." Hence, he explained, for some Anglican provinces this doctrinal reason "is seen not only to justify the ordination of women . . . but actually to require it."[58]

Since the area of women's ordination remains in dispute among the churches, it is especially heartening that Archbishop Runcie and Pope John Paul II commented directly on the question of women's ordination a few years before the publication of *Ordinatio Sacerdotalis*. Explaining that the ordination of women prevents Anglican–Roman Catholic reconciliation even where other progress has been made, they then added: "No pilgrim knows in advance all the steps along the path." Recommitting themselves to the full visible unity of their two communions, they continued: "While we ourselves do not see a solution to this obstacle, we are confident that through our engagement with this matter our conversations will in fact help to deepen

---

[56] Congregation for the Doctrine of the Faith, *Inter Insigniores: Declaration on the Question of the Admission of Women to the Ministerial Priesthood* (15 Oct. 1976), *Origins* 6 (1976–77): 519–20. Also at http://www.vatican.va/roman_curia/congregations/cfaith /documents/rc_con_cfaith_doc_19761015_inter-insigniores_en.html.

[57] John Paul II, *Ordinatio Sacerdotalis*, n. 4.

[58] Archbishop Robert Runcie to Cardinal Jan Willebrands (18 Dec. 1985), *Origins* 16 (1986–87): 157. Willebrands was president of what was then called the Vatican Secretariat for Promoting Christian Unity. Also at http://www.womenpriests.org /church/cant2.asp#runcie2.

and enlarge our understanding" because of the Holy Spirit promised to the church.[59]

By drawing a parallel between teachings on the salvation of non-Christians and the ordination of women I do not mean to suggest that they are the same kind of issue or that they have the same importance. But I do underline that neither issue was considered a source of division among the churches in the sixteenth century. The Reformation churches did not call women to ordained ministry in the sixteenth century, and Luther taught that native peoples in North America would go to hell because they had never heard of Christ. But each issue also does show how a shift in teaching by one community causes dispute and hesitation by another community about how the dialogue should proceed.

What is the way that such disagreements on these new sources of division can be overcome? While of course we should keep talking, we need a guide for our talks, one who will open up for us the meaning of the Scriptures as we walk along the road together. Here I think the warnings against relativism are vital: they remind us of the importance of the christological and trinitarian core of our confession. The basis of ecumenical dialogue is a common confession of the triune God and the incarnation of the word of God in Jesus Christ. These core teachings provide the norm by which we can discern whether the offerings of other churches are truly gifts or stones. Without a firm foundation in christological and trinitarian faith we not only lose the norm for such discernment, we also lose the reason for seeking visible unity with other Christians in the first place: proclaiming the Gospel to the whole world together.[60]

In fact, it is striking to me that a great number of the new issues causing division are questions related to trinitarian and christological questions. I already showed how discussions on women's ordination and on non-Christian religions draw directly on our teachings about Christ and the Holy Spirit. But debates about morality and voices from cultures where the church is young also raise questions about what it means to follow Christ. So while earlier sources of division among Christians demanded a deepening of our ecclesiology and

---

[59] John Paul II and Robert Runcie, *Common Declaration* (2 Oct. 1989), *Origins* 19 (1989–90): 317. Also at http://www.vatican.va/holy_father/john_paul_ii/speeches /1989/october/documents/hf_jp-ii_spe_19891002_dichiaraz-comune_en.html.

[60] Vatican II, *Unitatis Redintegratio*, n. 1.

sacramental theology, I think the new sources of division will push us to explore more fully our core doctrines about Christ and the Trinity.

2.2. *Rethinking the Understanding of Authority*

While the next generation of ecumenists faces new questions that divide the churches, it also faces the continuing challenge regarding authority. But if the new questions will spur amplification of our teachings about Christ and the Trinity, the continuing challenge likewise entails a further task: not just the reform of authority's actual exercise, but also the reconceptualization of authority itself, especially teaching authority.

Here I want to suggest a rethinking of the central doctrine about teaching authority that Catholics offer the church, the doctrine of infallibility. The Catholic doctrine of infallibility continues to pose grave challenges to our ecumenical partners, but the doctrine is also in some disarray within Catholic theology itself and thus needs rethinking even for that reason alone.

Some wonder whether infallibility is worth rethinking. They fear that the notion is too authoritarian, too patriarchal, or too historically naïve to be worth our time and theological effort. Like Limbo or St. Christopher, let infallibility be quietly neglected and then forgotten, they suggest.

But I would argue that infallibility, suitably rethought, provides an important insight into God's assistance to the church in its effort to preserve the Gospel. Understood at its deepest level, I think infallibility is a doxological doctrine about God's faithfulness. I think it also challenges those forms of relativism—so often a concern of Pope Benedict XVI—that question whether the church can know and teach the truth. Understood in this way, the doctrine of infallibility signals something important that Catholics can contribute to the ecumenical exchange of gifts: "the faithful transmission of the gospel and its authoritative interpretation," about which all Christians are concerned.[61] Hence I contend that rethinking infallibility is worth our time and theological effort.

Without reviewing the First Vatican Council's entire teaching on infallibility, let me note two reasons why I think Catholics spend so

---

[61] U.S. Lutheran–Catholic Dialogue, "Teaching Authority and Infallibility in the Church: Common Statement," in *Teaching Authority and Infallibility in the Church*, n. 23.

much time explaining again and again the meaning of that teaching. For one thing, the bishops at Vatican I spent months discussing papal *infallibility*, hedging it round with conditions for its exercise, but they spent only one week directly discussing the conditions for exercising papal *primacy*. On the latter, the council confirmed that the pope has universal, ordinary, and immediate jurisdiction over the local churches, but it specified almost no conditions limiting this jurisdiction.

In fact, the papacy in 1870 reflected the post-Reformation pattern of an increasingly centralized, pyramidal exercise of papal primacy. This pattern began to be countered only with Vatican II's emphasis on the collegiality of the bishops and the dignity of all the laity. I think many misunderstandings of infallibility flow from presupposing centralized, pyramidal papal primacy as the norm, even for the pope's everyday governance decisions, encyclicals, and ordinary theological opinions. In his book on papal primacy Klaus Schatz argues that papal infallibility was strenuously surrounded with conditions, but that papal primacy was left so vague both before and after Vatican I that an unwarranted significance, a kind of *ersatz* infallibility, accrued to the pope's ordinary governing and everyday teaching.[62] Even in their ordinary exercise of authority recent popes sometimes act as though they speak infallibly. Papal style can seem infallible even when papal teaching is not. Thus the *ersatz* infallibility of papal primacy reinforces misunderstandings of Catholic teaching about papal infallibility, which in turn becomes a serious problem in ecumenical work.

A second source of misunderstanding comes from the epistemology presupposed by Vatican I, with its emphasis on the unchanging and permanent character of the truth that may be grasped by human knowing. Bernard Lonergan labels such an account of human knowing "classicist," and in place of it he affirms a "historical-minded" account that recognizes not only the permanence of *truth* but also the historical development of *understanding*.[63] Without denying the permanence of meaning present in dogmatic formulations, Vatican II

---

[62] Klaus Schatz, *Papal Primacy: From Its Origins to the Present*, trans. John A. Otto and Linda M. Maloney (Collegeville, MN: Liturgical Press, 1996), 167–68.

[63] See above, n. 40. More broadly, see Frederick Crowe, " 'All my work has been introducing history into Catholic theology,' " 78–110, in idem, *Developing the Lonergan Legacy*, ed. Michael Vertin (Toronto: University of Toronto Press, 2004).

also appropriated such historical-mindedness when it taught that we change—we grow—in our understanding of the truth. *Dei Verbum* presented this growth as an uninterrupted conversation that Christ has with his bride, the church, as it is led into all truth by the Holy Spirit.[64]

Now, what would happen to infallibility if we could free it from these two problems: its confusion with papal primacy and its formulation in a classicist epistemology? What if infallibility were rethought in historical-minded terms and as a gift possessed by the whole church? It might now be conceived not just as a feature of the *content* of authoritative teaching but also and more fundamentally as a feature of the *process* through which the church discerns and proclaims the core teachings of the Gospel. More precisely, infallibility would be conceived as a key feature of the process of inculturating the core message of the Gospel—of effectively sharing it with every time, place, and culture. Still more precisely, it would be conceived as the *absolute reliability* of the process (and therefore of the result) of inculturation *insofar as* and *because* it is guided by the Holy Spirit.

On this reconceived notion, infallibility—absolute reliability assured by the guidance of the Holy Spirit—would characterize the integral process that includes not only the exercise of teaching authority by the college of bishops with the bishop of Rome at its head but also the entire church's discernment that a teaching proposed by pope, bishops, or council is or is not a genuine announcement of the Gospel. For, as Vatican II taught, the entire church cannot err in believing, since all of its members are anointed by the Holy Spirit.[65] In this interplay of magisterial teaching and ecclesial reception the magisterium would have the responsibility to discover and formulate the church teachings needed in a given situation; the entire church would then have the responsibility to recognize whether or not the teachings truly manifest the Gospel; and the Holy Spirit would mentor the exercise of both responsibilities.

I do not contend that what I have just suggested is the only way we might rethink the Catholic doctrine of infallibility. But I am convinced that some such rethinking is required in order to situate infallibility more clearly in history. Among other things, historically contextualizing infallibility more clearly might actually underline

---

[64] Vatican II, *Dei Verbum*, n. 8.
[65] Vatican II, *Lumen Gentium*, n. 12.

the conviction that links Catholic identity with defense of the truth, a conviction voiced by Pope Benedict XVI in his comments about ecumenism during his recent visit to the United States.[66]

2.3. *Anticipating the Future*

In this section I will be very brief, in part because I am talking about the unseen future. But talk about the future is appropriate for discussion of ecumenical dialogue. Ecumenism has an eschatological character because it anticipates the fulfillment of God's promise to heal the divisions within the church. Jesus prayed that all would be one, and Christians believe that his prayer will be effective. Dialogue between Christians, then, has a kind of built-in restlessness, a cognitive dissonance that anticipates and yearns for the church's healing. Yves Congar wrote that ecumenists of every generation have a desire for unity that gives their present belief a dynamic future-oriented dimension "in which their intention of plenitude is fulfilled."[67]

One place where I experience this restless anticipation is in dialogue with long-term ecumenical partners. I think such dialogue has more than a sentimental or anecdotal significance. I think it provides a means and foretaste of mutual acceptance by the churches. Because dialogue partners can listen to each other sympathetically over long periods of time without hostility or competition they can often discover aspects of the other's position that previously they distorted or neglected. In this way relationships between colleagues in the ecumenical movement foreshadow the relationships that can develop between churches once ignorant of or antipathetical toward one another. These mutual personal acceptances are a foretaste of the reconciliation of the many Christian communions. After the purification of memories, ecumenical partners can sometimes discover that "calm, clearsighted and truthful vision of things" of which John Paul II spoke.[68] Such reevaluation of one another's positions can evoke the shock of recognition I sometimes feel when I realize that my colleague

---

[66] Benedict XVI, "Ecumenical Prayer Service (18 April 2008)," *Origins* 37 (2007–08): 751–53. Also at http://www.vatican.va/holy_father/benedict_xvi/speeches/2008/april/documents/hf_ben-xvi_spe_20080418_incontro-ecumenico_en.html.

[67] Yves Congar, *Diversity and Communion*, trans. John Bowden (Mystic, CT: Twenty-Third Publications, 1984), 133.

[68] John Paul II, *Ut Unum Sint*, n. 2.

from another church tradition truly shares the very faith I am laboring to explain. Sometimes, of course, this includes the gift of criticism that I offer to the other church tradition or am offered in return. But such criticism seems a part of the ascetical disciplines that nurture ecumenical work.

I think ecumenism will continue to demand ascetical discipline from Catholic theologians, just as it does now. Ecumenists must regularly fast from the eucharist when not in full communion with the presider celebrating; they must spend their time and talents on lengthy study of positions they only gradually understand; they must endure the embarrassment and frustration that flow from the sins of both their own and their dialogue partner's church communion; and frequently their efforts are feared or suspected by members of their own church.

What has continued to nurture the foretaste of the church's healing has been prayer in common, and I am sure such prayer will remain at the heart of the ecumenical movement. This insight of Paul Couturier, founder of the Groupe des Dombes, seems even clearer to young ecumenists today. Their taste in Taizé-style common prayer, their exploration of earlier spiritualities, their widespread use of icons, and their persistent hunger for a common eucharist all point to the continuing importance of prayer in future ecumenical work. When these Catholic ecumenists of the next generation walk along the road together in dialogue with other Christians they will all find their hearts burning within them as their guide opens for them the meaning of the Scriptures, bringing them closer to the table fellowship of Emmaus. If we understand that *anamnesis* includes a kind of remembering that also points toward the future, perhaps we will not be surprised when the spiritual ecumenism of which the Second Vatican Council speaks becomes an even more central instrument for dialogue between Christians in the coming decades.

Conclusion

I began my reflections by noting some unfinished business needing attention by ecumenists, and then I considered the new business that ecumenists will face in the twenty-first century. Let me conclude by underscoring my conviction that this agenda, old and new, will increasingly be an agenda for the entirety of Catholic theology. Although I have talked mainly about colleagues who will be intensively engaged in ecumenical dialogue in the future, the reality is that all of us must cultivate keen ecumenical attentiveness if we are to retain our Catholic identity. The commitment of the Catholic Church to ecumenism is irreversible, and that means its effects on Catholic theology will be irreversible as well. All of us Catholic theologians will be responsible for ecumenical dialogue as the future unfolds. Fortunately, for this task—unlike the space travelers in *Star Trek*—we are assured of God's help.

Epilogue:
The Study of Theology[1]

Last year I was standing in line at the bank, waiting to be helped by the teller, when I overheard two young men talking to each other right behind me. They were discussing career options. The first one said, "I want something with constant opportunities for lifelong learning." "Yes," said the second, "and it should have global outreach." "Right," said the first, "and it should be meaningful." I almost turned around to them and asked, "Have you ever considered studying theology?"

This morning, as we honor those who have completed their programs of theological studies and have just graduated, it's a good moment to pause briefly and refresh our perspective on what exactly the study of theology is.

– I –

Let us begin with some comments made in the Letter to the Colossians, chapter 3. The author writes: "Set your minds on things that are above, not on things that are on earth, for you have died, and your life is hidden with Christ in God" (vv. 2-3). Our life is hidden now with Christ in God. And what has happened to us in this hiding place? Because we have put off the old self and put on the new self, the writer explains, our new self "is being renewed in knowledge according to the image of its creator" (vv. 9-10).

---

[1] Written by Margaret O'Gara in May 2012, as an address she hoped to deliver at the annual convocation of Regis College, Toronto, Canada, in November 2012 on the occasion of being awarded an honorary Doctor of Divinity degree. However, she died in August 2012. At the November convocation she was awarded the honorary degree *in memoriam*, and her address was read by Michael Vertin. Not previously published.

"Renewed in knowledge": *all* Christians are being renewed in knowledge, according to Colossians. But perhaps this phrase has special meaning for those of us *who study theology*—and here I include not just those here today who officially are still students but also those who are receiving their degrees. And I include faculty members as well, who must always be learning theology before they can be teaching it. For anyone who wants to minister or teach with proper accountability to God and each other, continuous study of theology is required.

– II –

So, studying theology allows us to deepen the renewal in knowledge that is happening to all Christians as they live in their secret hiding place with Christ in God. But *what exactly does it mean* to be renewed in our knowledge, for our knowledge to be made new? In the account of the beatitudes that is provided in the Gospel according to Luke (6:20-26), Jesus gives us some hint of how our knowledge can be turned upside down and become totally new. There we hear that people who now are hungry can know already that they will be filled. People who are poor today can see themselves in a new light: the kingdom of God actually belongs to them. The knowledge they had of themselves has been changed; it has been transformed. Those who are weeping today learn through the Gospel that someday they will laugh. And even those who are persecuted and excluded and reviled and defamed because of Christ are urged: "rejoice in that day, and leap for joy" (Luke 6:22-23). By renewing the knowledge of those hidden in God with him, Jesus Christ has turned their view of the world upside down. And he also has served woeful notice on those who are laughing and rich today: their perspective, he warns, is a false one.

The Colossians text gives us another example of this renewal of our knowledge according to the image of its creator. Here we read: "in that renewal, there is no longer Greek and Jew, circumcised and uncircumcised, barbarian, Scythian, slave and free; but Christ is all and in all" (3:11). This is an interesting list because it shows that the divisions imposed by our culture or even by our religion can conceal the deepest truth about ourselves as God our creator has made us. There is neither slave nor free, there is not even circumcised or uncircumcised, but Christ is all and in all. To say it again: the renewal of our knowledge means that what we think we know can be turned upside down, can turn out to be false. It must be replaced by the truth.

We have good news to announce, and we have to get it right. Sometimes that means turning even our initial knowledge of our Christian faith upside down. Theology helps us do that. Sometimes this overturning is tumultuous, a sudden breaking apart of the edifice of what we thought we knew about our faith, to have it replaced with a deeper and truer perspective, built on a more solid foundation. But usually the overturning is more gradual, a slow maturing of our understanding as we put aside the things of the child and become more mature in putting on the mind of Christ.

– III –

So theology helps us in the renewal of our knowledge. But once our knowledge is *renewed*, it must also be *shared*. The author of the First Epistle of Peter (3:15) tells us that we must always be ready to give an account of the hope that is in us. But that's where theology comes in. Theology is the discipline that readies us to give an account of the hope that is in us. For us who study theology it is not enough to *have* our hope in God: we must be ready to *give an account of* this hope. Theology can help us do that.

And the world is longing to hear a reason for hope. The hungry are eager to hear that food is coming. Those who weep are yearning for the end of their sorrows. People are aching to hear a hopeful word, and we Christians know that people in fact are hungering and thirsting for *God* and for the liberation that *God* wants and brings for the world. This longing has been put into all people by the God who made them, and nothing can take it from them. It is our privilege and our responsibility to respond to this hungering and this thirsting with a nourishing, a thirst-quenching Word.

– IV –

But learning theology in order to give an account of the hope that is in us brings with it a very broad responsibility to *be accountable*.

For one thing, we are accountable to the church *throughout the entire world*, in New Delhi and Munich, in Sydney and Rio de Janeiro, in New York and Nairobi and Tokyo and Toronto: to all the Christians living in all of the many local churches who live their faith in so many different ways but who believe together with the same faith that we share and celebrate here today. For another thing, we are accountable to *the past*. We are accountable to dead people, to all the Christians who have gone before us and whose understandings of the faith we must also take seriously: to Paul and Irenaeus and John Chrysostom and Augustine; to Francis of Assisi and Thomas Aquinas and Catherine of Siena and Julian of Norwich; to Martin Luther and Ignatius of Loyola and John Calvin and Teresa of Avila and John Wesley; to Dietrich Bonhoeffer and Karl Barth and Karl Rahner and Hans Urs von Balthasar and Dorothy Day and Bernard Lonergan—so many people to whom we must be accountable! For a third thing, we are accountable to *the future*, to those who will follow us in the faith: our children and their children, who will live in a world different from our own. We need to be seeking an understanding of the faith that can be heard and lived by them in a future that is likely to look quite different from the past and the present.

– V –

The need for theology to be accountable to the whole church, the entire community of Christians, past, present, and future, entails a further feature: theology at its best is a *collaborative* exercise, not a competitive one. Let me illustrate this point by referring to my experience as a member of the Anglican–Roman Catholic Dialogue of Canada (ARC) from 1976 to 1993, the first of several different ecumenical dialogues in which I have participated during the past thirty-six years.

Pope John Paul II, in his 1995 encyclical on ecumenism, *Ut Unum Sint*, said that ecumenical dialogue should allow us to arrive at a "calm, clearsighted and truthful vision of things," with a purified view of the past that would free us to proclaim the Gospel together, now and in the future. ARC certainly contributed to such a vision of things. How did it manage this?

The fact is that membership in the dialogue required a strong commitment to collaboration. It meant a willingness and ability to listen to and cooperate with fellow scholars who held very different views, and to continue this collaboration over many years. Even though other scholars and members of our churches saw no way forward, they turned to us and asked us to find a way. And that also meant that competition was effectively forbidden. Unlike some academic or scholarly settings where competition between scholars is encouraged and rewarded, members of ARC could not afford to waste time competing with each other. Instead, we had to figure out how to resolve the differences that were keeping us from being in full communion. What I learned from being on ARC serves as a counter-cultural model within academic circles. I learned that understanding and agreement are among the very highest goals of serious scholarship, not competition and individual display. I can still remember the heady experience, after hours of sometimes heated debate, when our whole group, from Oliver O'Donovan of Wycliffe College to Jean-Marie Tillard of the Collège Dominicain in Ottawa, came to a common breakthrough on the issue of infallibility. This experience was confirmed repeatedly when we could draft together, finding common words to say what each church communion meant. Competition would have been an utterly inadequate approach for achieving such a goal.

– VI –

Thus far I have argued (1) that studying theology is a deepening of the renewal in knowledge that is happening to all Christians (2) where that renewal involves having our initial expectations about what is true and what is false turned upside down, (3) that this deepened renewal prepares us for giving the world an account of the hope that is in us, (4) that it requires accountability to the entire community of Christians, past, present, and future, and (5) that at best it is collaborative rather than competitive. And so my final point should not be very surprising: (6) studying theology *takes time*. No wonder it requires that we engage with so many Christian thinkers past and present, that we consider so many perspectives, that we read such demanding articles and books, that we write such precise essays and dissertations, and that we give ourselves time to grow into what we are learning. The deepened renewal of our knowledge is not finished in a year, and in truth it is not finished in the three or six years of our degree study. The deepened renewal of our knowledge that is theology is the calling of a lifetime, and indeed of many lifetimes from one generation to the next generation in the church. But in fact, it's worth it: *theology is **worth** a life!* Let us take heart from that.

Margaret O'Gara:
Publications

1. "Infallibility and the French Minority Bishops of the First Vatican Council." *Catholic Theological Society of America Proceedings* 35 (1980): 212–16.
2. "Infallibility and the Contribution of Anglican–Roman Catholic Dialogue." *Catholic Theological Society of America Proceedings* 35 (1980): 234–39.
3. "August Hasler and Papal Infallibility." *Catholic Theological Society of America Proceedings* 36 (1981): 185–86.
4. "On the Way to a Truly Ecumenical Council." *One in Christ* 17 (1981): 335–39.
5. Anglican–Roman Catholic Dialogue of Canada, "Agreed Statement on Infallibility." *Journal of Ecumenical Studies* 19 (1982): 86–87. (O'Gara was one of three co-drafters.)
6. "Review: *How the Pope Became Infallible: Pius IX and the Politics of Persuasion*, by August B. Hasler." *Laval théologique et philosophique* 39 (1983): 120–21.
7. Roman Catholic Subcommittee of the Anglican–Roman Catholic Dialogue of Canada, "The Congregation for the Doctrine of the Faith's 'Observations on *The Final Report* of ARCIC,' April 1983: Remarks by the Roman Catholic Sub-Committee of the Anglican–Roman Catholic Dialogue of Canada." *One in Christ* 20 (1984): 272–86. (O'Gara was one of four co-drafters.)
8. "The Church as Sign: A Roman Catholic Response." *Mid-Stream* 23 (1984): 396–99.
9. "Infallibility in the Ecumenical Crucible." *One in Christ* 20 (1984): 325–45.
10. "Review: *Vatican I et les évèques uniates: Une étape éclairante de la politique romaine à l'égard des Orientaux (1867–1870)*, by Constantin G. Patelos." *The Catholic Historical Review* 70 (1984): 607–8.
11. "Pictures and Problems: A Response to 'The Ecclesial and Cultural Roles of Theology,' by Joseph Komonchak." *Catholic Theological Society of America Proceedings* 40 (1985): 33–35.
12. "New Directions for Ecumenical Dialogue." Collegeville, MN: Liturgical Press, 1986. (Cassette tape lecture.)

13. "Understanding 'A Certain Though Imperfect Communion' between Anglicans and Roman Catholics." *Mid-Stream* 25 (1986): 190–99.

13a. "Understanding 'A Certain, though Imperfect, Communion' between Anglicans and Roman Catholics." *The Ecumenical Gift Exchange*. Collegeville, MN: Liturgical Press, 1998, 93–103. (Reprint, with minor changes, of no. 13.)

14. "The Nature of Koinonia: A Roman Catholic Understanding." *Mid-Stream* 25 (1986): 339–50.

15. Disciples of Christ–Roman Catholic International Commission for Dialogue, "Agreed Account of the Eighth Meeting (1985): Mandeville [Jamaica]." *Mid-Stream* 25 (1986): 419–25.

16. "Reception as Key: Unlocking ARCIC on Infallibility." *Toronto Journal of Theology* 3 (1987): 41–49.

16a. "Reception as Key: Unlocking ARCIC on Infallibility." *The Ecumenical Gift Exchange*, 81–91. (Reprint, with minor changes, of no. 16.)

17. "The Meaning of Ecumenism." *Ecumenical People, Programs, Papers* [newsletter of the Collegeville Institute for Ecumenical and Cultural Research, Collegeville, MN], November 1987, 13–16, 25.

18. *Triumph in Defeat: Infallibility, Vatican I, and the French Minority Bishops.* Washington, DC: Catholic University of America Press, 1988.

19. "The Episcopate, the Universal Primacy, and the Growth of Understanding: A Roman Catholic Response to Robert Wright." *Quadrilateral at One Hundred: Essays on the Centenary of the Chicago-Lambeth Quadrilateral, 1886/88–1986/88*, edited by J. Robert Wright. London and Oxford: Mowbray, 1988, 47–54.

20. Disciples of Christ–Roman Catholic International Commission for Dialogue, "Agreed Account of the Ninth Meeting (1986): Cambridge [UK]." *Mid-Stream* 27 (1988): 414–19. (O'Gara was one of four co-drafters.)

21. Disciples of Christ–Roman Catholic International Commission for Dialogue, "Agreed Account of the Tenth Meeting (1987): Duxbury [MA]." *Mid-Stream* 27 (1988): 419–27. (O'Gara was one of four co-drafters.)

22. "Agreed Account of the 11th Meeting of the Disciples of Christ–Roman Catholic International Commission for Dialogue, Abbey of Gethsemani, Kentucky, 1988." *Mid-Stream* 29 (1990): 279–89. (O'Gara was one of four co-drafters.)

23. "Agreed Account of the 12th Meeting of the Disciples of Christ–Roman Catholic International Commission for Dialogue, Cardinal Casa Piazza, Venice, 1989." *Mid-Stream* 29 (1990): 290–303. (O'Gara was one of four co-drafters.)

24. "Listening to Forgotten Voices: The French Minority Bishops of Vatican I and Infallibility." *Theology Digest* 37 (1990): 1–13.

24a. "Listening to Forgotten Voices: The French Minority Bishops of Vatican I and Infallibility." *The Ecumenical Gift Exchange*, 45–62. (Reprint, with minor changes, of no. 24.)

25. "The Petrine Ministry in the Ecumenical Gift Exchange." *Grail: An Ecumenical Journal* 6 (1990): 51–71.

26. Catholic Theological Society of America, "Do Not Extinguish the Spirit" [Statement of Catholic Theological Society Members on the Twenty-Fifth Anniversary of the Close of the Second Vatican Council]." *Origins* 20 (1990–91): 461, 463–67. (O'Gara was one of three co-drafters.)

27. "Ecumenism and Feminism in Dialogue on Authority," 118–37, in *Women and the Church: The Challenge of Ecumenical Solidarity in an Age of Alienation*, edited by Melanie May. Grand Rapids: Eerdmans, 1991.

27a. "Ecumenism and Feminism in Dialogue on Authority." *The Ecumenical Gift Exchange*, 135–49. (Reprint, with minor changes, of no. 27.)

28. "Another Step on the Road to Unity." *Ecumenism* 103 (September 1991): 3.

29. Anglican–Roman Catholic Dialogue of Canada, "Agreed Statement of the Anglican–Roman Catholic Dialogue of Canada on the Experience of the Ministries of Women in Canada." *Ecumenism* 103 (September 1991): 4–24. (O'Gara was one of two co-drafters.)

29a. "Reflections on the Experience of Women's Ministries." *Origins* 21 (1991–92) 605, 607–17. (Reprint, with minor changes, of no. 29.)

30. "New Perspectives on the Unity of the Church." *Proceedings of the Catholic Commission for Intellectual and Cultural Affairs* 11 (1992): 35–52.

31. "On the Road toward Unity: The Present Dialogue among the Churches." *Catholic Theological Society of America Proceedings* 48 (1993): 18–40.

31a. "On the Road toward Unity: The Present Dialogue among the Churches." *The Ecumenical Gift Exchange*, 1–28. (Reprint, with minor changes, of no. 31.)

32. *The Church as Communion in Christ*. Report of the Disciples of Christ–Roman Catholic International Commission for Dialogue (1983–92). Indianapolis: Council on Christian Unity, 1994. (O'Gara was one of four co-drafters.)

32a. "The Church as Communion in Christ." *Mid-Stream* 33 (1994): 219–38. (Reprint of no. 32.)

33. *Rethinking Infallibility*. The Chancellor's Lecture, 1994. Toronto: Regis College, 1994.

34. "1994 Agreed Account of the Disciples of Christ–Roman Catholic International Commission for Dialogue [Meeting in Indianapolis]." *Mid-Stream* 34 (1995): 77–86. (O'Gara was one of four co-drafters.)

35. "Formation for Transformation: The Ecumenical Directory Sets a Big Agenda." *Ecumenism* 117 (March 1995): 23–26.

35a. "Formation for Transformation: The Ecumenical Directory Sets a Big Agenda." *The Ecumenical Gift Exchange*, 151–56. (Reprint, with minor changes, of no. 35.)

36. "Responses to Rome." *Commonweal* 123 (January 26, 1996): 16–17.

37. "The Holy Spirit's Assistance to the Magisterium in Teaching: Theological and Philosophical Issues," with Michael Vertin. *Catholic Theological Society of America Proceedings* 51 (1996): 125–42.

37a. "The Holy Spirit's Assistance to the Magisterium in Teaching." *No Turning Back: The Future of Ecumenism*, edited by Michael Vertin. Collegeville, MN: Liturgical Press, 2014, 101–23. (Reprint, with minor changes, of no. 37.)

38. "Shifts below the Surface of the Debate: Ecumenism, Dissent, and the Roman Catholic Church." *The Jurist* 56 (1996): 357–86.

38a. "Ecumenism, Dissent, and the Roman Catholic Church: Shifts below the Surface of the Debate." *The Ecumenical Gift Exchange*, 105–33. (Reprint, with minor changes, of no. 38.)

39. "A Roman Catholic Perspective on the Content and Authority of Councils of the Church." *Mid-Stream* 35 (1996): 433–64.

40. "Disciples of Christ–Roman Catholic International Commission for Dialogue Agreed Account [1996 Meeting in Bethany, WV]." *Mid-Stream* 35 (1996): 477–89. (O'Gara was one of four co-drafters.)

41. "*Apostolicae Curae* After a Century: Anglican Orders in Light of Recent Ecumenical Dialogue on Ordained Ministry in the Church." *Canon Law Society of America Proceedings* 60 (1998): 1–18.

41a. "Anglican Orders and Ecumenical Dialogue on Ordained Ministry." *No Turning Back*, 79–100. (Reprint, with minor changes, of no. 41.)

42. "Reconceptualizing Infallibility in Ecumenical Dialogue: Epistemology, Ecclesiology, and the Issue of Reception." *The Ecumenical Gift Exchange*, 63–79.

43. "Purifying Memories and Exchanging Gifts: Recent Orientations of the Vatican toward Ecumenism." *The Ecumenical Gift Exchange*, 29–44.

44. "Roman Catholic Theology Today: A Guide for the Perplexed in a Time of Renewal." *The Ecumenical Gift Exchange*, 157–74.

45. *The Ecumenical Gift Exchange.* Collegeville, MN: Liturgical Press, 1998. (Collection comprising nos. 13a, 16a, 24a, 27a, 31a, 35a, 38a, 42, 43, and 44.)

46. "Apostolicity in Ecumenical Dialogue: An Overview." *Mid-Stream* 37 (1998): 175–212.

47. "Disciples of Christ–Roman Catholic International Commission for Dialogue Agreed Account [1997 Meeting in Venice]." *Mid-Stream* 38 (1999): 79–86. (O'Gara was one of four co-drafters.)

48. "Disciples of Christ–Roman Catholic International Commission for Dialogue Agreed Account [1998 Meeting in Aibonito, Puerto Rico]." *Mid-Stream* 38 (1999): 145–53. (O'Gara was one of four co-drafters.)

49. "Catholicity and the Unity of the Church." *The Mike* [student newspaper of St. Michael's College, Toronto] 52 (1999): 11.

50. "An Exchange of Gifts." *Seminary Ridge Review* 3/1 (2000–2001): 42–57.

51. "Lutherans and Catholics: Ending an Old Argument." *Commonweal* 127 (January 14, 2000): 8–9.

52. "Entering the Rhythm of Ecumenical Dialogue." *Trinity College* [Washington, DC] *Alumnae Journal* (Spring 2000): 8–9.

53. "Counter-Evidence of Infallibility's Exercise." *The Jurist* 59 (1999): 448–68. (Article written in 2001; issue back-dated because of journal's temporary lapse in publication.)

54. "Disciples of Christ–Roman Catholic International Commission for Dialogue Agreed Account [1999 Meeting in St. Meinrad, IN]." *Mid-Stream* 40 (2001): 51–58. (O'Gara was one of four co-drafters.)

55. "Disciples of Christ–Roman Catholic International Commission for Dialogue Agreed Account [2000 Meeting in Halifax]." *Mid-Stream* 40 (2001): 148–58. (O'Gara was one of three co-drafters.)

56. Disciples of Christ–Roman Catholic International Commission for Dialogue, "Receiving and Handing on the Faith: The Mission and Responsibility of the Church (1993–2002)." *Mid-Stream* 41 (2002): 51–77. (O'Gara was one of three co-drafters.)

57. "Being a Global Church: Strengths and Challenges." Posted to www .bridgefolk.net on April 16, 2009.

57a. "The Catholic Church in the World Today." *No Turning Back*, 3–6. (Revised version of no. 57.)

58. "Reinterpretation and Reception [of the Doctrine of Justification]," 219–24, in *The Doctrine of Justification: Its Reception and Meaning Today*, edited by Karen L. Bloomquist and Wolfgang Greive. Geneva: Lutheran World Federation, 2003.

59. "Ecumenical Dialogue in Canada Today." *Ecumenism* 152 (December 2003): 30–32.

59a. "Ecumenical Dialogue in Canada Today." *No Turning Back*, 7–10. (Reprint, with minor changes, of no. 59.)

60. "Growing Up *Commonweal*," with Monica O'Gara. *Commonweal* 131 (November 5, 2004): 17–18.

61. "Understanding Infallibility," 519–34, in *Sapere teologico e unità della fede: Studi in onore del Prof. Jared Wicks*, edited by Carmen Aparicio Valls et al. Rome: Gregorian University Press, 2004.

62. "Three Successive Steps to Understanding Vatican I's Teaching on Papal Primacy." *The Jurist* 64 (2004): 208–23.

62a. "Understanding Vatican I on Papal Primacy." *No Turning Back*, 61–78. (Reprint, with minor changes, of no. 62.)

63. "Ecumenism's Future: What to Look for under Benedict XVI." *Commonweal* 132 (July 15, 2005): 11–12.

64. "A Roman Catholic Perspective on *Jus Divinum*," 226–46, in *The Church as Koinonia of Salvation: Its Structures and Ministries*, edited by Randall Lee and Jeffrey Gros. Lutheran and Catholics in Dialogue, Volume 10. Washington, DC: U.S. Conference of Catholic Bishops, 2005.

64a. "Divine Law: A Roman Catholic View." *No Turning Back*, 163–85. (Reprint, with minor changes, of no. 64.)

65. "Making Peace for Peacemaking." *Benedictine Bridge* [newsletter of Holy Wisdom Monastery, Middleton, WI] 17 (Ordinary Time 2005): 6–9.

65a. "Making Peace for Peacemaking. *No Turning Back*, 11–15. (Reprint, with minor changes, of no. 65.)

66. "Mixed Messages [On Ecumenism during the Pontificate of Pope John Paul II]." *Pro Ecclesia* 14 (Summer 2005): 261–65.

67. "The Significance of 'The Joint Declaration on the Doctrine of Justification' and the Next Steps in Ecumenical Dialogue," 27–41, in *The Gospel of Justification in Christ: Where Does the Church Stand Today?*, edited by Wayne C. Stumme. Grand Rapids: Eerdmans, 2006.

68. *That the World May Believe: Essays on Mission and Unity in Honour of George Vandervelde*, coedited with Michael Goheen. Lanham, MD: University Press of America, 2006.

69. "Introduction," with Michael Goheen, v–x, in *That the World May Believe*.

70. "The Theological Significance of Friendship in the Ecumenical Movement," 125–32, in *That the World May Believe*.

70a. "Friendship in the Ecumenical Movement: Its Theological Significance." *No Turning Back*, 28–37. (Reprint, with minor changes, of no. 70.)

71. "Two Accounts of Reception," 116–24, in *The Importance of Insight: Essays in Honour of Michael Vertin*, edited by John Liptay and David Liptay. Toronto: University of Toronto Press, 2007.

72. "Response [to Brad Gregory]," 59–67, in *Martyrdom in Ecumenical Perspective*, edited by Peter Erb et al. Waterloo, ON: Pandora Press, 2007.

73. " 'Seeing in a New Light': A Roman Catholic Perspective on Anabaptist Martyrs," 109–20, in *Martyrdom in Ecumenical Perspective*.

74. "Openness and Gift: Themes from Rahner's Theology." *Science et Esprit* 59 (2007): 373–86.

75. "Receiving Gifts in Ecumenical Dialogue," 26–38, in *Receptive Ecumenism and the Call to Catholic Learning*, edited by Paul D. Murray. Oxford: Oxford University Press, 2008.

76. "Ecumenical Dialogue: The Next Generation." *Origins* 38 (2008–09): 154–63.

76a. "Ecumenical Dialogue: The Next Generation." *Catholic Theological Society of America Proceedings* 63 (2008): 84–103. (Reprint of no. 76.)

76b. "Ecumenical Dialogue: The Next Generation." *No Turning Back*, 206–31. (Reprint, with minor changes, of no. 76.)

77. "Pray without Ceasing." *Bondings* [quarterly newsletter of the Oblates of St. Francis de Sales, Toledo–Detroit Province] 21 (Spring 2008): 6–8.

77a. "Pray without Ceasing." *No Turning Back*, 23–27. (Reprint, with minor changes, of no. 77.)

78. "Review: *Consensus of the Church and Papal Infallibility: A Study in the Background of Vatican I*, by Richard Costigan." *The Jurist* 68 (2008): 598.

79. "Table Manners: Christ's Lavish Hospitality." *Commonweal* 136 (February 27, 2009): 13–14.

79a. "Table Manners: Jesus' Lavish Hospitality." *No Turning Back*, 38–41. (Reprint, with minor changes, of no. 79.)

80. "Toward the Day When We Will Keep the Feast Together." *Pro Ecclesia* 19 (2010): 260–78.

81. "Old Wine, New Wineskins." *Bearings* [semi-annual publication of the Collegeville Institute for Ecumenical and Cultural Research, Collegeville, MN] (Autumn–Winter 2010): 22–24.

82. "Response to Kinnamon, Bouteneff, and Daniels." *Journal of Ecumenical Studies* 45 (2010): 296–98.

83. "A Fruitful Time: Early Years of the Anglican–Roman Catholic Dialogue of Canada (1976–93)." *Ecumenism* 182 (Summer 2011): 11–14.

84. Disciples of Christ–Roman Catholic International Commission for Dialogue. "The Presence of Christ in the Church, with Special reference to the Eucharist (2003–2009)." *The Pontifical Council for Promoting Christian Unity Information Service* 141 (2013): 28–43. (O'Gara was one of three co-drafters.)

85. " 'Seeing in a New Light:' From Remembering to Reforming in Ecumenical Dialogue." *The Jurist* 71 (2011): 59–76.

86. "Witnessing the Ecumenical Future Together." *Journal of Ecumenical Studies* 46 (2011): 368–77.

87. "Disciples of Christ–Roman Catholic International Commission For Dialogue: Sharing the Fruits," 236–48, in *Celebrating a Century of Ecumenism*, ed. John Radano. Grand Rapids: Eerdmans, 2012.

88. "Watching from the Sideline: Recent Lutheran–Anglican Agreements." *No Turning Back*, 124–47.

89. "Scripture and Tradition." *No Turning Back*, 148–62.

90. "Christ's Church Local and Global." *No Turning Back*, 16–22.

91. "Teaching Authority: Catholics, Disciples of Christ, and Lutherans." *No Turning Back*, 186–205.

91a. "Remaining in the Truth: Catholics in Dialogue with Disciples of Christ and Lutherans about Teaching Authority." In *Toward the Restoration of Unity: Ecumenical Achievements and Hopes on the Eve of 2017*. Festschrift in honor of Monsignor John A. Radano., edited by Donald Bolen and Nicholas Jesson. Grand Rapids: Eerdmans, forthcoming.

92. "Ecumenical Dialogue as a Process of Personal Transformation." *No Turning Back*, 42–57.

93. "The Study of Theology." *No Turning Back*, 232–37.

94. *No Turning Back: The Future of Ecumenism*, edited by Michael Vertin. Collegeville, MN: Liturgical Press, 2014. (Collection comprising nos. 37a, 41a, 57a, 59a, 62a, 64a, 65a, 70a, 76b, 77a, 79a, 88, 89, 90, 91, 92, and 93.)

Index

Anglicans, xx, xxi, 8, 21, 25, 33, 40, 52–54, 64, 79–100, 107, 117, 119, 124–47, 153–57, 166, 176–77, 180, 184–85, 210, 213, 215, 219, 221–25, 235–36

Anglican–Lutheran dialogues. *See* Lutheran–Anglican dialogues

Anglican–Lutheran agreements. *See* Lutheran–Anglican agreements

Anglican–Roman Catholic Dialogue of Canada, xx, 52–54, 221, 235–36

Anglican–Roman Catholic International Commission [ARCIC], 21, 33, 52–54, 64, 82–83, 91–96, 107, 117, 119, 140–42, 153, 154, 155–56, 157, 166, 176–77, 180, 184–85, 210, 213, 215, 219

Anglican–Roman Catholic International Commission, documents of: *First* Phase [all in ARCIC I *Final Report* (1981)]: "Eucharistic Doctrine" (1971), 91, 210; "Eucharistic Doctrine: Elucidation (1979)," 91; "Authority in the Church I" (1976), 64, 92, 93–94, 117, 140, 142, 155, 166; "Ministry and Ordination" (1973), 92–93, 141, 142; "Ministry and Ordination: Elucidation (1979)," 82; "Authority in the Church II" (1981), 52, 64, 93–94, 119, 142, 166, 176, 180, 184–85, 213; "Authority in the Church: Elucidation (1981)," 33, 119, 153, 155, 156, 219. *Second* Phase: *The Gift of Authority: Authority in the Church III* (1998), 21, 52, 154, 157, 215

Anglican orders, their status as illuminated by ecumenical dialogue, 79–100, 132–47

Apostolicae Curae (1896). *See* Leo XIII

apostolicity: and the role of bishops, their relationship, 127–32; of the church as a whole, 129–30; early affirmations of, 198; as asserted by the Reformers, 198–200; crucial for both Trent and Vatican II, 199. *See also* authority in the church; collegiality of bishops

Aquinas, Thomas, 8, 47–49, 88, 113

Augustine, 8, 87

Augustinis, Emilio De, 86

authority in the church: diverse structures of, all deficient but in different ways, 3–6, 17–19, 21–22, 52–54; reform of its exercise needed, 142–44, 212–17; reform of its structures needed, 52–54, 56; reconceptualization needed, 226–29; scriptural, 14–15, 148–62; papal, 61–78, 164–85. *See also* apostolicity; church, local and global; collegiality of bishops; ecclesiology; infallibility; papacy; papal primacy; reception

authority, teaching, xi, xxi, 10, 29–30, 142, 144, 186–205. *See also* authority in the church; infallibility

authority, governing, 54, 61–78, 164–85. *See also* authority in the church

Balthasar, Hans Urs von, 34

Baptists, 8

Bassett, Paul, 33, 149

Methodists, 17, 25
Michael Ramsey, 98–99
minority bishops at Vatican I: French,
65–67; German-speaking, 67–68
Monsour, Daniel, xxiii
Mouw, Richard, 33

Neumann, Johannes, 171
Nicea, First Council of, xiv, 155–56
Nicea, Second Council of, 135
Nostra Aetate (1965). *See* Vatican
Council, Second, documents of

O'Donovan, Oliver, 165, 236
O'Gara, Margaret: personal history,
xviii–xx, xxiv, 149–50, 206–7;
professional history, xix–xxii;
comprehensive list of
publications, 238–45
ordained ministry: reevaluation of
the historical data regarding it,
83–88, 96, 132–36; evolution in
Roman Catholic theology and
liturgy of, 88–90, 96, 136–39;
ecumenical agreements on, 90–96,
139–44
Örsy, Ladislas, 82, 178
Orthodox Churches, xii, xiv–xvi,
9–10, 18, 25, 80, 89–90, 104, 109,
121–22, 207–8, 209, 213–14

papacy: as a ministry of unity, 21–22;
potentially a gift by Roman
Catholics to other Christians but
first needs reform, 21–22, 52, 212–
17. *See also* authority in the church;
papal primacy
papal primacy: as taught by Vatican I
and episcopal collegiality as
taught by Vatican II, their
relationship, 61–78; discussed by
Vatican I for just one week, papal
infallibility discussed for months,
xi, 226–27; has tended to acquire a
simulated infallibility, 227–28; in

jurisdiction, and papal infallibility
in teaching, their relationship, 72–
75; and the issue of Anglican
orders, 84–85, 87; as part of God's
design for the church or not, 52,
93–94, 142, 164–85, 213; relatively
unexamined since the
Reformation, hence a fairly open
theological topic, 75. *See also*
authority in the church;
collegiality of bishops; infallibility;
papacy
Pastor Aeternus (1870). *See* Vatican
Council, First, documents of
Paul IV, 84–85
Paul VI, xiv–xv, 89–90, 98–99
Pontifical Council for Promoting
Christian Unity, xxii, 95–96, 107
peace: and peace-making, 11–15, 50–
51, 210, 219; and nonviolence, 13–
15, 51, 160–61, 214; and social
justice, 4–5, 6, 7, 13, 51, 213
Pentecostals, 25, 54–55
Peter, Carl, 167, 168, 169–70
Péguy, Charles, 221
Piepkorn, Arthur Carl, 125, 133
Pierotti, Raffaele, 86–87
Pius XII, 70, 89
Portal, Fernand, 28, 85
Pottmeyer, Hermann, 63–65, 67–68,
71–73, 77, 212
Presbyterians, 8, 25, 188, 195
Princeton Proposal, 222–23

Rahner, Karl, 70, 77, 153–54, 158–59,
168–71, 178, 180, 217, 220
Ratzinger, Joseph, 17, 81–82, 151–52,
159–60, 181–82, 212
reception: as ecclesial consensus
regarding a doctrine, 52, 70, 103–4,
108, 110, 115–22, 208; as needed for
magisterial teaching to be
recognized (though not
constituted) as authentic, 32–33,
73, 75–76, 102–3, 194–96, 202, 205,

219, 228; as recognition of the same faith in another person or community, 8, 31–34, 95, 202, 212; of Vatican II by the Roman Catholic Church, 35, 149. *See also* authority in the church; collegiality of bishops; doctrines, their emergence as normative; ecclesiology; Holy Spirit; infallibility

relativism, xii, 178, 211, 222–23, 225, 226; and realism, 112–15. *See also* doctrines, their emergence as normative; historicity

Ricci, Mateo, 161

Rouco, Alfonso Carrasco, 75–76, 77

Routhier, Gilles, 3–6, 61

Runcie, Robert, 98–99, 224

Ryan, Thomas, 35, 36

Saint John's Abbey, 3, 11, 148–49, 210

Schatz, Klaus, 67, 73–75, 77, 227

Schillebeeckx, Edward, 171

Schlabach, Gerald, xxv, 11–15, 50, 217, 219

Schlink, Edmund, 168

Scripture and tradition, their relationship, 14–15, 148–62

Sklba, Richard, ix–x, xxiii

Seasoltz, Kevin, 40

Suarez, Francisco, 168

Tavard, George, 35, 36, 51, 84–88, 96, 144, 157

teaching and learning, their relative priority in the church, 105–8, 115–22

theological discussion, three levels of: particular doctrinal problems and proposed solutions, 103–4, 115–22; general theological accounts of how a doctrine emerges as normative, 105–10, 115–23, philosophical presuppositions

underlying the general theological accounts, 110–15, 122–23

theology, why to study it, 232–37

Thils, Gustave, 65

Thompson, David, xi–xii, xxiii, 27, 30

Tillard, Jean-Marie, 9, 28, 32–33, 35, 63–64, 68, 70, 77, 79, 97–98, 146, 236

Toronto School of Theology, 7–8, 23–27, 53

Trent, Council of, 48, 103–4, 108, 162, 167, 199

truth and understanding: the first as unchanging but the second as developing, 113–22, 142, 151–62, 177–83, 186–205, 227–28, et passim. *See also* doctrines, their emergence as normative

United Church of Canada, 8, 25

Unitatis Redintegratio (1964). *See* Vatican Council, Second, documents of

unity of the church: as divinely willed, xiii–xviii, xx, 16, 80; as human task, xiii–xviii; and multicultural experiences, 9–10, 222; fostered by common prayer, 7, 23–27; fostered by common work for justice, 7; fostered by teaching and learning theology together, 7–8; addressing five distinct obstacles to, 44–55; earlier sources of disunity pertained to ecclesiology and sacramental theology, newer ones pertain to Christology and trinitarian theology, 225–26; diversity within the church not necessarily division, 9–10, 80, 130–31, 192, 202, 211–12, et passim

Ut Unum Sint. See John Paul II, documents of

"Margaret brought an unusual and welcome array of gifts to conversations between Mennonites and Catholics in Bridgefolk: theological acumen, seasoned experience in ecumenical encounters, wise reflection on discipleship, abiding joy, and a passionate desire for friendship. But perhaps what endeared her most to Mennonites was her love of hymn singing—a practice we cherish. Thus it is of more than passing interest to us that she chose a song phrase as the title of her work. Singing with her, we met on solid ground and found the grace to persist in difficult and strenuous conversations—no turning back. We miss her deeply and will treasure her written legacy."

— Rev. Marlene Kropf
   Anabaptist Mennonite Biblical Seminary, Elkhart, Indiana
   Co-Founder, Bridgefolk

"To read *No Turning Back* is like completing a primer on the second generation of Roman Catholic ecumenism. Margaret O'Gara's crystal clear prose takes us through many important ecumenical achievements of the last thirty-five years, illuminating significant agreements in convergence texts by pointing to the heart of the agreement and then clarifying the steps in reasoning that led to it. In every essay, she found the very small space out of which to forge the next step. A 'star' ecumenist, she nonetheless demonstrates how ecumenical work at best is always a communal effort. *No Turning Back* is generous in spirit, as all good ecumenical work must be, and deeply learned."

— Prof. Nadia Lahutsky
   Texas Christian University
   Disciples of Christ–Roman Catholic International Commission,
      1983–2002

"In this book Margaret O'Gara combines her acute theological acumen, sensitive pastoral intuition, and honest personal vulnerability in essays from her life in ecumenical dialogue. Her passion for the unity of the church is engaged with a deeply generous openness to the other and an intellectual rigor that are woven throughout each section. These essays, across the breadth of the theological and ecclesial landscape, will readily speak to interested beginners in ecumenism as well as those deeply immersed in ecumenical dialogue and its theological challenges. May they ignite a passion for ecumenism in a new generation of theologians and ecclesial leaders!"

— Rt. Rev. Linda Nicholls
   Area Bishop of Trent-Durham & Bishop Suffragan, Anglican Diocese
      of Toronto
   Anglican–Roman Catholic International Commission, 2011–present

"This set of essays by Margaret O'Gara is both a testament to her fervent personal commitment to the ecumenical task and an invitation to the 'next generation' to continue the work from which there is 'no turning back.' Intended for both general readers and ecclesial or scholarly specialists, the collection manifests the breadth and depth of Margaret's ecumenical engagement. It reflects the attentive and probing scholarship I came to expect from her as a colleague and dialogue partner: scholarship that opens up possibilities for fresh insights and understanding, but without sacrificing her identity and convictions as a Roman Catholic theologian. While she is deeply missed, her legacy as an ecumenist and theologian will forever be a gift to the whole church."

> — Rev. Cheryl M. Peterson
> Trinity Lutheran Seminary, Columbus, Ohio
> U.S. Lutheran–Roman Catholic Dialogue, 2006–2010

"Over a period of decades, Margaret O'Gara had the unique opportunity of participating in several official international and national dialogues, an experience relatively few others have had. Her interpretations of some achievements of these dialogues, plus the further insights about ecumenical progress she garners when comparing several dialogues, constitute an invaluable aspect of this book. O'Gara, with a profound commitment to Christian unity, recognizes that renewal within the divided churches is a key to ecumenical progress. And with deep Catholic convictions, she does not hesitate to give her views concerning areas in which renewal must be explored in the Catholic Church. These essays comprise an important collection for showing people devoted to the future of ecumenism some significant steps already taken toward Christian unity and the dedication necessary as the movement continues."

> — Msgr. John A. Radano
> Seton Hall University
> Pontifical Council for Promoting Christian Unity, 1984–2008

"In my life as a Pentecostal ecumenist, I have often felt alone. Margaret O'Gara is one of those unique ecumenical friends who walked beside me for over twenty-five years and enriched my life immeasurably. She was a unique gift to the whole church. With the publication of this volume, her husband, Michael Vertin, has joined Margaret in continuing her ongoing ecumenical exchange of gifts. One cannot read it without catching Margaret's love and passion for the Lord and his church. The first section contains much wisdom and instruction on how to conceive of and participate in the quest for visible unity. It will be especially valuable for students of ecumenism looking for guidance. But Margaret was also a very fine Catholic theologian who wanted to share the rich gifts of her Catholic tradition with others. The essays and addresses in the second part of the volume provide profound insight into how Margaret understood her calling to serve the church in the work of Christian unity from within her Catholic home. *No Turning Back* provides a picture of Margaret O'Gara, a model ecumenist, at her best."

— Cecil M. Robeck, Jr.
Professor of Church History and Ecumenics
Fuller Theological Seminary, Pasadena, California

"*No Turning Back* offers an exceptional introduction to the theology and practice of ecumenical dialogue. But best of all, it introduces readers to the *spirit* of ecumenism—Margaret O'Gara's spirit—which shines through even the more technical essays here. It is a spirit of warm friendship across lines of historical suspicion, creative persistence in search of fresh understandings, and even (dare I say it?) fun! All those who knew and now miss Margaret remember her doggedly hard work, but also her laughter, her infectious love of all God's fractured people, and the joy of companionship that can transform the long journey toward church unity into an adventure. Yes, Margaret had fun, and the delight of this posthumous collection of essays is that it introduces friends she never got to make to the adventure of ecumenism and the fun she showed us it could be."

— Prof. Gerald W. Schlabach
University of Saint Thomas, St. Paul, Minnesota
Co-Founder, Bridgefolk

"*No Turning Back* is the distillate of Margaret O'Gara's lifelong vocation of theologically informed and ecumenically oriented witness to the unity of Jesus Christ and his church. Knowing that the Lord of the church effects and guarantees its unity, she dedicated herself—relentlessly, sensitively, cheerfully—to the public, indisputable manifestation of that unity.

"Few ecumenical thinkers have possessed the author's theological expertise, and fewer still have found a place in their heart for Evangelicals, Pentecostals, and other Christians outside the orbit of the European church bodies. Her breadth, however, is matched everywhere by her depth. Her catholicity, critical assessment, and, not least, her self-criticism all are plainly evident.

"Recent and experienced participants in ecumenical dialogue alike will profit from this fine book. Clearly and cogently written, it will bring the newcomer up-to-date on page after page. Embodying decades of profound theological scholarship, it will augment the wisdom of the veteran. And its committed inclusiveness reflects the Lord whose crucified arms embrace everyone and whose dereliction finds no one God-forsaken."

— Rev. Victor Shepherd
Tyndale University College and Seminary, Toronto
Evangelical–Roman Catholic Dialogue of Canada, 2008–present

"These essays of the late Margaret O'Gara engage the theological foundations of ecumenism in Christ, the apostolic faith, and the dialogical process and teaching of the early councils, always with 'historical-mindedness' and interpretation of new contexts and signs of the times. The dynamics of old divisions (e.g., about justification, tradition, Eucharist, Petrine ministry) are probed and reconfigured in a new light, through careful representation of classic texts—including Vatican II, ecumenical dialogues, and convergence documents. We are in the presence of an ecumenical theologian *par excellence*, a veteran dialogue partner, and a brilliant educator: insistently hermeneutical, yet keeping the whole in view, finding the secret Scripture in ancient formula, dissenting voice, and dangerous memory. Systematic analysis of dearly held confessional forms is balanced by a nose for the crux, emergent consensus, analogous approach. The reader learns that unity is gift of the Holy Spirit, nurtured in prayer, discipline, repentance, and the joys of friendship. Michael Vertin's editing is flawlessly achieved and attuned to what is manifestly for him, as for the author, a labour of love in service of truth and communion. Individually, and as coherent *oeuvre*, the essays hearken to a future where the regeneration of the church and ecumenical reconciliation go hand in hand."

    — Prof. Geraldine Smyth, OP
      Irish School of Ecumenics
      Trinity College, Dublin

"Reflected in this collection of articles and addresses by Margaret O'Gara is an exciting vision of God's calling to the visible unity of the church in our world today. *No Turning Back* challenges all churches to take seriously Jesus' prayer 'that they may all be one' (John 17:21): not as a burden, but as a gift to be received and shared and celebrated. This book will serve to keep alive Margaret's deep commitments to an ecumenism that is grounded in theological integrity, honest dialogue, abiding prayer, and (most significantly) personal friendships."

    — Rev. Robert K. Welsh
      President, Council on Christian Unity, and Ecumenical Officer
      Christian Church (Disciples of Christ) in the United States and Canada